SHAKESPEARE
AND
THE ELIZABETHANS

About anyone so great as Shakespeare,
it is probable that we can never be
right; and if we can never be right,
it is better that we should from time
to time change our way of being wrong.

T. S. ELIOT

SHAKESPEARE
AND
THE ELIZABETHANS

by Henri Fluchère

Translated by Guy Hamilton

With a Foreword by T. S. Eliot

A DRAMABOOK

HILL AND WANG, INC. · NEW YORK

FIRST DRAMABOOKS PRINTING AUGUST 1956
SECOND DRAMABOOKS PRINTING FEBRUARY 1959

Library of Congress Catalog Card Number: 56-10718

Published by Hill and Wang, Inc.
By special arrangement with Longmans, Green and Co., Inc.
This volume was originally published under the title *Shakespeare*
All rights reserved
Manufactured in the United States of America

Foreword

IN WRITING *Shakespeare: dramaturge élisabéthain* the author had
no thought of addressing himself to an English-speaking audience.
As he tells us in his preface, the book emerged out of his lectures
to his pupils at the University of Aix-en-Provence during the years
of the occupation; and his modest intention, as he told me at the
time of its publication in France, was to introduce French students
of Shakespeare to the development of Shakespeare criticism in
England during the previous quarter of a century. For such a task
M. Fluchère was exceptionally well qualified. He had pursued his
English studies for several years at Cambridge University; he had
become bilingual; his knowledge of English literature was exact
and comprehensive; he not only knew all the more recent English
contributions to Shakespeare criticism, but was personally acquainted with some of their authors. His experience as a translator
(he had translated *Everyman* and my own *Murder in the Cathedral* into French) had given him an understanding of the corre-
spondences and what I may call the *reciprocal inadequacies* of the
two languages, which cannot be acquired in any other way. As
one of the authors whose work he has translated, I feel qualified
to pronounce this encomium.

My purpose in writing this preface, however, is not to praise
M. Fluchère as an interpreter of English literature to French readers, but to affirm the value of this book for English-speaking
readers and students of Shakespeare. Its author's qualities, as
scholar and critic, far exceed the requirements of his original purpose. I am not acquainted with any recent English work which
serves the same need as this of M. Fluchère—not only giving us a
conspectus of Shakespeare's drama as a whole, but exhibiting that
drama in its relation to the other masterpieces of the Elizabethan
theatre, and taking account of recent studies by English critics.
Even had he done no more than summarize the conclusions of
English criticism in the last twenty-five years, he would have
written a book useful to English readers. But he has done much
more: his book commends itself to us because of the value of the
author's own ideas, which are supported by his combination of
scholarship with understanding and experience of the theatre.

At the present stage of Shakespeare criticism, the critic who
would give a well-balanced interpretation of Shakespeare's total
work needs a number of qualifications not commonly found together. The ideal Shakespeare critic should be a scholar, with
knowledge not of Shakespeare in isolation, but of Shakespeare in
relation to the Elizabethan Theatre in which he is only one, though

5

very much the greatest, of the masters, and of that Theatre in
relation to the social, political, economic and religious conditions
of its time. He should also be a poet; and he should be a 'man of
the theatre'. And he should have a philosophic mind. Shakespeare
criticism cannot be written by a committee consisting of a number
of specialized scholars, a dramatist, a producer, an actor, a poet
and a philosopher: each of them would be incompetent without
sharing some of the knowledge and capacities of the others. Certainly, to be a poet or a philosopher is not enough. A poet is not
a qualified interpreter, unless he understands the particular technique of *dramatic* verse. In order to understand dramatic verse he
must needs have had some success in writing it; and if his dramatic verse is to be really dramatic he must acquire also the point
of view of the producer, the actor and the audience. To understand
Shakespeare he must understand the theatre of his own time—but
also the differences between the theatre of his own time and that
of Shakespeare's time; he should know the latter, not merely as an
antiquary, but from the point of view of the producer, the actor
and the audience of Shakespeare's time. For such understanding,
both scholarship and imagination are required. Nor is the philosophic critic, without the other qualifications, in better case than
the poet. The philosopher needs to understand the nature of poetry, if he is to avoid the danger of confusing the philosophical
ideas which can be elicited from a poem with a system of philosophical belief which can be attributed to the author. And it follows from what I have said above that he needs also to understand the special conditions of the stage, the peculiar kind of
reality manifested by those personages of the stage who strike us
as most 'real', if he is to avoid the error of analysing dramatic
characters as if they were living men and women, or figures from
the historical past.

Our demands upon the Shakespeare critic have, in our time, become exacting. The number of important specialized investigations historical, social, linguistic, and studies of imagery and symbolism in Shakespeare—have to be taken into account by the critic
who aims to consider the work of Shakespeare in all its aspects.
But perhaps more than any other single writer, Mr. Harley Granville-Barker by his Prefaces, illuminating the plays with the understanding of the producer, has suggested the need for a synthesis
of the several points of view from which Shakespeare can be
studied.

The reader will judge for himself of the proportions in which
M. Fluchère possesses all the qualifications I have named: but I
am convinced that M. Fluchère has been able, to an exceptional
degree, to put himself at one after another of these points of view.
In passing from one section to another of his book, I have been
struck by his comprehension of all the problems involved—whether
of the conditions of the theatre, of the particular conditions and

aims of the Elizabethan theatre, of the nature of dramatic poetry, or of the development of Shakespeare's style from first to last. And, incidentally, I have noted with admiration his penetrating remarks upon the work of Shakespeare's contemporaries, notably Ben Jonson and Beaumont and Fletcher.

T. S. ELIOT

Preface

THE READER MAY be surprised to find in this book no biography of Shakespeare—hypothetical or traditional—based on the latest documentation available to the research student. It neither discusses 'the Shakespeare mystery' nor assesses the respective merits of the six or seven unsuccessful candidates for the honour of the authorship of the great dramatist's Works.

I take Shakespeare's plays as I find them, following the canon established by English scholars, without trying to discover in them 'the key to Shakespeare's heart'. I examine them simply from the critical and aesthetic angle, after attempting to place them in the frame of the period when they were written and staged. In other words, only the Works interest me, not Shakespeare the man's actions, authenticated though they may be or reconstructed by methods ranging from the most patient erudition to the uncertain logic of attractive theories. I have neither the scholar's competence, nor the historian's ambition, nor a taste for 'sensational discoveries'.

Shakespeare the man and his mystery for too long have been pushing the Works into the background and distracting attention from what is infinitely more important: their greatness and their beauty, and the fact that there must be valid reasons for the consensus of opinion that plays like *Hamlet* and *The Tempest* represent the summits reached by the mind of man. I believe that the critic's task is primarily to seek the reasons for this beauty and this greatness, to explore the riches they contain, and to justify to the reader of to-day the significance of Shakespeare's permanence and universality.

Such an enterprise on the part of a Frenchman would be presumptuous if it ignored the advances made by English criticism in the last twenty-five years. I pay tribute to writers as various as T. S. Eliot, Dover Wilson, Granville-Barker, F. R. Leavis, L. C. Knights, and Wilson Knight, to mention only a few, whose work and analyses have constantly pointed the way for me. I should like my essay to incite the French reader to turn to their books for the more complete satisfaction of a well-conducted investigation, through the maze of characters and subjects, so that he can then re-read Shakespeare in the light of their numerous revelations and enjoy his poetry more profoundly.

The following pages, therefore, do not claim to be an exhaustive study; there are many gaps;[1] the *apparatus criticus* is modest. Too often I have had to omit or neglect important points and regretfully drop them.[2] This book is to be regarded as adopting a new standpoint, as blazing new trails, rather than as summing up results already obtained. It is a starting-point, not a terminus, an introduction, not a finished work; in short, a prelude to the developments with which I hope to follow up this first instalment.

I should add that the ideas in it formed the basis of my lectures at the University of Aix-en-Provence during the years of the German occupation.

H. F.

Oxford, March 1947

---

[1] Of the Poems and particularly the Sonnets, for example, nothing is said here, the present writer proposing in a later book to consider the similarity of their essential themes with those of the plays.

[2] Notably the last plays, which are among Shakespeare's best and most subtle, and which I have sacrificed in my conclusion only in order to deal more fully with them elsewhere.

Contents

SHAKESPEARE
AND
THE ELIZABETHANS

PART ONE

THE SPIRIT OF THE AGE

O what a world of profit and delight
Of power, of honour, of omnipotence . . .
Doctor Faustus

1

AMONG ALL THE artistic functions of language, dramatic
expression is obviously the most direct and the most living,
and it has had to conform with the strictest requirements.
Nowhere more than in the theatre has there been so much
talk of rules, and though French classical writers may have
declared that 'the only rule is to give pleasure', none of
them dared attempt to please outside the rules. The whole
vision of French dramatists is governed by the separation
of genres and the rule of the Three Unities. The whole
point of the Romantic movement was its revolt against this
law. Yet it concerned only a framework, not the content;
only a mould, not the substance. This framework and this
mould, however, were so austere and rigid that any attempt
to break them would look like altering the substance and
content.

For a long time it was not realized that the value of the
drama or tragedy, like a picture's, lies in the colours on
the palette, not in its wooden frame. The truth was so simple
that it blinded without illuminating. All that was needed was
to see that the drama's meaning is conveyed through words,
is a function of language, and, if it is to be anything, is
merely the aesthetic expression of man's experience at some
period of his existence.

The hero speaks. He speaks with words: here is the great
salutary truth which alone can get us out of the quandary.
The function of criticism, which consists in defining what
the hero is by what he says, is therefore to examine how he
speaks and whether the language he uses expresses appro-
priately his emotions in a given situation.

Any art-form which cannot reveal to us a state of human consciousness, whether emotional or intellectual, fails in its object. Through the drama, a work of art, it should be possible to discern the drama of Man. But this drama of Man achieves its deepest meaning and its real significance only if it is expressed in a work of art: the aesthetic expression and the dramatic expression can only proceed together, only fuse in an indissoluble unity, and only have validity one with the other, one by the other; so that an analysis which dissociates them is merely the artifice of a critic when he is trying to understand them better and to explain the pleasure they give him.

If, therefore, the critic tries to judge a play by studying plot, character and style separately, and then its human significance and philosophic content, it should be only for the sake of greater freedom in judging the total effect. It should never be forgotten that the play is simply a certain arrangement of words that is unique and cannot be imitated, and that it is its word-arrangement which, in the last resort, produces the total effect.

I think we have long formed in our minds a conventional idea of Shakespeare because we were unwilling (or perhaps unable) to recognize this very simple truth.

French reasons for admiring, mistrusting or even hating him[1] have fluctuated, it is true, at different times according to the degree of culture or the enlightenment of critical thought. He has been admired for his originality, the freedom of his plays from rules, the variety of his characters, the boldness of his style, and the magic of his poetry. He has been hated for the same reasons on the pretext of his wild exaggerations. With each generation come new aesthetic conceptions and its predecessor's tastes are revised. Thus the masterpieces of the past see themselves in the distorting mirrors of the centuries, and from glass to glass exchange smiles, often of sadness. For it is rarely that the critic says the right thing for the right reason. According as this point or that is emphasized, the target is hit or missed, even if care has been taken to set the work in its proper period and recover the conditions that produced it and gave it its physiognomy.

Nevertheless, we can believe in a certain constant of art, a certain stability in its various means of expression. This constant might be defined as the expression of a human

[1] Voltaire, it is worth noting, after having been the 'discoverer' of Shakespeare, violently attacked his first translator.

experience refracted through the prism of beauty; the stability might be expressed and doubtless justified by instinctive obedience to formal conventions valid for a given period.
The finished product would be a perfect balance between
the conception of the beautiful and the conventions of expression. Techniques sometimes survive, even when the succeeding epoch understands them imperfectly or not at all;
others, again, may be completely forgotten and then critical
judgment is doomed to go completely astray. This, I think,
is particularly true of dramatic expression in which—through
I know not what delusion, with its accretions of prejudice,
credulity, lack of imagination and the mere force of habit
—certain techniques continue to govern, if not the creative
artist, at least the critic, with an authority which old age
makes increasingly arid.

French critical habits towards Shakespeare have been, to
say the least, regrettable. Since Voltaire's remark about
'pearls in the dung heap', the French have constantly treated
him as a strange, abnormal, disorderly genius. He shocks
their Cartesian minds and sometimes offends their good
taste. The Romantics threw his extravagances in the teeth of
the Classics as a good joke. But the Classics, even when
they have become more lenient towards him, have not forgiven him. 'Bardolatry' is always suspect as a kind of
eccentricity. The lowest form this takes is shown by such
glosses as 'play upon words, untranslatable in French'; [2] the
highest form of admiration, by essays of an inspired lyricism,
like those of André Suarès. But of criticism worthy of the
name I find very little. Only a few specialists have achieved
it, and the worthy Taine himself, however much he may
carry us away with his enthusiasm and however sympathetic
his intentions, gaily plunges into mistakes.

The reasons for this French attitude towards Shakespeare
—of which Louis Gillet's essay represents the last word in
refined popularization and Léon Lemonnier's the latest
fashion in industrious and romantic orthodoxy—are not only
that the English themselves have shown us the way, or that
our inveterate French classicism frowns upon anything that
seeks success without regard to rules. The explanation is,
no doubt, that Shakespeare's greatest excellence, namely the
use he makes of the English language, either has been beyond our powers of appreciation or has not received from us
sufficient attention.

[2] So reads the footnote to the nonsense reply: *'Je crois que le merlan est
recuit sur la table,'* in P. Reboux and C. Muller's parody of a Shakespeare
play (*A la Manière de . . .* , Vol. I, p. 275).

For want of this critical ability to study the apparatus of his language, the French have tried to understand and define Shakespeare by externals—by what appears to them as far-fetched and unnatural in his plays. His prestige in the first place was opposed to something the French held dear. He was made a flag, a symbol, almost a myth. Shakespearian freedom was contrasted with Classic restraint, the variety of his characters with the uniformity of the French, the so-called realism of his style with the severe purity of the best French stylists, and the richness of his thought with the philosophic indifference of the tragic writers of the *Grand Siècle*. Hence the picture has been formed of Shakespeare the Romantic, the creator of inimitable characters, the lyric poet and great philosopher.

I should like to prove (even if it raises a smile in some quarters) that these hackneyed judgments will no longer bear examination. It seems to me that French criticism should now take account of the advance made by Shakespearian studies in England during the last twenty-five years —a decisive advance, a new stage in our knowledge of the greatest dramatist and the greatest poet of modern times.

To call Shakespeare 'romantic' is as meaningless as to talk of the 'romanticism of the classics'. These are empty verbal analogies, hardly to be excused by intellectual laziness or misapplied learning. The French drama of the Romantic period is no more like Shakespeare's than, for example, Sully Prudhomme's poetry is like the *Divine Comedy*. But, it may be objected, Shakespeare did not respect the three Unities any more than the Romantics did; he mixed genres as they did; his style is rhetorical poetry, like Victor Hugo's; there are clowns in both; there is the same meditation on the meaning of life and death—lyricism, violent passions, irony, sarcasm. All that is true, but these parallels are no more substantial than the shadows in Plato's cave.

We must get rid of deceptive labels: the word 'romantic' lost all concrete meaning as soon as it was applied to anything but its proper object. It has been defined and presented in a hundred different ways, like the words 'poetry', 'lyricism', 'realism' and many others: they serve the lazy-minded who cannot grapple with their difficulties or make their vague notions precise and clear. In my view it means no more than a kind of emotional disorder which inclines to dreaming and often seeks to move the reader by fraudulent means. Or let us call it a word that has fallen somewhat from its high estate: Shakespeare, Hugo, Delacroix, Wagner —all Romantics. Villon can also be included, and Chartres

Cathedral, Cervantes and Loyola, the Cathars and the Jaco-
bins, the Inquisition and Dostoievsky! But, seriously, Shakespeare is as far removed from Victor Hugo as Racine is from
Maurice Donnay, or James I from Louis Philippe, King of
the French.

Dramatic art, however, is a living thing precisely because
it is the expression of an epoch and a society. Any valid
art-form worthy of the name, I repeat, can only be that. Of
all instruments of expression language is the most complete,
the most subtle, and also the most exacting. For it is charged
not only with thought, but also with emotion in a form that
aims at being both beautiful and intelligible. Tragedy exists
only with the actors who perform it and the public to whom
it is addressed. The love of play-going merely shows man's
keen curiosity about himself—the self he knows or the self
he does not know, it matters not—man as he is, as he could
be, as he should be. And there has never been a Drama
(except, no doubt, that of the Greeks) which so perfectly
fulfilled its function as Renaissance Drama in England.

Elizabethan Drama[3]—and of course I mean Shakespeare's
also—is not a literary genre as French Romantic Drama is.
It is the voice of a whole epoch, talking in all possible tones
and ways, expressing through the mouths of its dramatic
characters the sum of knowledge, preoccupations, emotions
and ideas constituting what is called the soul of that Age.

Between the dramatist and his public contact is established
through the vehicle of language which carries this soul to
the knowledge of the audience, for its delight. The content
of the play, the story, the experience from which it derives
and on which it is based, has in itself no greater value or
importance than the form of its expression. Its only value,
indeed, lies in the latter. Neither the plot nor the *dramatis
personae* nor the philosophy nor even the poetry holds the
first place: there is a total effect produced by a happy
arrangement of all these elements in one indivisible whole.
If one could perceive the drama without taking duration into
account—but can one for a fugue, can one for a cathedral
which has at least to be circumambulated?—this coherence,
to which I shall revert shortly, would be obvious. Themes
follow each other, cross each other, are superimposed, and
from all this springs a major harmony giving the play its
distinctive individuality.

But all subjects are suitable, whatever they may be (just
as all the faces haunting the imagination of the stone-mason

[3] In this term adopted by French criticism I include Jacobean Drama also—
in short, the whole Stage production from 1580 to *c*. 1640.

may appear on the stone façade of the cathedral)—all, from the hackneyed themes of legend or history to the latest item of news from home or abroad. All may be taken by the dramatist for his characters—God, prince, gardener or stable-lad—since they form part of the world and pass for men; monsters even and angels, creatures imaginary or real. Their 'character' is simply how they behave in a given situation. In a menagerie, it is as curious to watch the behaviour of the lion as that of the tamer, and this behaviour which supplies the action of the drama takes shape in definite acts and gestures after the personage has outlined in speech the actual obstacles facing him in the real world around him. Speech explains, justifies, supports and prolongs his effort: alive, conscious, understanding what is done or to be done, language is an image of ourselves swept along into some act that cannot be undone and moving, through fortuitous episodes, towards the irrevocable end.

The essential problem for the critic seems to me, therefore, to be not literary classification for academic satisfaction, nor theoretical study of the various forms to which poetry and drama may have contributed, nor even the so-called psychological analysis of the characters which gives the mind the illusion of grasping a complex and fugitive reality; but rather the study of human experience refracted by the drama and shaped by the instrument of expression.

The time seems to me accordingly to have come to cease making a romance out of the theatre, as a romance has been made out of Shakespeare's life; or if it is done, let it be with more knowledge. It is no longer sufficient to call Shakespeare 'a universal genius' or 'the greatest dramatist of all time'.

To say that his supreme distinction lies in creating, better than any other dramatist, a throng of different characters is tantamount to supposing that character-creation is the dramatist's only business. To dilate upon his philosophy, to trace the curve of his thought, to try to deduce 'the man Shakespeare' from the vast accumulation of variegated phrases—truths and untruths—in his plays, is an equally illusory enterprise which can never achieve more than a relative objectivity. Victor Hugo's strange, ecstatic, bombastic declamations, Louis Gillet's elegant musings, Taine's sinewy, passionate eloquence, André Suarès's esoteric lyricism—all in their way do honour to Shakespeare's memory, but they sometimes disturb and irritate the reader.

Everything has been found in Shakespeare. Critics have even found what is not there, what he never intended to put

in (an obvious proof of the richness of his mind). It would
be exciting to catalogue the apocryphal sediments which each
epoch and school has left on the Shakespearian shore. Here,
I suggest, is a fine subject for young French teachers to offer
for their theses! It would produce some very curious conclusions about the somnolence or the ardour of the critical
mind down the ages and, no doubt, would help to throw
a sharper light upon the Protean Shakespeare whom so many
attempts have been made, hitherto in vain, to pin down.

2

For the past twenty-five years English critical studies of
Shakespeare have taken quite a new, indeed a revolutionary,
direction. Here, as elsewhere, traditional methods have been
abandoned. Writers are no longer content to describe, and
often to digress in describing: they seek to define by rational
analysis and research, standing away from the past. An
enormous amount of work has been done. The years between
the two wars were particularly fruitful and will be looked
back upon, in the future, as an outstanding period of criticism. The movement took root in university circles, and
Cambridge led the revival through men like I. A. Richards,
F. R. Leavis, William Empson and L. C. Knights. The foundations of the new attitude had been laid by T. S. Eliot,
Middleton Murry, Lytton Strachey and even Virginia Woolf.
Such magazines as *The Criterion, The Athenaeum, The
Calendar of Modern Letters* and *Scrutiny* spread the fertile
ideas in intellectual circles and increased the public interest
in problems of language, poetic expression and more generally in writing as a work of art. It was natural that a new
'evaluation' of great literature should be applied to Shakespeare; and Shakespearian criticism, which had made no
serious progress since Coleridge, has been carried forward
with a tremendous impetus.

I do not intend to speak here of erudite research regarding Shakespeare's personality, the mystery of his life, or the
genuineness of the plays attributed to him. I do not know
much about Homer or Aeschylus: the little I know is enough
for me since I have their Works. I have no taste for the
Stratfordian quarrel, and no desire to take sides for or
against the orthorox view. Such learned exercises are for
specialists, retired colonels, clergymen with a passion for
cryptograms, or adepts at detective fiction. The result of
hours spent in scrutinizing the typographical alignment of
first editions, in examining under a magnifying glass the

thickets of lawyers' notes or parish registers, is as disappointing as it may occasionally be picturesque. Of course, for
the biographer or the historian a minute knowledge of facts
is valuable, and no doubt it is a good thing that research
students should be passionately interested in hunting out
trivialities which some day will be put together and will reconstruct the complete fresco of a life composed of shifting
colours and unfinished lines. These patient and persevering
detectives have rendered, and will again render, invaluable
services, if only in raising problems! But it is not to them
that we must look to enrich our knowledge of Shakespeare's
Works.

There has also been a reaction against those nineteenth-
century critics who used Shakespeare merely as a splendid
pretext for writing about themselves, of whom the Romantics
Hazlitt, Lamb and, later, Swinburne were the most notable.
Brilliant writers in their different ways, moving panegyrists,
they told the stories at second-hand, copying the fine series
of Shakespeare's pictures, the 'incomparable gallery' of heroes
and heroines over whom they shed pitying tears. Their
attitude is that of disciples and friends who dole out their
emotion in well-timed essays full of the prestige of their
name and style: they for long stereotyped the 'right' attitude
and formulas to be adopted towards 'The Bard'. In so doing
they tell us more about themselves and their own day than
about Shakespeare. But, apart from Coleridge who remains a
great critic, the critical importance of these essays is largely
negligible.

Finally, there is the industrious academic group, torn between the duties of teaching and research, whose immense
labours and varied investigations are of very unequal value.
The professor may be a literary historian, a commentator or
a critic—very different functions which may reinforce each
other but are rarely found in combination. Shakespeare's
words, images, rhymes and rhythms have been counted; all
his allusions have been investigated, his sources probed, his
ambiguities explained, his incoherences justified; all Shakespeare's legendary or historical figures have been compared
with their originals; his text has been taken to pieces, the
prose analysed, the poetry scanned—in short, Shakespeare
has been so tortured, torn asunder in every direction and
ground down, so much paraphrased, scrutinized, sifted, measured by X-ray and seismograph, that there is not a syllable
or particle, not a subtlety of style or thought that has not
been detected and reported. Under this gigantic mass of
commentaries and glosses, learned or childish, Shakespeare

would have been buried had there not been more life in him
than in all those who have hunted him like a pack of hounds.
Shakespeare's amazing vitality has withstood all their assaults.
The reader tires of their commentaries more quickly than of
his text, and few consult, for example, the Furness Variorum
Edition.

Nevertheless, this enormous critical deployment has left
some positive results. In the first place, the text has been
established almost beyond a doubt. Glossaries and grammars
are available which make it easier to understand Shakespeare. Valuable works of reference facilitate the reader's
task. Analogies can be drawn, comparisons made, misunderstandings dispelled. In short, real critical work can begin.
It was thanks to this body of research that the striking
progress was made which in the 1940's produced an entirely
new attitude towards the Elizabethan period and the work
of Shakespeare. It is much to be desired that French criticism
should now take account of it.

Two or three roads seem to me to have led to the present
position, of which some specialists make perhaps too much,
and sooner or later they will be left behind. It would be
absurd to claim that the last word has been said. The mind
is always seeking new reasons for admiring Shakespeare and,
every time it finds a new one, thinks it the right one. That
would be a fruitful but dangerous illusion if one had to stop
there. It is precisely because the new orientation of Shakespearian studies opens up unlimited horizons that it is well
to take our bearings.

To begin with, the historical conditions in which the Elizabethan Drama flourished have been investigated with a more
informed interest. It surpassed in extent all literary expression until then known, except the Greek Drama. The theatre
seems to have been as necessary to the Elizabethan crowd
as bullfighting is to the Spanish crowd. Having no news-
papers, political meetings, clubs or other places of entertainment, the public frequented the play-house for information,
education and company. There, people laughed together and
wept together. They went there in search of dreams, of
morality, of politics, of sensation, and lessons in wit. They
were attracted by scenes of violence and bloodshed as well
as by subtlety and clowning and magic. In the theatre they
heard the great names of the past, the heroes of legend, the
heroes of their own day, lovers, assassins, eccentrics who had
gained notoriety.

Witty dialogues, political discussions, machiavellian confessions, cries of despair or of vengeance, admissions of

powerlessness or professions of faith were listened to with
passionate interest. So receptive was the Elizabethan audience that the observation of Hamlet in his famous soliloquy
(Act II, sc. ii) must be taken literally:

> . . . I have heard
> That guilty creatures, sitting at a play,
> Have by the very cunning of the scene
> Been struck so to the soul that presently
> They have proclaimed their malefactions. . . .

The theatre found its natural sustenance in the political,
economic and social conditions then prevailing. It was obsessed by religious or philosophical themes, conveyed through
the poetry of symbols and allegories, raised to hitherto un-
suspected heights, yet within the comprehension of all. Such
plays drew upon the whole range of human experience at
that time. They did not, like the Restoration Comedy of
Manners or the bourgeois drama of the eighteenth century,
mirror a limited society. They did not set out to be propaganda plays, defending ideas, assailing abuses or preaching
sermons as some twentieth-century plays-with-a-purpose have
done. Elizabethan Drama was not a philosophy, a moral
system, a social doctrine, but it took the place of them because it was, above all, dramatic *art*. Or rather, it acted
as a catalyst, transmuting the substance—thought or emotion
—into a work of art. Everything that happens on the stage,
through the mouth of a personage, becomes something else:
such is the great rule.

It is not surprising, therefore, that what the English call
the *background* of the Elizabethan Theatre has been carefully studied. The idea, of course, is not new, and many
critics since Taine have exploited it. But the comments it
calls for are made in the light of what is known of the
period and the environment. This knowledge had long been
fragmentary and erroneous, giving rise to arguments (which
entailed conclusions) that were highly coloured, to say the
least, and owed more to the imagination than to any real
concern for the truth. The contention, for example, that the
average audience of the Elizabethan Age—not to speak of
the 'groundlings', the porters, sailors, artisans apprentices,
men without a trade, in a word, the public of the Bear-
Garden—was gross and uneducated, has been shown to be
remarkably false, by the investigations of Mrs. Q. D. Leavis,
Mr. L. C. Knights and Mr. Louis B. Wright.

It would, indeed, have been strange had this mixed, un-
cultivated public been able to interest itself in plays which
for subtlety of language, profundity of thought, delicacy of

observation, poetic concentration and musical grace are equal
to the most remarkable poems of, say, Baudelaire, Mallarmé
or Valéry. For it is in these terms that the problem should be
presented. Whereas the three French poets whom I take for
purposes of comparison never imagined that their verses
could be read and appreciated by a tavern- or circus-going
public, Shakespeare wrote for the populace as well as for
the courtier. Let us not say that he alternates high poetry
and farce in order to please *successively* the Court and the
Pit. The Court equally with the Pit required clowning of
him, and the Pit—the groundlings, who stood in the rain
—appreciated, as did the favourites of Elizabeth and James I,
Hamlet's soliloquies, the precious verbal fencing of Rosalind
and Orlando, and the lyrical outbursts of Romeo. If the
reader has still any doubts on the point, let him think of
the *quality* of the songs scattered through almost all the
plays of the time.

No, there was no loss of continuity, no cleavage between
the cultivated public and the populace. Not that the latter
was educated in our sense of the word, but the unlettered
masses had not lost touch with the treasures of popular
culture handed down by oral tradition, folklore, legends, the
deeds of national heroes, the Old and New Testaments, the
cultural resources of the Guilds. Nothing came amiss to them
that had gone into the ballads, the songs, the pageants, the
old wives' tales, the school horn-books, the almanacks, the
sermons, the chapbooks, proverbs, anecdotes and jests.
The spoken English was salty and rich, bold, direct, full
of images. A grammar that was still uncertain, words with
various senses side by side with concrete terms with precise shades of meaning, enabled the Elizabethan to express
himself with a compact and allusive vocabulary that was
neither banal nor journalese.

All this wealth of language was at the disposal of a deep
instinct for its proper use, which is primarily to express all
the emotions. In time the instinct grew thin and anaemic,
polished by so-called classical culture, made respectable by
Society, by the coffee-houses, universities, drawing-rooms,
periodicals, 'best sellers' and finally (to complete the circle
of decadence) the modern Press and radio, until only a few
great writers can save it from final disaster.

It is of interest to note that Shakespeare began to be
bowdlerized [4] in the eighteenth century, that the Elizabethans were termed barbarians, and that when a great

---

[4] Bowdlerize: word formed from the name of T. Bowdler who expurgated
Shakespeare in 1818.

Romantic poet objected to the 'poetic diction' of the Classical, or rather pseudo-Classical Age, he claimed to be substituting for it the poetic style nearest to prose. But this prose which he imagined to be so near to poetry or vice versa, is as conventional in its platitude as poetic diction had been in paraphrase, litotes or metaphor.

Wordsworth's great mistake lay precisely in believing that there was no difference, or that there should not be, between poetry and prose. His intention was praiseworthy, for he aimed at ridding poetry of its colourless crust of stylistic conventions left over from the Augustan Age, which had ended by drying up all poetic vitality. Poetic expression had been polished and repolished until in the end it had lost all vigour. It had also moved too far away from spoken English. The Elizabethan 'barbarians' were not, indeed, guiltless of far-fetched, precious and extravagant turns of phrase —in a word, of conventions: I shall come back to this point —but what was natural to them was just this continual effort to follow their desire for expression through to the end. Whether the writer's bent be towards the elegant or the gross, to the rhetorical or the musical, he must in the end exhaust what he has to say; he must put into words, with all the passion necessary to carry conviction and arouse wonder, the excitement of his inspiration, the faith that sustains him, the joy that transports and the grief that lays him low. The means do not matter when the tongue is supple and rich enough, the mind sufficiently alert and the passion sufficiently strong.

Such a language the Elizabethan public understood and felt, because its own was likewise living and expressive, its mind equally alert. The dignity and quality of poetic language had not yet become hackneyed and insipid. The poets, it is true, were beginning to toy with the sweets of music that were to prove so attractively easy. Who can say how much good and how much harm a Spenser did to English poetry? The trouble is that he erected a veritable monument, a fairy palace of traceried architecture, an interminable vista of strophes, each on its alexandrine pedestal, and that through this gallery with its thousands of columns blew the melodious breezes of all his sober consonants, borne along with a rare refinement of expression. He held up this magic to be admired and imitated, but was there ever poetry more dead, more frozen, more like a world of darkened mirrors? Spenser raised very high the prestige of verbal art; he ennobled the poet's function, and gave it more splendour than it had ever had before. But he petrified it, successfully removing it so far from life that he has remained the cynosure, the unapproached model, the rich store-house where his successors have gone to admire his jewels and learn the secrets of his great art.

Spenser's poetry sought to be learned (he added, or caused to be added, glosses to his *Shepheardes Calender*), to be musical and no longer merely to *express* itself. (Possibly Spenser, for that matter, had nothing to express: not even love really moved him.) There was nothing dramatic about it; it was not *of the people*—not because it was difficult but because it was cold. There are in—and round—Shakespeare musical strains as sweet as Spenser's, but they are the voice of tenderness, for example, or of pity or love, or simply of admiration for the beautiful. They *express* an emotion, they vibrate, and the Elizabethan public was not deaf to these voices which made it vibrate in its turn, even if the language is difficult or 'barbarous'.

So there is, I believe, a *quality* in this public, as there is a quality in the language and a quality in the authors. These Elizabethan masses were perhaps actually an aristocracy in the sense that their culture had its roots deep in the past, in memories of the race, in that fertile soil—the consciousness of a people destined for high adventures, physical and spiritual. Such a consciousness is wakeful, embracing at once the past, the present and the future of the nation. It takes an insatiable interest in everything, especially in those experiences allegorically represented in a lust for the possession of things—love, ambition, patriotism; the desire for vengeance or conquest, property, power, even destruction, including self-destruction. Elizabethan authors knew this well, for poetic expression was *their* supreme venture, and for their themes there was God's own plenty.

No subtlety, no grandeur was beyond them, and their impetus carried them through to the end. No nicety, no vigour of language could stop them. Their range was boundless, their idiom ready for any purpose. They did not trouble to digest the matter they offered, and often the nut was hard to crack. But the public had good teeth, and it had a joyous appetite for everything. Hence the rich content of Elizabethan literature, its epic or its suave tone, conquering, arrogant—anything could be essayed, from virtuosity to rhetoric, from eloquence to farce. And all the preoccupations of the age are to be found in it.

Thus, close bonds were formed between the Drama and the living thought of a people ready for poetic marvels. The great political, economic and social changes of the end of

the sixteenth century were not ruled out, and the new social
ideas can be seen breaking through the pages of some of the
greatest Elizabethan dramatists. The themes of order, authority, royal power, political virtue or Machiavellianism, even
of democracy; of gold and the acquisitive instinct; of government, war or peace, poverty or wealth; religious, philosophical, metaphysical, supernatural themes—everything is found,
again and again, in this Elizabethan giant. Here the philosopher, the historian, the economist must come to the help
of the literary critic, and the latter has had to revise his
judgments in the light of their discoveries. The novelists, the
pamphleteers, writers of memoirs, preachers and moralists
of the time have been carefully studied, and they have added
to our direct knowledge a host of details which it is impossible to neglect. So a picture has been built up gradually,
more and more complete and complex, yet easily understood,
in which the phenomenon of the Drama's flowering finds its
natural place. The great currents of thought, the passionate
curiosities, the secret fears which haunted or passed through
the minds of the Elizabethans can now be read, no longer
as filigree work in the dramatist's texts but as the tormented
inspiration of these works. Roughly half a century (1580-
1640) saw the Drama open, expand and die. It was a period
of transition, one might almost say of revolution. Old beliefs
crumbled, old values collapsed; a new world came painfully
to birth in enthusiasm and distress, now bubbling over with
hope, with the pride of conquest and measureless ambition,
now suffering unspeakable nostalgias, agonizing soul-tortur-
ings and blackest despairs.

On the one hand there was the will to power which
would assert its empire over space, time, matter and even
God; on the other, consciousness of failure which the weaknesses and contradictions of human nature made inevitable,
even in the hour of the most brilliant triumphs, so near is
victory to defeat. Hence the cries of joy, the wails of anguish,
bursts of laughter, calls to revolt, melodious ecstasies, prophetic fears that fill to overflowing the tumultuous torrent of
Elizabethan literature. The writers who undertook to instruct and move their contemporaries reflect, more perhaps
than those of any other period in history, the complex soul
of their age. Men of flesh and blood, breath and movement,
they thought and felt, hoped and cursed, were elated and
terrified, like a soul which, not yet parted from the body,
nevertheless already apprehends the parting: the split between spiritual values which are breaking up and material
values that weigh heavily upon them.

The splendid humanism of the end of the fifteenth century
and the beginning of the sixteenth century (Sir Thomas More
was beheaded in 1535 and Erasmus died a year later, overwhelmed by his presentiment of the coming collapse) was
shattered by the repeated assaults of the Reformation (which
aimed at liberation but destroyed religious unity), of the
Wars of Religion, of the rising economic rivalries, and of the
materialism that was soon to triumph. All were conscious,
more or less clearly, of the revolution in progress: the clear-
sighted were those who tried to express the spiritual fraud
that was already taking shape, and was assuming its crafty
and dogmatic form in the sharp aphorisms of Bacon.

The study of the dramatists, so happily rounded off by
knowledge of Elizabethan conditions, thus enriches and completes what we know of the historic facts. Shakespeare,
though immortal, is not outside time: he is not a *lusus
naturae*, a solitary giant, inventive and inspired, but someone who flourished between two precise dates—1590 and
1610. At any other moment of history he would not have
been Shakespeare. This does not mean that he was merely an
echo or a reflection, more melodious, more luminous than
another would have been. His greatness does not consist
solely in the fact that he surpassed his contemporaries in
the originality, the variety or the depth of the themes that
he treated. It was, as will presently be seen, different. He
was absolutely, magnificently, gloriously a man of his time.
It is by setting him in that age, in the midst of its currents
or ideas or emotions, against its aesthetic background, among
all the contradictions and disconnected notions revolution-
izing the Elizabethan's picture of the world—it is by setting
him in that dawn-light which knows the dusk is coming and
fears the dark while longing for the roseate hues of a new
day, that we perceive his full brilliance.

I am not much inclined to the view that the curve of
Shakespeare's production follows merely the incidents of his
life. I know that it makes for tidiness to think of his career
as a dawn exuberant and full of promise, a sad and disappointed maturity and finally a haven of serenity: light comedies and lyrical tragedies followed by dark dramas and then
romantic plays in which the poet allows kindness, indulgence
and forgiveness to be stronger than the cruelty of fate. The
Sonnets, it has been said, give the key to Shakespeare's
heart. But what has 'Shakespeare's heart' to do with an
appreciation of his Works, since there is still controversy over
the question whether the Sonnets are the tortured expression
of a genuine sorrow or mere literary exericses in the taste of

the day? Any biographical explanation of these Works must be a matter of conjecture and chance, and hence merely imaginary. The essential lies elsewhere. One clear admission, one page of a diary would be more useful to the biographer. As for the critic, what is it to him whether the Dark Lady's name was Mary Fitton or not? The mystery is not whether Shakespeare was deceived, but why, if he was, he wrote as he did.

How much imaginaiton would be required really to believe that Shakespeare projected into his plays the result of his bewildering meditations in close relation with his own experience—Lear's demented fury, Hamlet's sorrowful madness, Othello's fatal jealousy, the love of chaos that gives so bitter a twist to Macbeth's utterance! Shakespeare was indeed all his characters in the sense that he created them out of nothing, breathed life into them upon the stage, made them speak as they would speak if faced with the situations in which he placed them or with the characters that he gave them: this is the domain of *art,* not of the poet's *life.*

Shakespeare undertook to write plays for a given public, at a given period, not to relate his own life-story or to deliver up his 'heart'. The graph of Shakespeare's plays follows rather that of the soul of his age.

3

From the Elizabethans properly so-called to the Jacobeans, of whom Ford is without doubt the purest and the most representative, there is a remarkable correspondence between the events, currents of opinion, moods of the day and the themes handled by the dramatists, the subjects they chose, the atmosphere in which their plays are steeped. English critics divide sharply into three phases the development of the Elizabethan's attitude towards the problems of his life and destiny.

First, there is the Elizabethan period in the strict sense when the plays of Greene, Kyd, Peele, Marlowe and the young Shakespeare flowered. A radiant cult of life, a firm faith in the possibilities of man's conquests, an exuberance of mind directly corresponded then with the upward movement of a society enjoying full prosperity. Between *Tamburlaine* (1587) and *Hamlet* England laid the foundations of her coming pre-eminence by crushing her great Catholic rival (The Armada, 1588), by assuring for a time the stability of the Throne (execution of Mary Queen of Scots, 1587, and of Essex, 1601), and by paving the way for her colonial expansion, with men like Raleigh, Drake and Hawkins.

The Merchant Companies flourished, spices brought wealth, the mirage of Venetian opulence became for the City a palpable reality. In the middle of the century (1566) Sir Thomas Greham had founded the Royal Exchange, and already the City had become so rich that it could fit out twenty men-of-war to fight the Spaniards in 1588. The Merchant Adventurers who for more than two centuries had been competing with the Hanseatic League for the European markets, ended by sweeping the board, securing the revocation of their foreign rivals' privileges and their expulsion from the City in 1597. Burghley, stubborn, realistic and crafty, concerned himself with the kingdom's material interests, just as the Queen sided both with the great pirate captains, sharing their spoils, and with the 'little people' whose loyalty and industry she loved.

Immense prospects opened up at sea, markets were won, enemies defeated; past glories were studied, and the English felt a new emotion rising within them, which was to fertilize the national conscience—patriotism. The poets were to rival those of the Renaissance abroad (Spenser and a host of sonnet-writers established the reputation of English poetry round about 1590). Hakluyt assembled tales of voyages and adventures (*Principal Navigations, Voyages and Discoveries of the English Nation*, 1589). Hooker raised the first monument of Anglican thought (*Laws of Ecclesiastical Polity*, 1594). Bacon undertook the reform and systematizing of scientific thought. And finally, the dramatists took up all these themes, while a group of essayists and poets founded literary criticism in the midst of this great fermentation of the national spirit (Sidney's *Apologie for Poetrie*, 1595). England was becoming conscious of her greatness. Threats to her security had been disposed of; wealth was flowing in to her; every kind of hope seemed permissible.

The most obvious qualities of the Drama in this upward period are, then, a robust tone, simplicity of outlook, a marked taste for violence or, on the other hand, for an exotic fairyland. They were soon to be replaced by more complexity, but as yet there was none of that subtle irony which, even in the horrible bloodshed of the pessimistic Drama of the 1600's, was to make its unhappy heroes bitter critics of human destiny. The personages of Tragedy were still all of a piece: brave, bloodthirsty, bent upon conquest, murder or madness; simple to the point of childishness but robust and healthy. Nor is the tragic *tone* dominant even in the plays which can most justly be termed tragedies. Blood flows, but the soul remains unsullied: the murdering and massacring are almost light-hearted. Love, death, time, space, solitude are not enveloped in the evil miasmas spread by a tortured conscience, nor darkened by all the contradictions inherent in these simple, eternal themes. The horror might almost be said—if the expression still has any meaning—to be chemically pure. The hero plunges, raging, into blood, in the night, as a bear falls upon the dogs, and no one questions either the chain that binds him to the stake or the claws and fangs that tear the quivering flesh to pieces; no one asks why this flesh suffers so. The condemned man goes to his doom with the unconscious grandeur of his instinctive insolence, which is akin to the fanatic's blasphemy and often echoes the accents of his despair.

In this first period there are no soliloquies, like Hamlet's, in which questions are asked and dilemmas appear insoluble: 'to be or not to be', or 'the native hue of resolution is sicklied o'er with the pale cast of thought'. All the thought is violently, frenziedly concentrated upon action. Ghosts play their part to the full—they are implacable. The deceived lover does not forgive—he avenges his shame in blood. The criminal hunts out his victim till he can kill him. The injured party clings to his revenge with incredible tenacity. Ambition exults with joy at each new conquest, as the executioner over each head that falls. Whether it be Kyd's *Spanish Tragedy* (?1589), Shakespeare's *Titus Andronicus* (1592) or Marlowe's *Jew of Malta* (?1590), the climate is the same: that of a world where violence knows no fetters, where passions are wild beasts, decked out with no unwonted graces, where action is held up by obstacles only to be precipitated the more violently.

But, despite appearances, all this violence and cruelty inspires neither pessimism nor discouragement. The tragic hero is not weighed down by his failure: he boldly continues exploring all forms of life, undeterred by the mutability of his fortunes. Only Marlowe's genius—to which the later Elizabethan Drama was to owe so much, alike in form and content—an almost prophetic genius, shows beneath the exuberant pride of his personages some hint of the secret feeling of defeat which was to form the background of Jacobean Drama.

The vigorous life which asserts itself so forcefully in the passionate rhetoric of Kyd or Marlowe, monotonous and unsubtle, often stiff and mechanical, having neither discipline in its vigour nor control over its impulses, is not merely displayed in the Drama proper: it also makes itself felt strongly in a great variety of forms in the newly discovered and immediately exploited sphere of the Chronicle Play. Here the English people becomes conscious of itself and its mission. To increase its confidence in its future, it delights in the spectacle of its past triumphs. The stage offers it a mirror reflecting the portraits of kings and knights who made some stir in history and whose names are far from being forgotten. Here also problems of domestic or foreign policy are discussed, the mysteries of government elucidated, the characters of kings and great lords shown in action, the secrets of war and peace unveiled, the virtues and vices of the country's rulers brightly illuminated.

It must, moreover, be admitted that English History from the Hundred Years' War to the beginning of the Renaissance lent itself admirably to dramatic poetry. What intrigues, murder and bloodshed; what great, tortuous or passionate characters; what arrogant, ambitious and fierce nobles, kings dethroned, brothers at enmity with each other! But also, what dashing, picturesque heroes! The gallery of historical personages and their adventures (of Elizabeth with her incomparable strength of character and guile no one dared yet speak except in hyperbolic terms that would embarrass the goddesses themselves; but her brutal and crafty father still lived in the memory of the people) offered the playwrights a wealth and variety of characters and problems which twenty years of stage-productions could not exhaust.

From Peele to Shakespeare and from Marlowe to Fletcher, most poets were tempted by the Chronicle Play, which they either wrote as straightforward history or, taking some historical fact, combined with a romantic plot. The transition is easy from the primitive technique of the early Mystery or Morality Play to the historical piece since the latter was often, at first, merely a more or less skilful selection from the chroniclers' stories or from popular legends handed down by oral tradition.

Coherence of character and credibility in the linking of facts, which should follow from them logically and naturally, were not immediately achieved. But, in spite of occasional passages of turgid eloquence, excessive chauvinism and even systematic misrepresentation of historic truth, these plays met a need and fulfilled a well-defined function. They satisfied popular curiosity, enhanced patriotic feeling and clarified the ideas on which British citizenship was to be fostered. Already the disputes that were to divide the sovereign and the subject, the people and its representatives, were taking shape,

although it was not realized how soon they would become
acute. Already the conflict had begun between virtue and
vice in politics, between justice and the abuse of power,
between legitimacy and usurpation. From all this was emerg-
ing, in vague outline but with occasionally precise and
brilliant details, a conception of government, of hierarchy,
of order, of the ideal sovereign.

Faced with the practical problems of success or failure,
of the stability of dynasties, of the fragility of favour, of
violence and trickery, of the inevitability of the facts themselves, the dramatists, possibly without knowing it, were
drawing up and offering for their listeners' consideration, a
political system that was to come slowly to maturity in the
course of years. They extended their historical investigations
beyond the English shores, crossing the French or Italian
frontiers, and finding in Classical, especially Roman, History
the same questions and preoccupations as in their own. But
these questions were always temporal: unlike the Greek
Drama, in which of course history was fused with legend
and quickened by mythology, the Elizabethan Chronicle Play
did not rise to a metaphysical examination of man's destiny.
Its problems, even when posed and discussed in abstract
terms, concerned the immediate present. It was left to the
Drama proper to raise and enlarge the vision, no doubt because its characters could be stripped of their historical
armour, already relegated to the museum of the Chronicles,
and could stand forth undisguised, simply as men, confronted freely with the problems of experience.

But if the Elizabethan heard with rapture the English-
man's first declaration of patriotism on the lips of the dying
John of Gaunt, or wildly applauded *The Famous Victories of
Henry V*, he unreservedly enjoyed the more exotic charms
of the fantasy or the romantic play. Fairyland, even when
drawn from an outmoded mythology or draped in an elaborate and precious scholarship, rarely leaves English soil.
Lyly's diaphanous myths and fragile allegories act themselves out beneath English arbours, even when his matter
derives from the Classics and his thought from Italy. His
gods and goddesses, his princes and his lovers, talk like
refined courtiers, with wit and subtlety, significantly antici-
pating the great comedies, lively in style, sprightly in
rhythm, that would soon be written by Shakespeare.

Lyly gave Comedy its tone and style, as Peele gave it
grace and humour, saving it from romantic disorder whether
in gentle pastorals, like his *Arraignment of Paris* (1580), in

which Elizabeth received the apple promised to one of the
three goddesses, or in amusing parodies, like the fantastic
Old Wives Tale, in which satire of romantic incoherence is
combined with a keen sense of rustic realism and a marked
taste for playing tricks with the subtleties and sonorities of
the English language. As for Greene, he, though borrowing
from Marlowe in his versification and general style, developed and enriched romantic comedy, skilfully constructing for it a realistic and familiar setting, intensely human
in feeling.

Thus Lyly, Peele and Greene, each in his own kind, prepared the ground for the flowering of Shakespeare's brilliant
comedies, in which realism and grace, wit and emotion,
combined convincingly in a closely-knit and swiftly-moving
plot. Already in these three predecessors (all university
men), the manner of expressing feelings was as important
as the feelings themselves, and their concern with *expression*
raised the status of popular drama very considerably. What
we find in these comedies is a taste for realism and poetry,
a mixture of the strange and the homely, an alliance of grace
with tenderness. They aimed at exploring the recesses of
the human soul in which the motives of actions lie concealed,
and at giving the exploration an artistic form. The place of
honour is given to love as the mainspring of the plays, but
there is also a touch of satire and irony, a sense of humour
that already can laugh at itself; and all this in an atmosphere of wonderful, unclouded, unrestrained gaiety.

Popular taste favoured these comedies as much as the
history plays or the horrific tragedies. There was an equal
appetite for exploring the national consciousness, for sounding the depths of passion's slaves, or for the diverting fantasies of a lively imagination.

4

It would, however, be arbitrary merely to divide the periods
of Elizabethan Drama into watertight compartments. Corresponding with the first phase of the Theatre was a time when
spiritual unity still powerfully aided the conquests of imagination and exercises in poetry. The earlier productions were
based on certainties. They put forth branches gay with
flowers or stained with blood. They explored a vast field of
experience, delayed by no cunning obstacles, disturbed by
no irritating spur of doubt. Yet one man there was, a restless
genius, eaten up with ambition, who, despite the tremendous

vitality of his heroes, was already preparing and determining the atmosphere of collapse and confusion that was to mark the Jacobean Drama.

Marlowe's work is contemporary with Kyd's: he shared with Kyd the favour of the public, and, more than Kyd, gave form and substance to the Elizabethan Drama. The most impetuous of the early group of writers, the most eloquent, the most tragic, and without doubt the greatest poet among them, he nevertheless was already, in spite of his boundless pride and lust for conquest, gnawed by a sense of failure.

All his plays are borne along by a tremendous afflatus. His heroes are conquerors who aim at the essence of conquest. Before the Scythian shepherd, Tamburlaine, thrones are swept away 'like dead leaves', space is vanquished, the earth is brought into subjection, kings become his beasts of burden. He is drunk with power, authority and prestige beyond those ever enjoyed by any tyrant. He exults in his frenzied appetite for power—'a god is not so glorious as a king'—as if he had it in him to surpass human possibilities. Though, however, the idea of a Fate stronger than Fortune's most favoured sons may not be a clear element of disillusion; though his cruelty, his capacity for pleasure, may be incredible, his ambition insatiable, his victories over his enemies unparalleled —all these are bounded by the limitations set to man's nature. This is the one thing real and indubitable when all his verbal delirium has exhausted itself and the simple fact of experience remains. He cannot, for example, find words adequate to describe the beauty of Zenocrate, the woman he loves, or the futility of rebellion or laments over death. Above all, his immense labours and his ranting dwindle to nothing when death comes to Tamburlaine in his turn. He has hurled defiance at the heavens in vain.

The Jew of Malta offers another aspect of the greed for power: the covetousness of Barabbas turns, naturally no doubt, towards riches. The lyricism with which he enumerates his jewels and his gold, all in supple, sensuous rhythm, is more directly effective than the flaming rhetoric of Tamburlaine. The play opens (and Ben Jonson's *Volpone* has an echo of it) with Barabbas gathering up in his arms these glittering splendours. But his passion for riches is not avarice, nor is it, like Volpone's, accompanied by joy in having acquired them by ignoble trickery: it is the pure ecstasy of knowing that all the wealth of the world is pouring into his coffers which are already full to overflowing, of computing the value of the cargo that is sailing towards him:

> Why then I hope my ships . . .
> Are gotten up by Nilus winding bankes:
> Mine Argosie from Alexandria
> Loaden with Spice and Silkes, now under saile,
> Are smoothly gliding downe by Candie shoare
> To Malta, through our Mediterranean sea.
>   *The Jew of Malta*, Act I.

In his turn this seeker after the Absolute, whose ruling passion is the acquisition of riches, is baffled by Fate; and this, not merely because the vicissitudes of the plot bring about his ruin after his mad, spiteful pursuit of revenge, but because Marlowe himself, once he has stated the theme, cannot or will not preserve the play's unity. For it starts on a fine lyrical note, then deals with the human problem of Christian justice towards the Jews: is it right to despoil Barabbas, and if so, how will he behave? But after the second act the play loses itself in theatrical devices, which proves, I think—though I have no means of judging whether it is a sequel or an interpolation by another writer—that Marlowe's own mind is divided by a growing sense of failure.

But it is chiefly in *The Tragicall Historie of Doctor Faustus* that the painful clash between two irreconcilable worlds can be seen. Faustus's ambition repeats and completes that of Marlowe's other two heroes. It concerns the physical as well as the spiritual world. Faustus barters his soul for unlimited power. His thirst for power and knowledge is insatiable: he has exhausted all the resources of human science, Medicine, Law, Theology, Philosophy. He wants to amass the most exquisite riches:

> Ile have them flye to India for gold,
> Ransacke the Ocean for orient pearle,
> And search all corners of the new found world
> For pleasant fruites and princely delicates.
>   *The Tragicall Historie of Doctor Faustus*, Act I.

He wants to vanquish time and space, to rid himself of the ills that flesh is heir to—obesity, weight, advancing years— to control men's minds, to know all the secrets of Creation, to drink at all voluptuous fountains. But in practice, in spite of some magnificently soaring lines—

> Was this the face that lancht a thousand shippes?
> And burnt the toplesse Towers of Ilium?

his lyrical exaltation collapses, each time, its wings clipped. Of beauty, he can capture only the shadow; of riches, only the outward attributes; of science, only the maleficent exer-

cise; of power, only the conjuror's dexterity. Neither space
nor time nor matter nor death is vanquished. Everything
escapes him, slips through his fingers, especially the supreme
satisfaction of feeling himself assured of his ephemeral
conquests.

Proud Faustus is the most uneasy of men, the frailest conqueror, the most sorrowful of atheists, uncertain of his
uncertainties. Here indeed is the weak man, terror-stricken
by his own audacity, irresolute at the very moment when he
boasts of his inflexibility, hurling defiance at God and Devil,
but immediately mad with terror, choosing now the soul,
now matter; incapable of grasping the unity of the world,
of making a synthesis between this soul which he cannot
repudiate and this matter which imposes on him its laws.
He hopes, then renounces; summons, then rejects; brags and
trembles.

It is truly a 'Tragicall Historie', not because it ends by the
hero's death but because it is like the culmination of a long
debate, broached over three centuries before, between the
spiritual world and the everyday world. Faustus flutters about
like a caged bird, dashing his head against the bars. The sun
refuses to stand still, his body to decompose, his soul to be
annihilated, God to grant him pardon. In the end, everything
flees before him: only death and damnation remain. Is it,
then, sinful for man to aspire to be like God, to succeed in
the physical world in overcoming his own weakness, to acquire possessions for their enjoyment, power in order to
exercise it, and knowledge so that this power may be further
increased; to aim at extending his power even beyond the
physical world? Is it a sin of pride to deny his own frailty,
his dependence on divine laws, his submission to what
transcends him? The worst sin is to refuse to perceive the
unity of Creation, to pursue two Absolutes which are not
interchangeable but closely linked, and then, when all has
been tried unavailingly, to rush bull-headed into one impasse
or other of this dilemma.

The play sounds almost like a Morality: Faustus or Everyman, the tragic accents are the same. But whereas the gradual
stripping of Everyman does not reach his inmost conscience,
the living heart where the miracle of repentance takes place
and which can be touched by grace, Faustus in his fool-
hardy grandeur casts immortality to the winds but cannot
rid himself of anguish:

> Why then belike
> We must sinne, and so consequently die.
> Aye, must die an everlasting death.

He affects to be concerned only for this world, yet the other disturbs him. At each impulse towards repentance his heart hardens:

> I do repent: and yet I do despair.

What does this despair mean but the admission that neither pride nor rebellion nor ambition can solve the moral and metaphysical problem? It is a religious problem, presented by man's dual nature, which will always confront the dramatists preoccupied with action, conscience and man's ultimate destiny.

Marlowe's work is therefore clearly differentiated from the humanism of the end of the fifteenth century, mentioned above—the humanism which had so happily tried to reconcile the new thought derived from the experience and contemplation of Antiquity with the spiritual life slowly built up by more than ten centuries of Christian experience and meditation. The balancing-point, always unstable, which the great humanists of the Renaissance had reached, at the cost it might be of martyrdom to crown their labours and sacrifices, had now been left behind. Marlowe's 'atheism' merely meant that he clearly realized this spiritual overdraft: he drew a blank cheque on the future, but he was secretly apprehensive. This ardent pragmatist, this bold thinker, ready for any violence, who was a man of his age, in the forefront of the pioneers of Elizabethan England's temporal salvation, freed the Drama once and for all from the Church's control. He also heralded, and paved the way for, the tragic greatness of his immediate successors. For it was a liberation accompanied by weeping and gnashing of teeth.

The Church, mistress of the Medieval Theatre—its mother indeed—gave birth to a prodigal son who never again returned to the fold. The Mysteries and Moralities, performed in front of, or even within, the cathedrals, went round the country on movable stages which were set up in inn-yards. As the spectacle became more varied and the leader of the troupe took all life for his province—all life, all history, all human experience—he came to need a special place, more adaptable to his manifold requirements, and hence regular theatres began.

The spectacle was no longer dictated by the needs of edification and preaching; its religious mission evolved towards profane ends. It took time for the spiritual split to come, but it was in the theatre that it first took place. Thinkers and poets, however eager to find a meaning in life, escaped less easily from the gilded cage of spiritual unity.

Between the world of practical experience and that of inner experience it is always easy to pass—the bridges are not broken. The most ardent and exacting realists, great travellers, soldiers, statesmen, for whom the world is a battlefield where danger is their constant companion, can die edifying deaths and pass calmly from the illusory universe of their combats to a universe of dazzling certainties, the still intact Kingdom of God. They do not die with bitterness or defiance on their lips, thinking that their life, if they have failed in their earthly ambitions, entitles them to call God to account.

The Parable of the Talents has thus still a meaning for us. It is the servant's duty to make the talents entrusted to him bear fruit, but he knows also that he must render an account to his lord in order to enter into the full enjoyment of his gains. So died Raleigh, after the stormy life of an explorer, soldier, statesman and poet; so also the unruly Earl of Essex, and so, the admirable Sir Philip Sidney. Nor is it certain that even Bacon (so bent upon worldly success, so hot for truth, founder of philosophic pragmatism, the man who ranged first the data of experience controlled by reason, who moreover wrote a text-book for *arrivistes* in which double-dealing seems to be the mainspring, and religious morality the last thing he thought of) did not preserve his soul intact when the hour of death came.

Marlowe's heroes claim to fight their battles only in the physical world. But their dazzling victories have the fleeting quality of things temporal and they rebel in vain against the survival, in the darker depths of their consciences, of the feeling that there is another presence, a spiritual world of which the world of their own activities must have been only a reflection. It is hardly surprising that Marlowe's 'atheism' was considered dangerous. It brought about a re-doubtable cleavage between the material and the spiritual world—a cleavage that made the great tragic heroes of his successors writhe in the agony of the interdict that was laid upon them. Between Faustus and Macbeth, as will be seen presently, the difference lies not in the nature of their suffering but in the quality of it.

The world, at any rate, was henceforward cut in two. Life on earth offered vast possibilities for every sort of adventurer to exploit without being over-scrupulous as to means. Freed, or so he imagined, from religious dogma and the restrictions it imposed on his thought and actions, man became in some sort his own god, at the cost of making himself his own executioner. Nothing would any longer impede his bold curiosity, his vaulting ambition, his perverse pride.

Let this world, his domain, at least make a perfect, coherent, unassailable universe. But it was not so, for how could the existence of evil be denied, or suffering, or death, or the contradictions of his nature? The exaltation of the first victories soon gave place—as the cold light of day undeceived minds that had been fevered by the struggle and the too swift triumph—to an immense disillusionment.

5

The second period of the Drama opened, roughly, about the time of Elizabeth's death. This was the great period, containing Shakespeare's masterpieces and characterized by the change of atmosphere that was foreshadowed in Marlowe's plays. By the more clear-sighted it had been foreseen some years before the Queen died that the legacy would prove a difficult one. The consciousness of the sixteenth century was in its death-throes with hers: the Elizabethan realized that everything was going to be brought into question, that nothing was settled, that profound political and social changes were imminent, and that a period of instability, confusion and uncertainty was beginning. Ten years had elapsed since the crushing defeat of the Armada, yet the war dragged on, with alternate successes and reverses and, occasionally, sudden panics like that of August 1599, when a Spanish invasion was again expected.

The overseas expeditions of 1595, from which Hawkins and Drake failed to return, and of 1597 which exposed the incapacity of Essex, the loss of Calais to the Spaniards, were hardly compensated by the striking achievement of the capture of Cadiz. Ireland, in open rebellion, had been neither subdued nor pacified in spite of the size of Essex's expedition (more than 16,000 men—an enormous force for that time). The alliance with Henri IV against Spain was highly uncertain, and England feared to find herself fighting alone in an interminable war against an enemy who could not be given a knock-out blow. The continuance of the war meant not only a vast expenditure and loss of human life, but also the terrorizing of England by bands of arrogant soldiers, the incessant threat of invasion, danger to the country's institutions, especially to religious stability, which had been won at the cost of such bloody persecutions and which a Catholic victory would destroy.

This distant and unspectacular war—for apart from the victory over the Armada, the sacking of Cadiz and the siege of Ostend, it had no great military achievement to show—

is not usually associated in people's minds with the Elizabethan Age, yet the men of that age lived through it. It affected nobles and commoners, and many writers took part in it. Sir Philip Sidney lost his life in it, Donne went on the Cadiz expedition, Ben Jonson fought in the Low Countries, and Spenser saw from close quarters the horrors of war in Ireland. If the initial victories aroused popular enthusiasm and caused Talbot's speeches in *I Henry VI* or the Bastard's last lines in *King John* to be wildly applauded, a few years later, Falstaff—a parody of a hero—could treat military glory very differently. With weariness and disillusion had come cynicism.

The day of eager progress, of simple exhilaration, of idle amusement, in a word, of youth, was over. A great queen had had the stamina to live on, but England had aged. Elizabeth's dazzling display, her jewels and her brocades, her six thousand dresses; her great lords who went to their death blessing her, influenced by love of her, of glory, of luxury; the beauty she incarnated, the chivalry she inspired, the poetry she adorned, the music she delighted in—everything that was done for her, because of her, passed and disappeared with her. A whole civilization lay in ruins at her death.

The Tudors gave to the sixteenth century the stimulus of Henry VIII's appetite for pleasure, Mary's bloodthirstiness, Elizabeth's suave, mannered, ornate stiffness. A coquette she was, but, with good reason, implacable: sure of herself, she had a high conception of her station. She knew that she was the last of her dynasty and that, after her, less firm hands would guide the country to perilous destinies. Not that she doubted England's greatness, but it would be an England seeking salvation by other ways than hers. Nothing could be more pathetic than Elizabeth's attitude of stiffening in resolute refusal to meet death. Yet the hour struck and the odd, ugly, timid Stewart came to make his bow before the bed where she lay in state.

James I brought in his train a whole galaxy of grimacing demons to drive out the old Elizabethan fairies—the confident certainties, the optimism, ardour and wonder. Now, there was to be doubt and regret, distress and disillusionment, above all, anxious curiosity, irony, satire and that grinning hyena, cynicism. The joys of discovery were to be disputable and disputed; the paths to success, tortuous and perilous; hope, to flutter like a bat; the spirit of adventure, to lose for a time that hardihood, that love of danger, that break-neck air which it had worn in Elizabethan days, that mad temerity of the illustrious sea-dogs. The men who grew

up in the declining years of the Elizabethan Age continued
to produce, but in a changed atmosphere: reaching manhood,
they were animated, under the prevailing influence, rather
by a critical spirit than by a taste for discovery. After great
epochs, as after wars, the spiritual balance-sheet of the past
is drawn up.

The drama, as was to be expected, thrived on this investigation: more than ever, it was in the theatre that the complex consciousness of the new age would find expression
and, no doubt, would be forged. The themes tackled would
be more numerous, the investigation more critical; emotion
would gain in depth and intellect in clarity. The poets themselves would no longer be content to embroider upon Petrarchan and Platonic themes a sophisticated or mannered
poetry: they were going to set themselves to solve in their
own terms the insoluble contradictions presented by the
simplest concepts and sentiments, in the light of the new
experience which, as we saw above, implied the duality of
the physical and the spiritual worlds. The so-called metaphysical school, working on parallel lines with the dramatists
but with rarer and more esoteric gifts, posed the same problems and experienced the same anxieties. The intellectual
tension produced in some of the metaphysicals a compression
of language which rivalled that of the best dramatists: Donne
is as great a poet as Shakespeare.

The legacy of Elizabethan thought may be said to be
contained in Bacon's formula: 'I have taken all knowledge to
be my province.' But this ambition for knowledge was applied
to definite ends: 'Studies serve for delight, for ornament, and
for ability.' The world is a field of experiments and man is
created to succeed. What matters is the technique of success.
Agreed, the Jacobeans would say, but what would be the
use? To fall, to die is inevitable. Briefly, their themes were
two, one political, the other metaphysical: how to succeed,
and how to face death. The meaning given to life is determined by the way in which these themes are treated: a
radiant optimism or an uneasy defeatism, a pragmatism full
of detours but sure of itself, or an uncomfortable half-light
where lurk doubt and despair. But these alternatives are
found side by side with, and intertwined in, the Drama which
continually drew nourishment from recent tradition, memories
of the remote past, discoveries and aspirations of the contemporary world.

More than any other man of his age, Marlowe left his mark
on the Drama, for he had intellect and a sense of form. He
left behind the heroic figure of Tamburlaine, with his bound-

less pride and indefatigable zest, all of a piece and finally
vanquished only by the bludgeon of Fate. But Marlowe left
also such calculating intriguers as Barabbas in the second half
of *The Jew of Malta* or Guise in *The Massacre at Paris* and
Mortimer in *Edward II*. On the one hand was the superhuman challenge to destiny, on the other, cruel, treacherous
strife—two aspects of the tragic mode which were to lead
to infinite developments. Marlowe was not strictly this mode's
inventor since, to some extent, one aspect of it derives from
Seneca and the other had already taken shape in Kyd's
Lorenzo. But it was Marlowe who breathed life into both
kinds by the strength of his inspiration and the lyricism of
his poetry. From then onwards these two types of character
dominated the whole of Jacobean Tragedy, and they deserve
to be looked at more closely.

In a world where success is the essential mainspring of
action, it is natural for men to look for a technique of promo-
tion. The tragic character moves towards a goal, encounters
external obstacles which provide the incidents of the drama
and internal obstacles which shape his behaviour. He fights
against the world and against himself. In other words, there
is the resistance of matter and the resistance of moral conscience. From these clashes the action results. We say the
character is alive inasmuch as the clash in his conscience
takes precedence and conditions the action. No one before
Marlowe had dared to throw off the moral law or, in doing
so, to look for noble reasons justifying himself in the eyes
of man and God.

The tragic hero is essentially virtuous or, if he sets himself
against the moral law, it is because the fates have a special
hatred of him. *Quos vult perdere Jupiter prius dementat.*
At a later period they would have been said to 'lack Grace'.
But the transgressor would be pursued by the Furies. In Seneca
Hercules who massacres his own family is stricken with
madness and recovers his senses only after sinking into a
long torpor and indulging in terrible lamentations. The curse
of the gods falls upon Orestes and Oedipus: it makes their
grandeur; they are criminals led by divine hands. Neither
of them is deceived as to the meaning of his destiny. Orestes
flees, Oedipus puts out his own eyes. But cruel though their
world may be, it preserves its balance and its unity. The
unwritten laws remain strongest of all. Antigone is greater
than Creon. Man collapses but the gods stand erect. The
boldness of thought, the movement of revolt among the Greek
tragic writers do not go so far as to question the order of
the universe. On the contrary, for them sorrow has a re-

deeming virtue. The Classical world did not really feel it
was crumbling until the time of Seneca's Tragedies, nor the
modern world feel it was free until Machiavelli's day.

What a strange collocation of names to assist an inquiry
into the Jacobean Drama—that of a second-rate dramatist
remembered only in histories of literature, and that of a
politician who made a failure of his life and whose reputation
is somewhat unsavoury! On this point my own convictions,
formed long ago, are confirmed and strengthened by the
profound observations of Miss Ellis-Fermor.[5] If some meaning
is to be found in the plays written between Marlowe's day
and Webster's, it is from 'the melodramatic hotch-potch' of
Seneca (as it has been unjustly called) and the Florentine
Nicolas Machiavelli's manual on the conduct of princes (the
sincerest and most precise ever written) that we may receive
most assistance.

6

The vogue and influence of Machiavelli were the result of a
misunderstanding. For how can it be supposed that the
Elizabethan dramatists were attracted from the first by his
harsh thinking, his calculating though bold cast of mind, his
materialism apparently insensible to the highest, most disinterested aspirations of the human soul, his implacable examination of motives, his cold, deliberate assault on the
citadel of medieval thought, the absence of all excitement
in the controlled passion of his grave appeal to the Italian
people for unity? His influence and vogue continued to grow
throughout the Jacobean Age, and the 'Machiavellian' character—the villain of melodrama—embellished and developed,
became one of the essential dramatic types, often the mainspring of the plot, the bearer of messages, possessed of a
philosophy, great stature and impressive character. Sometimes he achieved the heights of stoicism. Originally, he was
nothing but the typical villain, or the diligent, cruel thruster,
subtle and full of stratagems, like the Vice of the Morality
Plays. He could, indeed, like Kyd's Lorenzo, speak in the
accents of tragedy, but he had no coherent philosophy of
life. He helped the plot along, but was far from being the
life and soul of its incidents. Here again, however, Marlowe
proved himself a bold precursor, taking over the Machiavellian system, deformed though it was by the time it reached
him, and breathing life into it.

[5] Una Ellis-Fermor, *The Jacobean Drama.*

A French translation of *The Prince* had appeared in 1553 and a version in Latin (the language of the educated and the philosophers, let us not forget) in 1560. Moreover, Innocent Gentillet, by his *Discours contre Machiavel* (1576), had added to the celebrity of the doctrine, even though he had considerably deformed it. *The Prince,* written by an Italian for Italians, nevertheless represents the first and most sagacious attempt of modern thought to set man free from the tutelage of medieval thought, alike in the political, the social and the religious spheres. Medieval thought had supplied a complete explanation of the world. Social forms, political conceptions and institutions were backed by metaphysical ideas which, whatever the real state of affairs, were valid for everybody. The code of honour, for example, was the same for the sovereign as for the meanest of his subjects. The virtues were indivisible, as fragrant in the poor as in the rich. Knight and churl thought the same of death. The Divine Right of Kings admitted of doubt neither for the usurper nor for the supplanted, and the executioner knelt before his victim.

The miracle of faith achieves and preserves spiritual unity, which keeps its balance—constantly threatened by the possibility of excesses which Christian dualism seems to allow—despite all trials and assaults. The corruptible body and the immortal soul are reconciled at the moment of their separation, for so God's immutable decrees ordain. For Machiavelli these are outworn forms of thought, contradicted by historical evolution and by the contemporary state of affairs. The moral and the social systems of the Middle Ages were no longer in accord with the facts. Politics and metaphysics were two divergent activities, the apparent unity of which was maintained only by lies and hypocrisy. To discern men's true nature, the naked reality must be grasped and abstractions discarded: it was no longer a battlefield between the body and the soul trying to bring it into subjection (those two enemies whom the humanists had temporarily reconciled). Rather it was 'a source of energy thrown for a time into the social world and carried by a secret power towards goals which are not so much steady aims as illusions that man erects for himself, to satisfy his irreconcilable need for action'.

The author of this phrase, which I quote from his introduction[6] to a recent edition of *The Prince* and which might have been written about a hero of Marlowe's, adds the following passage from Machiavelli:

[6] Yves Lévy's Introduction to Machiavelli's *The Prince* (Cluny edition).

In misfortune he (Man) is afflicted, in good fortune he is bored. And from both these feelings spring the same effects; for whenever men do not have to fight from necessity, they fight from ambition which is so strong in the human heart that it never leaves them, however high the station they reach. The reason is that Nature so created men that they can desire everything yet cannot obtain everything.

Man, then, is born for action and not for meditation nor to lose himself in the maze of self-analysis and repentance. It was on the forms of this action that Machiavelli was now to throw a crude light. To say that the Florentine's first quality was candour may seem paradoxical: Machiavellianism came almost from the very first to mean lying and hypocrisy. But Machiavelli wanted to free from this hypocrisy the conscience of man, the man who interested him most, namely the man of action, the head of the State. He based his rule of conduct on a frank acceptance of the wicked and vicious nature of men: 'men do not go in the direction of Good unless they are forced to by necessity',[7] or again 'as it is my intention to write things profitable to those who will hear them, it has seemed to me more proper to follow the truth of facts than certain speculations . . . the life one leads is so different from the life one ought to lead that he who leaves what is for what ought to be done effects sooner his ruin than his preservation; for whoever wants to make wholehearted profession of being a good man cannot avoid being destroyed among so many others who are worthless.'[8]

Later, but on the same page, examining the ways, vicious or virtuous, by which the Prince may win blame or praise, but concerned above all for the good conduct of government, Machiavelli adds: 'And especially let not the Prince fear to incur blame for those vices without which he cannot easily preserve his States; for if one considers everything carefully, one will find something which *seems* to be virtue, and to follow it would be ruin; and something else which *seems* to be vice, but ultimately security and prosperity come of it.'[9] Although these formulas have not the brutality of the famous *Oderint dum metuant,* the Prince, faced with the alternative of being loved or feared, must resolutely prefer hatred to love:

Here a question arises whether it be better to be loved than feared or feared than loved. I answer that both are necessary, but as it is very difficult to unite them in one person, it is

[7] *Discorsi,* I, 3.
[8] *The Prince,* Chapter XV.
[9] ibid.

much safer to make oneself feared than loved if there has to
be a choice. For one thing can generally be said of all men:
that they are ungrateful, fickle, dissimulating, cowardly, greedy
of gain. While you shower benefits upon them, they are all
yours, they offer you their blood, their goods, their lives and
their children, as I said above, when there is no need of
these; but when matters are urgent, they object. And the
Prince who relies solely on their word is lost if he is totally
without other resources; for friendships acquired by bribery
and not by greatness or nobility of mind deserve to be tested,
but their promises are not kept and they cannot be used at
need. Men have less scruple in harming one who makes himself loved than another who makes himself feared, for love is
maintained by a bond of obligation which, because men are
wicked, is broken when an opportunity of private advantage
offers; but fear is maintained by a dread of punishment which
never fails. Nevertheless, the Prince should make himself so
feared that, if he does not win friendship, at least he avoids
enmity.[10]

The whole of Chapter XVIII is also full of terrible dynamite.
Never before had the human mind turned such a crude and
destructive light upon the moral conscience. Until Machiavelli's day men had secretly repudiated the sins they affected
to indulge. Before God's Judgment Seat they disavowed and
cursed them. But for Machiavelli the dual nature was not
that of angel and beast but of man and beast. It is 'necessary
for the Prince to know how to act the beast and the man',[11]
and Machiavelli finds a new meaning in the fable of Chiron
the Centaur, on which 'some great nobles of time past' had
been brought up:

Having thus for teacher one who was half-beast, half-man
simply means that a Prince must know how to use both natures, and that one cannot endure without the other. Since,
therefore, a Prince must know how to use the beast, he
should choose the fox and the lion, for the lion cannot defend
himself against the snares or the fox against the wolves, and
so he must be a fox to discover the snares and a lion to
make the wolves afraid. Those who rely merely on the lion
do not understand what they are about. The wise lord cannot keep faith when such observance may be turned against
him, and the causes which led him to promise no longer exist.
If all men were good, my precept would be void; but as they
are bad and would not keep faith with you, you need not
keep faith with them either. . . . And even, I shall make bold
to say that to have them (the virtues) and always to observe
them is harmful, but that pretending to have them is useful;
just as to appear merciful, faithful, humane, upright, religious,
and to be so but with a mind so framed that, should you re-

[10] ibid., Chapter XVII.
[11] ibid.

quire not to be so, you may be able and know how to change to the opposite.[12]

It is legitimate, therefore, and much more profitable that the Prince 'who organizes a Republic and ordains its laws, necessarily presupposes that all men are evil and will try to exercise the malignity of their instincts whenever a favourable opportunity offers'.[13]

This realistic interpretation of society, not content with raising bad faith to a principle of government, is logically led to take the most sacred things and make them serve the same purpose. Thus religion itself must be merely a means of making peoples more docile and easy to govern. Christianity, which had brought about the immense revolution of love and established moral progress upon the major virtue of charity, finds itself reduced to being the instrument of a prince as if it were idolatry or superstition. Machiavelli's pitiless analysis makes him responsible for this decline of the high virtues of old—courage, high-mindedness, resolution, firmness of character—for realistic and immediate ends, virtues of which only the palest reflection subsists among modern men who have too long been taught that their kingdom was not of this world.

> Our religion (says Machiavelli[14]) has glorified humble and contemplative men more than men of action. It has, in fact, proclaimed that the sovran good lay in abject humility and the despising of things human; whereas the other (the old religion) placed it rather in high-mindedness, in vigour of body and all those other things which tend to make men valiant. And if our religion never recommends force to us, it wants us to be readier to suffer than to do a great deed. This way of life, consequently, seems to have debilitated the world and to have delivered it up to wicked men. They are sure to have control of it, knowing that most men, to get to Heaven, think more of submitting to blows than of avenging them.

And Machiavelli puts in the forefront of the Prince's qualities that famous *virtù*—at once strength of character and resolution, intelligence and clear-sightedness, courage and promptness of decision—which will enable him to fulfil his high duty as chief in the most difficult circumstances. In the complicated, subtle or brutal play of historic facts which Machiavelli refers to under the vague term 'Fortune', success belongs to him who makes up his mind with lightning speed and has an almost instinctive sense of the best conduct

[12] ibid., Chapter XVIII.
[13] *Discorsi*, I, 3.
[14] *Discorsi*, I, 2.

to adopt (mistakes are fatal, as we see in Caesar Borgia), and an unlimited ambition for his country. It is known that the historical model for the Prince was Caesar Borgia, a man of decision if ever there was one, and utterly unscrupulous. The amazing career of the young *condottiere* filled Italy with the fame of his insolent successes and afforded Machiavelli the most realistic and—till he made fatal mistakes—profitable example of that *virtù* which was to assure Italy's salvation.

Now it was at this point that the doctrine of the Prince was misinterpreted by its Elizabethan admirers. Moved by a blazing patriotism, the first Italian to have imagined and felt in his inmost heart the need for uniting and unifying an Italy divided into twenty principalities tearing each other to pieces, ravaged by faction, a battlefield for foreigners whose greed was whetted by the least sign of weakness or dissension, or the slightest hint of an invitation to intervene —Machiavelli wrote with the aim of uniting and unifying this Italy under a strong and capable leader. He sought nothing but a political solution for a problem apparently insoluble until this unity had been achieved. We have only to read the admirable Chapter XXVI of *The Prince* to feel the quivering of hope which raises the normally cold, analytical style of Machiavelli to the most moving eloquence:

> This opportunity, therefore, should not be allowed to pass, that Italy may see her liberator at last appear. I cannot sufficiently declare with what great affection he would be received in all these Italian cities which have suffered from foreign invasions, with what thirst for revenge, with what stubborn faith, what devotion, what tears. Where is the gate that would be closed against him? Where, the people that would refuse him obedience? Where, the envy that would hinder him? What Italian would refuse him homage? [15]

If only the Medicis had understood!

The Elizabethan dramatists failed to remember this grandiose vision of a country aspiring to unity in blood and tears, or to associate political realism—immediately baptized 'Machiavellianism'—with historical necessities. But they remembered the interpretation—pessimistic to the point of cynicism—of the world and the characteristics of the ambitious, brutal hypocrite who intends to make his way in life by any means. They remembered the amoral basis of the doctrine, when it had not even the burning temptation of patriotism as a justification. Any man of well-tempered character, whatever his station in life, and for purely selfish motives, could now claim for himself the rights of the Prince.

[15] *The Prince,* Chapter XXVI *ad fin.*

Machiavelli, the cleric who betrayed humanism and whose treachery was to echo down the centuries of history, filling some with alarm, and others with enthusiasm, believed that he was engaged in a work of piety. In fact, his work proved to be merely a breviary of *arrivisme,* compared with which Bacon's, coming later and much more timidly, was simply an elegant missal. The first result of circulating *The Prince* outside Italy was that English dramatists were given a corpus of doctrine and a personage who would put it into action.

We can understand now the attraction which this doctrine and this man had for minds which were setting themselves to probe the motives of human conduct, and that it was entertaining to bring on to the stage personages driven of necessity to action by the law of this genre, especially in an age of growth, spiritual restlessness and unparalleled curiosity. The powerful lever of ambition raised the new world and here the fact was recognized. English history, reports from abroad, contemporary news-items provide a hundred examples of men brought thus into prominence by *virtù,* made subtle by their craftiness, cruel by their cynicism, yet admirable by their courage. They lived on lies and audacity, hurling defiance at Fate, flouting both human and divine law, rising to great heights and then, like young Mortimer, knowing how to die stoically. This brings them into line with the Senecan hero who is the obverse side of their medal. 'Base fortune', cries Mortimer when he is led out to execution,

> Now I see, that in thy wheele
> There is a point, to which when men aspire,
> They tumble headlong downe: that point I touchte,
> And seeing there was no place to mount up higher,
> Why should I greeve at my declining fall?
> *Edward II,* Act V, vi

Machiavelli haunts Marlowe, so much so that he asks him to serve as Prologue to his *Jew of Malta,* and Machiavelli-Prologue is surprised to find himself playing this strange part: 'But whither am I bound', he exclaims after a tirade of personal apology more or less full of 'Machiavellian' phrases:

> Though some speake openly against my bookes,
> Yet will they reade me, and thereby attaine
> To Peter's Chayre . . .
> I count Religion but a childish Toy,
> And hold there is no sinne but Ignorance . . .
> Might first made Kings . . .
> *Prologue to The Jew of Malta,*
> spoken by Machiavelli, *passim.*

He bethinks himself that he has come not to read a lecture in Britain but to present to the public the personage of Barabbas who owes his fabulous wealth as much to his own industry as to the application of the Florentine's principles. Moreover, Barabbas is really only a melodramatic degradation of the rascally Machiavelli type, cruel with frenzy, just as Mortimer is drawn with cynical pride and only the grossest traits: 'Fear'd am I more than lov'd;—let me be fear'd', he exclaims arrogantly.

The Duke of Guise in *The Massacre at Paris*, who owed his bad reputation in England as much to his fanatical Catholicism as to the part he played in the Massacre of St. Bartholomew, is no doubt the most finished study of the Machiavelli type that Marlowe attempted. Double-dealing and insensitive, cruel to the point of committing atrocities, clear-minded and calculating, he has, in addition, the purpose (*virtù*) for great designs:

> . . . at last I have learn'd
> That perill is the cheefest way to happiness,
> And resolution honors fairest aime . . .
> That like I best that flyes beyond my reach.
> *The Massacre at Paris*, Act I

He covets the diadem with a 'quenchless thirst', and the burning grandiloquence of his opening monologue, from which these lines are quoted, equals Tamburlaine's own. But he has, furthermore, intelligence and contempt for fools:

> For this, this head, this heart, this hand and sworde,
> Contrives, imagines and fully executes
> Matters of importe, aimede at by many,
> Yet understoode by none.

He dies with the same grandeur as Mortimer, a curse on his lips, haughtier than Caesar, regretting only that his vengeance escapes him.

It is difficult to say how far Marlowe's own thought is identified with that of the pseudo-Machiavelli, to whom he is the first to give an essential part in his Drama. But the strange fascination is to be noted that this sinister personage had for Marlowe and others, and the persistence with which Marlowe's example was followed. On the whole, it is not so much the dramatic value of the Machiavelli type which drives the play and compels the attention, as the human experience of which he is the active symbol that carries the play's message. For him life has a certain meaning and his acts are merely the application of his principles. The dramatist puts this interpretation to the decisive test of facts, and almost always the result is failure.

'Men can desire everything yet cannot obtain everything.' Once raised to the summit of power and glory, riches, pleasure and crime, they fall rapidly and inevitably. Was the world wrong, then, or the theory? Were there still spiritual values which Machiavelli had made the mistake of neglecting? Had everything to be brought into question again? Would even that be useless? For the personage to preserve his human value and be psychologically credible, or simply possible from the dramatic point of view, he must end with a cry of rage and a curse, or by a death-bed repentance, an abjuration: this might not save him from being struck down like a wild beast, but at least the salvation of his soul, or what remained of it, would be assured. The hero plunges into damnation or the equivocal mists of a possible redemption. In any case, the proof is there: Machiavelli's system has been put to the test and has failed.

The period of blasphemous negation, of carefree cynicism and of stoicism insulting over weakness or cowardice, is also the period which gives even melodrama the most authentically dramatic note: the ultimate recognition of the spiritual values marks the fruitless but moving return to an order of things that has been abolished. This is virtually the road travelled between Marlowe and Webster: from an arrogant gaiety that has nothing to repudiate, down to that flabbiness of soul which, after all the struggle and the tension, comes to terms with pessimism and faith. Such, it may be, are the human ills 'that flesh is heir to'.

The Machiavelli type, the man of iron, absolute, incorruptible, is much more a creature of the imagination, imperfect and fallible, than a dramatic reality. There is no perfect example unless it be Webster's Cardinal in *The Duchess of Malfi*. Greene objects to this 'pest'. Chapman merely sketches its superficial traits. Ben Jonson at once perverts it with refinement and surpasses it. Shakespeare, who is also an heir of the Marlowe tradition, sometimes, like Marlowe, carves out a Machiavellian villain—a Richard of Gloucester grinning over his victories or fighting frenziedly to his last gasp: 'A horse, a horse, my kingdom for a horse!' At other times, with the lightest of touches Shakespeare will sketch the Don John of *Much Ado about Nothing*. Or again, using his own technique, he will draw an Iago limited in scope and inadequately motivated, an evil thing gnawing at the flesh of Othello whose eyes not even the dazzling light

of grief and grace can open. Or yet again, as in *King Lear*,
the fact of Edmund's bastardy is introduced, like Richard
III's deformity, to combine in one minor personage the
colourful blemishes of the soul and Fate.

But Shakespeare is too clear-sighted, his vision embraces
too many diverse objects, to regard the Machiavelli type
as anything more than one experiment among many. If some
of his great heroes, such as Macbeth, are tinged with Machiavellianism, it is merely a trait, not a complete picture, and
their greatness lies elsewhere. In none of Shakespeare's Machiavellian characters does the tone of their language, the
quivering passion of their speech, lead us to suppose that he
considers their solutions of life's problems valid. But the
personage cannot be ruled out even if he appear only to be
ridiculed, punished or pardoned in the end.

Webster, on the contrary, is the Jacobean who is most
interested in the Machiavelli type. Flamineo, Bosola, the
Cardinal and Romelio are, after Marlowe's, the most finished
and detailed portraits of it that we possess. They are, it is
true, merely supernumeraries to the major characters whom
Webster creates full of ardour and bearing the heaviest re-
sponsibilities in face of life's moral and metaphysical problems. But these supernumeraries are not the traditional,
technical accidentals, thrown in to complicate the plot or
to enhance by contrast the greater brilliancy of the major
characters. They are alive, active, individual, clear-cut and
not lacking in *virtù*. We feel that Webster wants to probe
the full extent of their experience and their philosophy of
life. His curiosity in regard to them is as keen as Marlowe's
but less passionate, more discriminating. Marlowe seizes upon
the Machiavelli type with the undistinguishing appetite of a
starving youth, and the headstrong mind of one who has not
yet discovered the depth of his disillusionments.

Webster seeks to rebuild a world hopelessly divided, and
he strives for truth, not for conquest. His own mind seeks
in vain to escape the dichotomy. The quality common to all
his personages, even among the humblest, is indeed resolution, courage and what is nowadays called 'pluck'. But light
comes only slowly to them, thanks to the clash between
action and thought, the thought convulsive at first, even
when premeditated, and gradually gaining self-knowledge
which brings out their real nature and the real meaning of
life. Then the result may be a blinding revelation ('mine
eyes dazzle', says Ferdinand beside the dead body of his
sister, in *The Duchess of Malfi*), or a plunge into madness
and remorse (the lycanthropy of Ferdinand, the sudden con-

version of Bosola), or again the tardy revelation that all hope of atonement and salvation is illusory.

Other characters remain steadfast in the old faith, in the midst of swirling violence, and regard with terror, disgust or anger aberrations that destroy the soul. This sound but timid and powerless reaction in the course of the play triumphs in the end over the debris of accumulated treachery or brutality. When the protagonists have been vanquished the Chorus expresses satisfaction and takes charge of the future, but how many corpses litter the stage! The moral is that, after all, it is far from certain that the Machiavellian interpretation of the universe, however attractive it may be to man torn by the anguish of action, offers a coherent system, despite the tenacity with which the characters try to answer life's problems, and in spite of the stoicism that crowns their career they are hurled into the abyss or enveloped in the cold mist of death.

In this lies the supreme effort made by Jacobean thought to assimilate an unsatisfying and unhealthy doctrine, the essence of which it fails to grasp, but which answered an urgent need for co-ordinating in one new system the revolutionary data of a disappointing universe. Under the form of Machiavelli man reappears and, with him, pity, anguish, grief. The mask is torn, the grimace contorts the face even when man clenches his teeth and exhibits, like Webster's Cardinal on the threshold of eternity, the supreme elegance of reticence:

> . . . How tedious is a guilty conscience . . .
> When I look in the fish-ponds in my garden,
> Methinks I see a thing armed with a rake
> That seems to strike at me.
>   *Duchess of Malfi*, V, v.

7

The Jacobean world was out of joint. Machiavellianism, no doubt, was the only response that it could offer to the demands of reason if it hoped to avoid sterility and despair. But the response proved powerless to reconcile irreconcilables. Spirit, Matter—the two co-exist and, like the emanations of some subterranean fire which the piling up of lava cannot extinguish, the nostalgic smoke of the inner flame pierces the uneven crust of imperfect resolution. Weariness creeps in, discouragement oppresses those who do not plunge heart and soul into Matter, and who are beset by ingratitude, injustice, treachery, violence and cruelty. The best of characters are weighed down by the consciousness of imperfection, of the impossibility of a perfect world. There are so many pitfalls, such a swarming of vice, a sabbath of witches riding men's foul egotisms, a mad rhythm of passions in pursuit of power and pleasure, ending dizzily with the hero crushed against the wall.

Stygian darkness and sulphurous vapours, blood-baths, lightning flashes of madness, the tortures of Tantalus, the rock of Sisyphus in a nightmare landscape, a universal falsification of values, crime and suffering, evil everywhere triumphant—to say of such a world, in 1602, that 'there's something rotten in the state of Denmark' would indeed be a euphemism. The breath of defeat which passed over this darkened world was to blow up into a hurricane, sweeping all before it on the blasted heath where Lear is stripped of all. It was night—the night of the Senecan tragedy, with its powerful poetry revived and *felt* by the Jacobeans.

Oedipus's partial suicide, the 'shower of blood' streaming from his blinded eyes, is the self-inflicted punishment of one who is appalled by his own crimes: it redeems him and raises him to the stature of the gods. Gloucester's bloody eye-sockets radiate horror for horror's sake, like the gloomy banquet of Thyestes, Hercules's blind massacre or Medea's sadistic cruelty. How, then, could death fail to be hailed as a liberator to be desired, to be loved, to be rushed towards: 'Out, out brief candle' . . . 'the rest is silence'?

Seneca, indeed, had already been the darling of the Elizabethans. Far more than the Greeks, he had been their classical model, the god of the theatre, upon whom the dramatists had fixed their wondering gaze. In imitation of him they had forged their weapons, and as pupils they had sat at the Master's feet. But, as often happens to imitators emulating their admired exemplar, they were deaf to the powerful accents of his voice: they could not understand its inner meaning. They copied externals rather than absorbed the spirit.

Here was robust, violent, realistic tragedy, full of wise saws which the Latin rhetors and philosophers had made so familiar that they had lost their real significance. It was Tragedy carefully studied in its form, very learned, adorned by subtle and vigorous stylistic effects; its rhetoric now thunderous, now polite; its characters unbridled in their passions, gigantic in stature, raised to sublime heights by the enormity of their legendary crimes or sufferings; besmeared with blood, wrapped in horror, hunted by fatality; at the mercy of their rage, their revenge, their love, the haughty familiars of Death. Superhuman personages, tragedy of the sublime, rhetorical poetry on the verge of bad taste and the grandiloquent—in short, drama that attracts and dazzles, an unchallenged model which fixes the limits and the laws of tragedy.

But the Jacobeans dragged Seneca, so to speak, out of his own time, separated him from his period and ignored the deeper reasons which made his tragedies what they are. It was not their spirit which appealed to his imitators but their technique, the forms of style, the rhetorical figures, the word-play, the trappings. Seneca served them as a store-house of stage properties, a retail-shop for the mannered or the sublime of which he is a master. Passages rather than plots were borrowed from him, surface elaboration rather than depth of feeling, *sententiae* rather than philosophy, and all the tricks of style from hyperbole to stichomythia, not to mention anaphora and antithesis, the precious or the bombastic, the subtle or the pompous. There was less of his essence, less re-creation of his particular vision of the world from which the Elizabethan Drama in its fruitful period of growth obviously had no need to borrow.

In appearance, from *Gorboduc* (1561) to *Titus Andronicus* (1592) or *Richard II* and *Richard III* (1592-5), including of course Kyd's *Spanish Tragedy* and Marlowe's play, it was the same forces which impelled Tragedy—curiosity and admiration, terror and pity, above all, horror (which Seneca overdid), clutching at the heartstrings and curdling the blood. In all his plays there are atrocious crimes, unnatural passions, personages superhuman in their hate and their evil, frenzied tyrants, kings and queens in captivity or exile, bloodless ghosts crying out for vengeance, necromancers, fortune-tellers and soothsayers, innocent victims, tortured victims defying death, arrogant criminals, brothers at enmity with each other. It is a joyous orgy of the horrible, which does not yet raise great problems or oppress the mind: such a chain of fury and crime, so close to earth, is an exuberant invention: it provides no answers to harrowing questions about the meaning of life, the reality of the universe or ideas of good and evil.

Or, again, there were simple learner's imitations like those of Daniel, or Kyd's translations adapted from Garnier, Seneca's French follower.[16]

Seneca's great shadow falls across the whole half-century of preparation for Tragedy, and none escaped his influence. But, once the stage of initiation was passed, Seneca was

[16] For example, *Cornelia* (1593).

turned to again, though with clearer and more penetrating
eyes. His dark sun with its blood-red rays still shone with
sustained brilliance, and now his light harmonized with the
uncertain twilight of the threatened years at the close of
the sixteenth century and the troubled dawn of the seventeenth. His bag of tricks had been emptied, all the old
tragic writer's devices were now familiar and it was realized
that there was still matter and thought and poetry to be
found in him.

The stoic attitude to suffering and death is the only one
that can save the criminal hero, ill dealt with by destiny,
from an ignominious end. The 'tragic' speeches, the rivers
of blood rumble and flow no longer merely for the sake
of effect. It so happens that Seneca's ideas, expressed in
'sentences' full of wisdom and disillusionment, correspond
with those of the Jacobeans about the fall of man, dis-
abused as they were by a Machiavellianism which had failed
to assure the hero's salvation. Seneca sounds the death-
knell of a decadent society, of a collapsing metaphysical
system, a debased morality, an empire in ruins. His tragedy
is a twilight of the gods as well as of men. The fire of
Rome is reflected in it; one feels in it 'the morbid and
depraved taste of Nero's contemporaries for fine crimes and
unnatural passions',[17] the anguish and the doubt obscuring
faith in an immanent justice. The innocent perish without
valid reason, the gods themselves are chained by Destiny
(they are perhaps not even immortal: *et mortis dominus
pertinuit mori*),[18] humanity is decadent and nothing can
save it; the Golden Age, long disappeared, is merely a sad
theme for nostalgic regrets.

The end of the world, on the other hand, threatens fallen
humanity—a preoccupation common to Seneca the philosopher and Seneca the writer of tragedies. It was a theme
which haunted his contemporaries also:

> A day will come when all the laws of the universe will be
> overthrown: the South Pole will crush all Libya, all the land
> of the nomad Garamantes; the North Pole will crush all that
> is beneath it and that the dry Boreas beats down upon; and
> the trembling Sun will be dislodged from the sky, bringing
> light to an end; the heavenly palace in its fall will bring down
> East and West, all the gods will perish and collapse in the

---

[17] Léon Herrmann, *Le Théâtre de Sénèque* (Les Belles Lettres), p. 469. I
refer the reader to this excellent study of Seneca which, however, to my
mind does not do sufficient justice to the poetry of the great Latin tragic
writer.
[18] *Hercules Furens*, 1. 565.

general chaos. Last of all, Death will pronounce the final sentence of extinction against itself.[19]

The Chorus in *Thyestes* takes up the theme and develops it with powerful poetry:

> The Sun at its setting is surprised to find the Dawn: he forces darkness to arise before Night is ready; no stars come out, there is no light in the firmament, nor does the Moon dispel the inspissated gloom. Whatever this portent may be (would it were really night!), our hearts tremble, stricken with intense fear lest the whole universe collapse in fragments in the general ruin, lest chaos should come again and overwhelm both gods and men, and earth and sea be engulfed with the wandering planets scattered over the sky. . . . So, out of all the generations it is we who have been found deserving of such a fate, to be crushed in the fall of the disrupted heavens! It is we who are caught by the end of the world! O cruel destiny that we should be born to such misfortune, whether we lost the Sun or drove it away. But a truce to our laments. Fear, begone! . . . Not to consent to die when the universe perishes with us is to be too avid of life.[20]

Here is indeed complete despair, the ultimate dead-end where man's only recourse is to the stoic acceptance of his destiny. 'Fear, begone!' The atmosphere is so charged, the darkness so thick, heaven and earth so thrown out of their courses, that the hero moves in a slime of mud and blood, whence the only possible issue, the supreme test, is escape into nothingness; the only salvation, complete contempt for death: *contempsit omnes ille qui mortem prius*.[21] We are at the extreme limit of what gods and men can desire, or will undergo: to rush into vengeance, like Atreus or Medea, with but one regret—that the imagination cannot invent a yet more atrocious crime—to destroy the loved one, a Dejanira or a Phaedra, because love and jealousy can be satisfied, like hatred, only by destruction; to throw oneself upon one's sword—*libet ire in enses*—or, like Hercules, rear one's own funeral pyre and offer to the devouring flames one's battered limbs, one's heart consumed by the crueller fire of shame and despair, to triumph finally over the gods themselves and Fate—*Inferna vice rursus, Alcides, loca*.[22]

And the gigantic figure of Hercules towers over the gods in their assembly, a symbol of Wisdom triumphant through courage and through scorn of evil, suffering and death itself which, once it comes, is nothing. Moreover, the chorus of

[19] *Hercules Oetaeus*, ll. 1102 *et seq.*
[20] *Thyestes*, ll. 822 *et seq.*
[21] *Hercules Oetaeus*, l. 443.
[22] ibid., l. 1976.

Trojan women declares in accents equally moving, if less
consolatory: 'After death there is nothing—death itself is
nothing, only the ultimate bourne of our dizzy career. O
avaricious ones, quit your hopes, quit your fears, O anxious
ones! . . . Greedy time and chaos swallow us up. Death
cannot be divided; it is an evil that is inherent in the body
and that does not spare the soul either.' [23]

Seneca's mind, like that of the Jacobeans, is profoundly
divided. This sage, who narrowly missed greatness, lived in
a world of evil, the clear-sighted and disillusioned observer
of a great empire's impending fall. The only spiritual values
still operative in the immense disorder that afflicted the
soul were those which steel it and make it greater through
suffering and through indifference to Fate. The virtuous hero
may believe in the survival of his virtues at the very heart
of his trials and may throw down to annihilation the challenge of his own greatness. But he who is passion's slave
and finds in their frenzy alone that touch of the sublime
which makes the superman, is doomed to spiritual self-
destruction.

The morality is terrible and it was not understood or felt
by Seneca's early admirers. Gradually they drew level with
him. Tamburlaine is immoral with his every breath. He
does not deliberately work out his destiny; he is like Victor
Hugo's Hernani, a driving force. A joyous, healthy tyrant,
sated with victories and cruelties, he has neither desire nor
leisure to probe his human imperfection. But Macbeth enters
upon crime with cunning, muffled steps. He needs to intoxi-
cate himself with delirious words, and his invocations—
though less rhetorical, more fraught with meaning than those
of Medea or Atreus—have all the equivocal sound of the
enchantress's which are echoed by Lady Macbeth, or of
the dreadful son of Pelops, generator of appalling crimes.

Now it was no longer a question of pillage or of imitation.
Seneca's thought, scattered through many works, popularized
and presented in a normal setting, is of less importance for
its content than for its tone. The lyric note which appeals
more directly than the moral aphorisms, sounds differently
in the Jacobeans, but it sounds in all of them. It colours their
vision of the world, it exacerbates their passions, it governs
the plots and their *dénouements*. Invective, invocations,
incantations; soliloquies in which the hero analyses himself,
probes into his own motives, reaches his decisions, apostro-
phizes the cruel or the protecting gods; disillusioned reflections, cries of despair, rhetoric no longer purely hollow

[23] *Troades*, ll. 397 *et seq.*

but seeking to express the very substance of the soul's drama
—all this is to be found in Jacobean plays. The atmosphere
is heavy, thick, charged with threatening symbols. Everywhere a gale blows, bracing the will of the strong, sweeping away the weak, devastating every prospect. There is no
denying it: the tone is one of utter despair.

At great crises, confronted with the insoluble problem of
his triumph or his fall, of his triumph *in* his fall, the
Jacobean hero mocks, curses, wilfully mutilates himself. He
resorts to inflammatory words, flashing images, a breathless,
sustained rhythm, for the supreme justification of his attitude. The stars, the seasons, witchcraft, Nature, disease provide him with metaphors which best give him the fullest
understanding of his malady. He conjures with stars, Hell,
fallen gods, cataclysms, hurricanes. He attains that profound
reality of things which poetry alone can reach and which
alone can reach us. So the bombastic and brutal old Seneca,
the vampire who sucked blood from the Greek tragic writers,
borrowing their very scraps and making something magnificent out of even their defects because, no doubt, he expected
Tragedy to express and ennoble his own misfortunes—
Seneca became in his turn a veritable inspiration. The
Jacobeans drew life from him also, carrying still further
than he the magnitude of horror, but altering its images,
re-creating for themselves that dangerous universe where a
malevolent fate and passion overpower man's strength.

Thwarted love loses itself in the brutal emptiness of death,
degenerates into a perfidious or mad tyrant, a 'green-eyed
monster' in hot pursuit of his prey, preparing with refinement his own destruction; ambition welds crimes together,
link by link, into an infernal, blood-bespattered chain, and
step by step moves towards the abyss; revenge lights its
torches, rears its furious locks, while grisly shades, rising
from their graves, utter in harsh, strident tones, their ineluctable commands to the hesitant and terrified—everywhere
crime leading to crime, to blasphemy, to annihilation. And
those heroes who are unsullied are too frail of spirit to resist the incessant onset of evil. Some, of finer metal, discard
their integrity and fall to cursing in their turn, like Timon of
Athens. Others, less robust, find their escape only in madness, as for example Lear, the fond and foolish old man
whose reason is blinded by the revelation in a lightning-
flash of his daughters' wickedness; or Ophelia, who is reduced to a pathetic, gentle madness by the sarcasms of
Hamlet's despair. Others, again, whom one might have
expected to be more resistant and implacable, are van-

quished without knowing it in the chiaroscuro of their conscience—and Lady Macbeth seeks to wash the spot of
blood from her little hand. But all of them see chaos, universal disorder, love baffled, honour betrayed, evil triumph-
ing over good, the hideous crushing the beautiful, ignominy
besmirching virtue, suffering and death sure of their powerless victims.

Such are the fundamental themes. They are found again
in the tragedies of Chapman whose ambitious heroes, frantic
individualists, brought low by Destiny, aspire to some kind
of an apotheosis; in Marston, who depicts vigorously, if
somewhat incoherently, characters owing as much to Machiavelli as to Seneca, and who borrows here and there a passage, a run of images which obscure the background of his
picture; in Middleton who, despite his sense of comedy and
his penetrating analysis of feminine character, brings to
inevitable destruction criminals who are not ennobled by
their sufferings. Webster, full of *sententiae,* a divided mind
if ever there was one, master of the pathetic and the horrific,
curiously enamoured of Machiavelli—Webster, whose characters all go to their death with head held high and resolution in their hearts, tries, unsuccessfully, to pierce the mist
of nothingness which shrouds their end. Tourneur, the
most terrible, the most Senecan of them all, for whom the
stars certainly do not shine, insensible to pity, to sympathy,
even to nostalgia for the Beyond, manœuvres his personages
in the thickest darkness, traversed by baleful gleams, peopled
with rotting corpses and ghosts, ruled by a Nature (invoked interminably by d'Amville, 'the atheist') whose laws
devour his victims, driving them to their agony and the
executioner to his own punishment.

If Webster exposes to the horrified eyes of the Duchess
of Malfi the corpses of her children, they are only wax-
figures, worthy of a theatrical Madame Tussaud's. Tourneur
goes still further: he clothes a real corpse, a woman's, attractively, not forgetting rouge on the grinning lips, and
especially not forgetting poison; and in the shade that lends
itself to guilty passions, he offers the lustful Duke-assassin
the lascivious skeleton of his beloved for his convulsive
embraces. This libidinous appetite, tempted by a corpse in
a foul-smelling night, under the eyes of a sadistic, macabre
monster thirsting for vengeance, exceeds in horror the rage
of Medea cutting up her own children. It is a ghastly nightmare, that makes the blood run cold, in which the voices are
metallic and supernatural; a nightmare performed by madmen in an atmosphere of sulphur and death.

Like all his contemporaries, Shakespeare also yielded to the strange attractive magic of evil. A superficial and boisterous Senecan in his Elizabethan period, with *Titus Andronicus* for example, he came to share the spiritual disorders and negations of his day. Hamlet's bitter arguments, Angelo's ambiguities, the invective of Thersites or Timon, Lear's furious sarcasms, the sublime disgust of Macbeth—all this proceeds from the same mood. The conflict between good and evil, ugliness and beauty, innocence and crime, purity and impurity, hope and disgust, love and hate, order and disorder, natural laws and the anarchy produced by the passions—all is resolved in Shakespeare's so-called 'dark period' with an infinite despair.

But Shakespeare could transform this incomprehensible universe. The expression of its metaphysical sickness is always subordinated to a situation from which there is no way out, yet the sickness is as deep-seated, as absolute as it well can be. The heart is fretted in its very substance, Nature's laws are turned upside-down, a being is pulled up by the roots. This human malady attains superhuman proportions; neither faith nor reason can survive it. It is not enough to say with Hamlet 'The time is out of joint': epic deeds must be insulted (Thersites), modesty debased (Angelo), Athens, the city of eternal wisdom, cursed (Timon), the elements defied (Lear), innocence assassinated as it was by Othello, and a Macbeth must descend into the hell of fear, destroying himself, utterly despising life.

8

Thus the atmosphere of Jacobean Drama was fixed in a despiritualized world where, for the time being, the road to hope was denied by the excess of evil. Swept off its feet by the passion for conquest, the Elizabethan Age had bravely trampled underfoot its scruples and apprehensions to secure the triumph of a conception of life full of promise but destined to fail when brought to the test of facts and passions. The impetuous and prosperous Machiavelli type of the early days becomes the Senecan hero, whose traits he already foreshadowed. The double-dealer is enticed into a dark and bloody ambush, and emerges from one horrible night only to enter another, more redoubtable because unknown. The world escapes him and the fatality of evil makes of this Knight of Imposture a martyr of destiny. If some feel regrets or remorse, if they raise their eyes towards the distant constellations of which they dimly perceive the

half-extinct fires, most of them scan the darkness in vain to
find the gateway to salvation.

The thousand doors of death open on the same emptiness.
The same dizziness seizes all. Once he becomes a prey to
the world of matter, Man is completely engulfed in it, and
such clear vision as remains to him increases his torture,
for this world by itself cannot satisfy. One must either
perish in it or attempt the spiritual adventure, repudiating
what one has been and wanted to be. What was unity cannot be content with a compromise. The gulf is too deep
and too wide to be crossed by a casual step: it can only
be over-leaped, without a backward glance. The heavenly
solutions lie elsewhere; further on there is peace. The profane turns its back on the religious without possibility of
reconciliation, and the religious sheds the profane if it wishes
to preserve itself unspotted from the world. Thus the
separation is achieved, the schism completed.

The theatre is the blazing forge where, with weeping and
gnashing of teeth, brothers at enmity consummate their final
quarrel. Marlowe struck the first blow; the Jacobeans finished
the task. Man, wanting to be God in a universe made for
him, risks losing both the kingdoms which he unwisely
separated. The choice has to be made between being
accursed or being redeemed. The first sigh of repentance is
given by Greene at the end of the Elizabethan Age in his
confessions which, it seems to me, are sincere. But the
warning came too soon, or too late. The experiment had to
be made: once committed to the course set by Marlowe,
his successors were bound to go through with it to the
end. They did so. Thus, independence is won, not without
ruin and at the cost of infinite sacrifices.

Driven from the theatre, religious feeling lost ground also
in the philosophic sphere where, first, Bacon, then Locke
and the empiricists—even the idealists—left it but little
hope of recovery. Science also dropped away from religion,
like a ripe fruit, and, outside the ardent group of the playwrights, the pure poets themselves had to choose between
profane exercises and divine inspiration. Donne, after a
stormy youth, abandoned the worldly life: recovering his
faith and washed in the waters of repentance, he reserved
for the service of God the purified poetry of his maturity.
Those who had not wavered in their religious convictions
had put on the strong armour of faith against the assaults
of corruption. Horrified by the insolence of carnal and
intellectual sin, they too turned their backs upon the world-

liness of their day and paved the way for the gloomy Puritan
revolution.

It must be remembered that the first victims of the Round-
heads were the unruly playwrights.[24] It is not enough to
say that their entertainments were a danger to morality:
they were especially so to the mind. Many a trumpet
sounded the charge against Marlowe's 'atheism', but at least
the risk was worth running for the sake of the beauty
gained by his creations. Beauty, however, was the *bête noire*
of the Puritans and remained dangerous: they did not realize
that the tragic period of blasphemy, of disgust, of the refusal to accept life, had passed. There were, of course, other
dangers. Whether or not there had been a breach between
the two generations, whether the theatres had been closed
or not, the dramatic hero was tending to become an Alman-
zor.

For peace of mind was gradually replacing distress.
Twenty years of tension, of extravagant hopes and bitter
disillusionments put a serious strain upon the metabolism
of a generation, even the Elizabethans. The succession to
the throne seemed to be assured, prosperity to have returned, the dangers of revolution and invasion to be removed. The drama of life had turned to tragi-comedy in
which men skirted death without being caught up by it.
If Raleigh's head rolled on the block as late as 1618, that
was because there was an old account to be settled, dating
from 1603. Raleigh, moreover, died, as Essex had died, like
a true Elizabethan. But the notorious trial of Bacon was
merely a case of corruption, at the end of a reign; it did not
involve any inner conflict over the life beyond the grave.

The policy of reconciliation with Spain—pursued first
secretly, then openly, by James—cost Raleigh his head; but
at any rate it had the advantage of keeping war away from
English soil, even if it dealt an irremediable blow at Catholic
prospects in England. The days of the brilliant freebooters'
exploits were over; there were no more Sir Philip Sidneys
to meet chivalrous deaths on the new battlefields of the
Thirty Years' War. James lowered the Crown's prestige but
Parliament thereby gained. The problems now were no
longer spiritual or metaphysical but political and economic:
the spark set to the Puritan revolt was Hampden's determination to pay no taxes that Parliament had not voted.
The colour of heroism was becoming subfusc, the authority

24 The theatres were closed by the Long Parliament in 1642 and not re-
opened until the Restoration in 1660.

of statesmanship degenerating into mere politicians' intrigues; there was caprice instead of firmness in high places. Life was, indeed, still lived with a plume and a brave air—with too much of an air, even when bespattered with the blood of a King.

But it would take us too far to explain how Jacobean Drama ceased to dash its head against the wall of imperfect propositions and solutions. The bitterness of black-hearted heroes was finally dispelled. The scintillating golden hair of the Elizabethans—dulled for a time by Commonwealth clouds—was resplendent again on Buckingham's wig. The end of this age was, indeed, golden in colour. On the yellow sands of Prospero's isle died the dark waves of anger and despair, crime and treason. Ariel led the revels. There was music in the air: it flowed in the heart of Caliban, it moved Prince Charming and led him by its sound to the crossroads of Beauty and Virtue, reconciled by Love. Conspiracies, storms of passion, envy's sharp tooth, the taste for blood, the bitter quarrel with Time and Space, the pangs of mortality, the challenge thrown down to Fate—all are resolved in episodes from which the sting has been drawn.

Shakespeare had been the darkest of the pessimists, as satanic as Marston, as self-divided as Chapman, bloodthirsty as Webster, sinister as Tourneur, mordant as Ben Jonson. But he had escaped damnation by the vigour of his lyrical gift and, no doubt, by the superior balance of his genius. Now, without repudiating his past experience or finding in romantic unreality a quiet refuge for his weary, battered spirit, he glided gradually towards serenity. At the same time that Timon of Athens (1607) uttered his frenzied curses, Cleopatra's suicide was preparing the way for a reawakening of the sense of immortality. Despite their weaknesses and even their defects, Antony and Cleopatra, the most splendid of Shakespeare's heroes, restored the divine element in human love and gave a new lustre to high ambition. Then, from *Pericles* (1608) to *The Tempest* (?1611), anguish progressively gave way to a calmer vision of a world where values that were excluded before, recovered their position. There was still complexity, but its colour had changed. Jealousy remained blind and violent, but the beneficent forces of chance and of men forestalled its deadly blows. Folly was as vile and cruel as ever, but purity evaded its clumsy traps. Treachery, finally, was replaced by the miraculous, and the magic formula no longer confused, in the lightning of a murky sky, the antagonistic aspects of fair and foul. Prospero's anger amounted to no more than the rumblings of a summer storm, in a sky that was once more blue, over a scented and tuneful island.

Others afterwards went further than Shakespeare into the pastoral forest with its romantic incidents where tears have the glint of moonlight and hearts are oppressed in the stifling heat of the stable. Beaumont and Fletcher created an unreal world which tragedy rarely touched and where realism had no place. Twenty years earlier Marlowe had been able to free himself from the influence of Spenser's music which for a time had attracted him, because he had a fiery spirit, a spiritual ambition that could not be satisfied by smooth language. But now the ever-present ambition seemed to be to satisfy nostalgic longings for the beautiful. Even in Tragedy the tragic atmosphere was no longer breathed: only the illusion of tragedy survived when blood flowed under daggers flourished by heroines who found their sins revolting.

The famous Scene ii of Act V of *The Maid's Tragedy,* which carries the dramatic tension so skilfully foward to the stabbing of the libertine king by Evadne in his dissolute bed, strikes us as a *show* of crime arising less from a blind exasperated passion than from the requirements of the subject. How different is the raving of Macbeth in King Duncan's antechamber from the cool, self-possessed soliloquy of Evadne! She feels not a shudder of terror. 'The night grows horrible and all about me like my black purpose', she may say indeed; [25] but it is no longer the night of Inverness, with its evil spells, its horrors lurking in the dense silence. It is a fine and even vigorous scene. But Evadne, however ferocious she may be, is somewhat remote from her crime and her suffering, in those vague regions where *human* suffering and crime lose the colour of reality; they become illusory and touching but do not destroy our faith in the hero who is not responsible for what he suffers.

The narrowest of lines separates tragedy from the tragi-comedy which Fletcher invented and defined. In tragedy people die; in tragi-comedy they skirt death. This is both too much and not enough to say. For surely *Measure for Measure* is a tragedy even though no one dies in it, and there is a world of difference between this play (which defies classification) and the 'tragedy' of Evadne. *Measure for Measure* thrives on the theme of sin and corruption: an equivocal evil attracts and pollutes those who by vocation or professed faith are pure; the impure desire twists the judge's immobile face into a grimace, and the terror of

[25] *The Maid's Tragedy,* Act V, ii.

defilement deforms the virginal features of Isabella more than fear of death. Death, to serve as a bogy, springs from the burning words of Claudio who fears it more, and more cravenly perhaps, than does any other of Shakespeare's creations.

The theme of *The Maid's Tragedy* is also that of the horror of sin and in it the stain is washed away in blood. But it requires the vehemence of a brother—reversing the Claudio-Isabella situation—to awaken the sense of purity and to drive the sinning Evadne to action. Nor, even when the sin is at last revealed, does it cause any distress. The spirit does not grieve under the burden of insoluble contradictions: it has become simple, almost joyful again— the spirit of the dramatist and that of his heroes alike.

It is in tragi-comedy that Beaumont and Fletcher score their successes. Here, indeed, no ambiguity is possible: we are in the fairy-tale world where credibility is no longer bound by the same conventions. I know (and I shall return to this point) that our sense of the credible is severely strained in all the plays of the Elizabethan Age, not only as regards their incidents but particularly in regard to the motives which impel the characters to action. But if the absence of logical continuity in a character's behaviour destroys neither his unity nor his credibility in most plays of the time, it is because neither the plot nor the characters' behaviour requires to be logical. The author pays no attention to psychological probability which is a necessary law of the Classical drama.

In tragi-comedy, on the other hand, Beaumont and Fletcher seem anxious to avoid the reproach of motiveless behaviour in their personages so as to make the liberties taken by their imagination more credible. That Evadne should be changed into a woman bent upon avenging her honour seems surprising enough after Melantius, her brother, has merely pretended to intimidate her.[26] But what are we to say of the fact on which the whole plot of *Philaster* turns, namely the dangerous (but not fatal) jealousy felt by Philaster about Bellario, his mistress's page, who is a woman in disguise? In the forest where the plot becomes involved—a forest foreshadowing the sumptuous scenery of the operas to come—the noble steel of the sword traces moving patterns on the skin but it does not plunge straight

---

[26] *The Maid's Tragedy*, III, i—especially after the admission 'I love my life well' at the end of the scene between the King, her lover, Amintor her husband and herself.

into the heart. Death is no longer the terrifying mystery which made Claudio tremble.

Compare Claudio's terror when he is faced with death:

> Ay, but to die, and go we know not where;
> To lie in cold obstruction and to rot;
> This sensible warm motion to become
> A kneaded clod; and the delighted spirit
> To bathe in fiery floods, or to reside
> In thrilling regions of thick-ribbed ice . . .
>
> *Measure for Measure,* III, i.

with this quiet acceptance of a poeticized death:

Philaster:

> Oh, but thou dost not know
> What 'tis to die.

Bellario:

> Yes, I do know, my lord:
> 'Tis less than to be born; a lasting sleep;
> A quiet resting from all jealousy,
> A thing we all pursue; I know, besides,
> It is but giving over of a game
> That must be lost.
>
> *Philaster,* III, i.

Weariness of life is content with the soft repose of sleep. Bellario, pursued by Philaster, takes refuge in the forest and stretches himself exhausted on a grassy bank:

> A heaviness near death sits on my brow,
> And I must sleep. Bear me, thou gentle bank
> For ever, if thou wilt. You sweet ones all,

(he says to the flowers on which he lies)

> Let me unworthy press you: I could wish
> I rather were a corse strewed o'er with you
> Than quick above you. Dulness shuts mine eyes,
> And I am giddy: oh, that I could take
> So sound a sleep that I might never wake!
>
> IV, iv.

Evil vanishes like a bad dream, under the king's hand raised in blessing, and a vaguely happy ending closes the agitation of the play. Such a note is as smoothly unreal as the discreet and well-behaved distress throughout the play. At the end the king says:

> Last join hands in one. Enjoy, Philaster,
> This kingdom which is yours, and, after me,
> Whatever I call mine. My blessings on you!
> All happy hours be at your marriage-joys,

That you may grow yourselves over all lands,
And live to see your plenteous branches spring
Wherever there is sun! Let princes learn
By this to rule the passions of their blood;
For what Heaven wills can never be withstood.

V, v.

What, finally, are we to say of the pastoral properly so-called—of the exquisite *Faithful Shepherdess*? Here is to be found all the seductive style of Spenser stripped of its archaic affectations, an even smoother enchantment of the ear, if possible, clear and limpid as a stream, an entertainment that is merely restful, the supreme luxury of the many-jeweled Jacobean Drama. Deprived of the support of the robust Beaumont, Fletcher yielded to the silvery magic of the moon and tears and virginity. He draws upon a mythology that raises no problems: his personages are so diaphanous that the wonder is they should have a drop of blood in them to be pricked. Even the Satyr with his magic is no traditional character leading the revel, but the unsubstantial and subordinate shade of an outworn pagan pageantry.

Chastity is here no virtue, not even a symbol, but merely an exquisitely melodious poem. It is surprising that Lamb should have complained of Fletcher's 'mixing with this blessedness such an ugly deformity as Cloe, the wanton shepherdess'—as if Cloe, who distinctly and maladroitly seeks less ethereal pleasures than Clorine or Amoret, could, whatever her sensuality, pollute a play in which love is an air played on a flute, grave and slow, in the chiaroscuro of a half-magic forest, full of unreal apparitions. The debate between purity and pollution, virtue and vice, which used to be masked by angry, threatening tones, is now an elegant fencing-bout between chastity and lust—but the chastity is tender and plaintive, and lust pursues its object indolently. Everything takes place in undefined regions of a melodious dreamland, in the escapism of a well-conducted fairyland, without caprices or surprises, an idealized world embracing nature and humanity, emotions and ideas, distress and spiritual conflict.

This 'semi-dramatic' poem, as Swinburne called it, full of flowers and nestlings, languid and velvety in its beauty, a pastoral masterpiece, surpasses its literary prototype, Guarini's *Il Pastor Fido*, which Daniel translated in 1602. Daniel himself had tried his hand at this genre, somewhat prematurely, in 1605 with *The Queen's Arcadia* which he called 'a pastoral tragi-comedy'. But by 1605 the day of the Sidneys and the Spensers was over: Peele's freshness,

Lodge's light, witty dialogue, Greene's unbridled romanticism, Lyly's exclusive taste for the euphuistic and the strange
had been succeeded, as we have seen, by more serious concerns. The energy of the dramatists sought other outlets than
the pastoral, 'semi-dramatic' poem. Such perfect pieces as
those of Fletcher, Thomas Randolph (*Amyntas*), and—im-
probably enough—Ben Jonson himself (*The Sad Shepherd*)
had to wait till the Elizabethan fire, vitality and unease had
died down. Their publication became possible when the
substance of the drama, the truth—not logical but human
—of the characters counted for less than the form in which
it was contained.

Since Spenser's *Shepheardes Calender* (1579), Lyly's
Euphues (1578) and Sidney's prolix *Arcadia* (written *c.*
1580, published 1590), pastoral themes had constantly appeared on the stage, even at the height of the 'dark' drama.
Escapist themes always contain an element of disillusion and
sentimentality; they are a protest against anguish, violent
passions, severity of thought, and the intolerable tension of
a mind seeking to resolve its own contradictions. They prefer country retreats, far from the Town and the Court, in
parks that open upon pasture-land where, following Theoc-
ritus and Virgil, the shepherd's life can be idealized. There,
there is no longer ambition, conflict or danger. The idyllic
vision is loaded with the scent of flowers, with soft melodies,
with nostalgia of Paradise. The rustic transformation is facili-
tated and embellished by such marvels as gods and goddesses
sailing over lawns and making shadows dance to the strains
of an invisible orchestra. Pan and Juno are there; we even
catch sight of Iris's scarf and of Diana the chaste whose
hounds mingle with the fairy rounds familiar to the local
peasantry.

These glimpses of a clear sky come sometimes in the
middle of the most sombre drama: for example, within the
sinister walls of Elsinore the Queen may describe the touching landscape where Ophelia pursues her dream till she
drowns:

> There is a willow grows aslant a brook
> That shows his hoar leaves in the glassy stream;
> There with fantastic garlands, did she come,
> Of crow-flowers, nettles, daisies, and long purples.
> *Hamlet*, IV, vii.

Or in *The White Devil*, when we have supped full of horrors, Cornelia's funeral dirge over the body of her son
comes as a pathetic escape from the tragedy that surrounds
us:

Call for the robin red-breast and the wren,
Since o'er shady groves they hover,
And with leaves and flowers do cover
The friendless bodies of unburied men.
Call unto his funeral dole
The ant, the field-mouse and the mole,
To rear him hillocks that shall keep him warm.
                                    The White Devil, V, iv.

But these shafts of light are not thrown upon the plot
like superfluous adornments. The descriptive poetry is subordinated to the drama, the pastoral theme to the human
characters. Irony and even realism temper, in Shakespeare,
what might be embarrassing in pastoralism. If *A Midsummer Night's Dream* remains pure entertainment, at the end
of which we rub our eyes to make sure whether we are
awake or not, it is different with *Twelfth Night* where irony,
raillery and sometimes humour considerably complicate the
critic's task. Finally, in the famous fourth act of *The Winter's
Tale,* Shakespeare's experience shows itself so rich and complex that, within this pastoral world, there is still a world
of difference between the flesh-and-blood Florizel or Perdita
or the old shepherd and the melodious Fletcher's slight and
fragile creations.

From beginning to end *The Faithful Shepherdess* is pure
entertainment. Its poetry is all on the surface without any
subtlety to complicate it. When Milton, some twenty years
later, came to celebrate virtue in his *Comus* (1634), he
remembered Fletcher's limpid-flowing verse but he did so
at least in protest against sensual seductions. The Platonic
equation of beauty with virtue, reinvigorated in Milton's
music, sounded a new strain: his ardent spirit was nourished
by his lyrical gift and the conflict between chastity and corruption took a new meaning. For Puritanism, which began
to show itself by the middle of the sixteenth century one
among many of the Elizabethan Age's restless movements,
at first stifled by more vigorous intellectual forces and more
exacting passions, gained ground and took root as time
went on. It withstood mockery, satire, official persecution.
It came to have ardour and the audacity to assail its foes.

Refusing to compromise with Sin, with anyone who might
welcome, encourage or tolerate it, Puritanism had a horror
of beauty, sensuousness and sensuality. The extravagant display of James's Court, the sumptuous Masques where immorality ruled—sensual spectacles if ever there were any,
in which the Theatre delighted and which ultimately ruined
it—were repugnant to Puritans. The stage appeared to them

a school of corruption and lies, a vast industry of debauchery, an ever-increasingly degenerate activity.

For after the point of balance where Shakespeare's experience stopped, where all the varied phases of his stormy career contributed to his reconciliation with life, the drama may be said to have declined. The vigour that it lost in the tragi-comedy or the pastoral it could not recover in intensity or even in diversity. Pure tragic themes were watered down with doubtful elements, and there was no longer a stable scale of values. Often the hero was by turns tragic and comic without any justification in the facts for this twofold character, and without his succeeding in fusing it in the fire of action. The tragic hero loses some of his strength, the comic some of his naturalness, and both some of their dramatic power. The action is overloaded with sensation, such as rape or incest, even unconsummated, in order to whip up a flagging inspiration. Without conviction and therefore without convincing, writers resorted to the most violent and spectacular effects to intensify a drama that tended to become external. Atrocities were now calculated rather than instinctive, the emotions often intolerable because not fitting into the tragic universe which had formerly breathed life into them. Nor is it certain that the plea for chastity was sincere, so patent occasionally was the dramatist's own indecision which sometimes exaggerated and sometimes introduced a rather crude form of irony.

9

Nevertheless, there is Ford, the last of the group. His case is curious: praised by some, blamed by others, heir to the great Jacobean tradition at the moment when the crisis that characterized it was passing and was giving place to the taste for pleasant and well-contrived entertainment, Ford retained the love of passionate dramatic action, of characters who choose the hard path of fidelity to themselves. But he curiously reduced the sphere of drama properly so-called. The themes of ambition, revenge, jealousy, the conflicts between duty and passion, vice and virtue, life and death, are still found in his plays, but they do not provoke loud uproar as did those of his forerunners. They do not form the active element in the movement of the play: they remain discreetly veiled, sometimes even smothered.

The external violence, the intentionally melodramatic incidents, the choice of subject even (*'Tis Pity She's a Whore*, for example, where Ford takes up the theme of Beaumont

and Fletcher's *A King and No King* but boldly makes his
hero and heroine commit incest) expose Ford, unjustly in
my opinion, to the charge of decadence. If he is decadent it
is not at all because Giovanni breaks into the banqueting
hall with Annabella's bleeding heart on the point of his
dagger, nor because Orgilus traps Ithocles in a chair 'with
an engine', the arms of which close upon him and immo-
bilize him within an inch of his enemy's weapon.[27] Neither
is it because Orgilus opens his veins on the stage, or Fer-
nando takes poison and the Duke stabs himself before the
open grave of the unfortunate Bianca.[28] We have seen
effects just as spectacular in the great period of English
Drama, and these effects do not indicate in Ford any irre-
sistible impulse towards melodrama or any wayward poverty
of dramatic invention.

If Jacobean drama becomes decadent, it is in its ideas
much more than in the way they are worked out. Drama was
no longer the vehicle or favourite mouthpiece of contemporary thought and anxieties. Rather, contact had been lost
between the dramatist and the lively mind of his time. The
public no longer brought to the stage the alert interest, the
exigencies, the constantly shifting influence of an audience's
collective personality: it had found other channels of expression for its new preoccupations. The dramatist was now
expected to provide only entertainment, not any spiritual
nourishment. Moreover, the number of those who regarded
the theatre with suspicion was growing daily, and strangely
enough, after always being in the forefront of intellectual
enterprise, it was now suspected of reactionary corruption.

Since James I's reign, it had been the Court alone which
protected the companies of players who had become the
property of the King and Queen. And with Charles I, whose
popularity had been short-lived, the companies became still
more official. Hence, mistrust of the King, soon developing
into hatred, reacted upon the theatres. The Puritans re-
doubled their attacks and found more favour with the public. The year when Ford published, if he did not have
performed, his best plays was also the year—1633—when
William Prynne launched his redoubtable pamphlet against
the theatres and actors. His invective far exceeded the de-
nunciations of Stephen Gosson and Philip Stubbes.[29] *Histrio-*

---

[27] *The Broken Heart,* IV, iv.

[28] *Love's Sacrifice.*

[29] *The School of Abuse* (1579), Gosson's pamphlet, was dedicated to Sir
Philip Sidney and encouraged him to write his famous *Apology for Poetrie.*
Stubbes, *The Anatomy of Abuses* (1583).

mastix is a venomous, vulgar and pedantic assault upon
authors, players and public alike, in the name of morality,
religion and law. It sought to prove, with the authority of
Scripture and the early Fathers of the Church, that 'plays
are criminal, pagan, dissolute, impure spectacles . . . and
that the profession of dramatic poet or actor, and the fact
of writing, performing and going to see plays is illegal,
infamous and unbecoming for Christians'. Actresses (recently
introduced at Court where the Queen's Ladies-in-Waiting
and Henrietta Maria herself amused themselves by acting)
were described in the pamphlet as 'notable whores'. Magis-
trates who failed to move against the theatres were taken
severely to task, and the author went so far as to evoke the
shady character of Nero.

The Court, of course, reacted vigorously. Prynne was
arrested, lost his ears in the pillory, was sentenced to a
heavy fine and perpetual imprisonment. As an old offender
(but that was on a purely religious charge) he even had
both cheeks branded, but the publicity surrounding the
whole affair gave the mad pamphleteer notoriety. It was no
longer the people but the Court who defended the stage.

There was no popular rising to set Prynne free, but neither
was there any to cut him to pieces. The political and social
ferment from which a bloody revolution was soon to emerge
had its centre elsewhere than in the theatre. The dramatists
had lost the intellectual supremacy, the title to admiring
wonder which they had kept for some years after Shakespeare's death. Their social role may be said to have drawn
to its close when they confined themselves to holding up a
mirror to their contemporaries—sometimes a faithful mirror
in which they could see their daily life reflected, and sometimes a magic mirror wherein they could see the fleeting
colours of false heroism blend with the romantic tints offered
to them as a substitute for life.

Can it be said that Ford was already suffering from that
depressing disaffection which was to leave the dramatist to
play only the debased part of an idle entertainer of the
rich? No: the question, no doubt, did not openly arise for
him. But, as I observed above, he considerably narrowed
the frontiers of the drama. I am almost tempted to say that
his tragedies anticipated in some sort Racine's stripping off
of inessentials—that they were moving towards that state
of the drama in which exclusively the purity of human
passions, irrespective of time and space, is responsible for
their fate. It may seem paradoxical to talk of purity in
connection with a play like *'Tis Pity She's a Whore,* the

subject of which is incest between a brother and sister. But
who can forget:

> Et Phèdre, malgré soi, perfide, incestueuse. . . ?

Giovanni, inflamed by Annabella's beauty, seeks in vain
under cover of a pseudo-Platonic sophistry, to justify his
incestuous passion:

> It is a principle which you have taught,
> When I was yet your scholar, that the frame
> And composition of the mind doth follow
> The frame and composition of the body:
> So, where the body's furniture is beauty,
> The mind's must needs be virtue; which allowed,
> Virtue itself is reason but refined,
> And love the quintessence of that; this proves,
> My sister's beauty being rarely fair
> Is rarely virtuous; chiefly her love to me:
> If hers to me, then so is mine to her;
> Since in like causes are effects alike.
>> *'Tis Pity She's a Whore,* II, v.

Yet he feels weighing upon him that fatality of love which
bears Phèdre to her doom:

> Lost! I am lost! my fates have doomed my death:
> The more I strive, I love; the more I love
> The less I hope: I see my ruin certain. . . .
>> I, iii.

Similarly Tecnicus—who corresponds to the Friar in *Romeo
and Juliet*—says to Orgilus in *The Broken Heart*: 'Tempt
not the stars; young man, thou canst not play with the
severity of fate.' [30] It is in the fatality of passion that destiny
lies, and however clear-sighted, good and virtuous men may
be, they are never beyond reach of its blows.

Possibly such a conception was arbitrary in the England
of 1630, if it did not find its counterpart in at any rate an
implicit acceptance of the doctrine of Grace, which could
redeem Phèdre in the eyes of the great Arnauld. But among
men who no longer threw down this insolent challenge to
fate, as the great ambitious figures of the earlier Drama had
done, this disinterestedness, I had almost said this modesty,
which is essentially anti-romantic cannot but make them
nobler in misfortune and sometimes in crime.

Ford's characters, allowing for a few unconvincing ones,
jealous or hypocritical, whose role is secondary even when
they may seem essential to the plot,[31] have precisely this

---

[30] *The Broken Heart,* I, iii.
[31] For example, Fiormonda or D'Avolos in *Love's Sacrifice.*

quality of restrained heroism, of discretion in the expression of suffering, of calm assurance in courage, which makes them particularly grand as tragic heroes. Annabella, beneath the threats and brutality of a Soranzo mad with rage, keeps her dangerous secret and sings her song: '*Che morte piu dolce che morire per amore!*' Calantha in the famous second scene of Act V, more stoical in Lamb's words than the Spartan boy who let a beast, hidden beneath his tunic, gnaw out his bowels, hears without flinching, in the middle of a dance, that the three beings dearest to her—father, friend and betrothed—are dead, and she goes through all the remaining steps of the dance before facing her misfortune with her full stature. Penthea in the same play, married against her will to a jealous husband, buries in the depths of her heart the secret of her love for Orgilus, and, once she is married, resists the burning importunities of her lover:

> . . . my true love
> Abhors to think that Orgilus deserved
> No better favours than a second bed.
> > *The Broken Heart*, II, iii.

and she lets herself go mad and die, after doing her brother (who is responsible for all her suffering) the last service of winning Calantha's heart for him. Bianca in *Love's Sacrifice* clings desperately in the presence of death to the heroic lie of her chastity, so as to spare her lover the vengeance of her husband.

Violence is powerless against such spirits, resolved never to give way under grief, nor to yield to the blackmail of annihilation. They do not know what terror is. They welcome death with an indifference which does not even treat it as a liberator:

> My glass of life, sweet princess, hath few minutes
> Remaining to run down; the sands are spent [32]

but as a sacred priestess of peace:

> Thoughts of ambition, or delicious banquet,
> With beauty, youth, and love, together perish
> In my last breath, which on the sacred altar

---

[32] *The Broken Heart*, III, v. The whole scene is one of unsurpassable beauty, in which the calm accents of Penthea's next speech:

> > On the stage
> > Of my mortality my youth has acted
> > Some scenes of vanity

are heard in an atmosphere suddenly made more tense by the invisible presence of death.

> Of a long looked-for peace—now—moves—to heaven.
>   IV, iv: death of Ithocles.

Excessive suffering wrings from them no grandiloquent
cries: their anguish is resolved with rare simplicity, faintly
tinged by a restrained longing for the world to come:

> Pleasures, farewell, and all ye thriftless minutes
> Wherein false joys have spun a weary life!
> To these my fortunes now I take my leave.
> Thou, precious Time, that swiftly rid'st in post
> Over the world, to finish up the race
> Of my last fate, here stay thy restless course,
> And bear to ages that are yet unborn
> A wretched, woeful woman's tragedy! [33]

All through the tragedy this serene assurance sustains
them (even Giovanni, whose more impatient youth at times
reminds us of the fiery Romeo), and makes them accept
the tyranny of their passion. It gives them an unknown
strength, a chivalrous courage of rare quality. Never before
had love been raised to such a pinnacle of omnipotence, at
once so free from sensuality[34] and so exacting. It is as if
unwillingly, with implacable tenderness, it can reach its
full height only by destroying the object of its affections,
and then be precipitated in its turn into the abyss. Giovanni
stabs Annabella, the Duke in *Love's Sacrifice* kills Bianca,
Orgilus sacrifices Ithocles, and these appalling deeds are
done without anger, without raving, but with an immense
pity in the heart, an immense love for the victims. 'She's
dead, alas, good soul', says Giovanni, and he adds, a few
lines below:

[33] *'Tis Pity She's a Whore*, V, i—death of Annabella. Or again, the death
of Giovanni, faithful to the end in his terrible love:

> Death, thou'rt a guest long looked for; I embrace
> Thee and thy wounds: O my last minute comes!
> Where'er I go, let me enjoy this grace,
> Freely to view my Annabella's face.
>
>   ibid., V, vi.

[34] The scene where Giovanni declares his love to Annabella (I, iii) is one of
the purest and most tense that I know (apart, of course, from the chaste
wonder of Shakespeare's Miranda):

> O, Annabella, I am quite undone!
> The love of thee, my sister, and the view
> Of thy immortal beauty have untuned
> All harmony both of my rest and life.

And Orgilus (*The Broken Heart*, I, i) tells his love of Penthea in these
words:

> A freedom of converse, an interchange
> Of holy and chaste love, so fixed our souls
> In a firm growth of union, that no time
> Can eat into the pledge . . .

> Fair Annabella,
> How over-glorious art thou in thy wounds,
> Triumphing over infamy and hate.
> > *'Tis Pity She's a Whore*, V, v.

Orgilus has the same cry of admiration beside the body of his friend Ithocles, whom he has held responsible for the death of the woman he loved:

> Farewell, fair spring of manhood!
> > *The Broken Heart*, IV, iv.

There is so much nobility in such cries that one hesitates to use the cruel word sadism. Yet in Ford it is always the loved one whom love sacrifices, compelled to pursue an absolute beyond its reach, and realizing itself perhaps in this destruction. The conventions, the code of honour, of chastity, of justice—these are the restraints necessary for ordered human relationships, which passionate love has to submit to, without forgoing its own nature. Ford's lovers do not fall from their high estate. They make no renunciation. They rarely discuss their fate; still more rarely, their passion. Calantha contrives the remarkable feat of belonging body and soul to Ithocles without a single admission of it passing her lips until she is dying: 'They are the silent griefs Which cut the heart-strings; Let me die smiling.' [35]

This precedence given to love over all the other passions, this reticence in suffering, this welcome offered to death without any thought of metaphysical rhetoric, this calm acceptance of a fatality that brings ruin upon the lovers—these are the elements of Ford's greatness. The problem of evil does not present itself to him in terms of conventional morality, and the problem of success does not present itself at all. Victim and criminal alike are made greater by sacrifice, and what matters is not that justice should be done but that the murderer should accept it in his heart with a wild joy. 'Think on thy life and end, and call for mercy', says the Cardinal to Giovanni after he has been stabbed, and Giovanni's reply is: 'Mercy! Why I have found it in this justice!' [36]

The Duke of Pavia's attitude is the same when he tries to kill himself on learning that his victim had remained chaste: 'Lords, do not care for me, I am too wise to die yet',[37] which implies that he wishes to prepare a self-punishment

[35] *The Broken Heart*, V, iii.
[36] *'Tis Pity She's a Whore*, V, vi.
[37] *Love's Sacrifice*, V, ii.

which will leave nothing to chance. A sudden revelation
comes to them which brings them peace and greatness.

It is only in this tragic climate that Ford is at ease, and
this is my reason for suggesting that he reduced the scope
of Drama. Deep though his knowledge of the human heart
was, his experience was confined to abnormal or extreme
cases, all of the same complexion, the same tension. The
dramatist no longer took the whole of life for his province,
all knowledge for his field of experiment. His curiosity was
concentrated on the points of brilliance with their 'hard,
gemlike flame'. The flux of matter moving all round him
escaped his penetrating but limited vision. Ford's comedy
when he attempts it is appallingly jejune, and what is
generally called his realism is dull and devoid of interest.
He invents neither situations nor dramatic effects. He does
not, like his predecessors, pose agonizing problems which
absorb the play's substance and nourish it in return. The
spectator can be interested in Ford's characters only if he
regards them as ideal figures transcending ordinary humanity and becoming objects of contemplation and aesthetic
satisfaction. Their inner life is simple but so intense that
if it gave itself free rein in expression instead of being
understated and reticent the play would be submerged beneath floods of romantic rhetoric.

But Ford's art lies precisely in well-bred restraint, in the
economy of the means he employs. There is no undisciplined
excitement, no noisy boisterousness, but a sustained effort to
keep the expression within bounds, to muffle the shouting, to
reduce the gestures to a minimum. The passions consume
their own smoke and the heart swells till it ends by breaking.
We seem to be transported to an imaginary world, a world
of transparent, frozen imagination from which good and
evil have been excluded, in the sense that suffering and
emotion are co-eternal and suffering arouses neither revolt
nor pity. Ford's personages move with superb mastery. The
faith that animates them cannot be subdued by misfortune.
They are doomed but make no boast of their heroism. They
dominate quietly and calmly, without a cry of defiance,
without a wince of pain, because in the inhuman order of
things which is their human lot, they can work out their
destiny only by this complete adherence to the suffering
that liberates man.

To go further was hardly possible. It is in this sense that
Ford marks a conclusion. The tragic spring is run down,
exhausted or, one might say, broken with Calantha's broken

heart. Even had the theatres not been closed ten years later, what follower, what successor could have taken up Tragedy where Ford had left it? The wheel had now come full circle. All sources of inspiration had been tapped, all themes had served, all characters and situations had been used. During the fifty-odd years between *Tamburlaine* and *The Broken Heart,* between Marlowe's joyous freshness and Ford's burning intensity, consuming Tragedy in its white flame, the stage had achieved a miracle: it had given living expression to a dynamic society.

This stage was not a luxury, nor the mirror of luxury, but a workshop where thinkers, poets, moralists laboured with ardour and courage, with a willing and co-operative public as subject for their experiments. Interlocking of themes, diversity of characters, complexity of situations, hope involved in an impasse of stoic perplexities, the anguish caused by the conflict of contradictions; a love of eloquence, of verbal extravagance, of refined poetry; a robust digestion for the strongest as well as the daintiest dishes; in short, a passion for life, for action and simultaneously for enjoyment, for feeling themselves alive and active—all this is to be found in the drama of the Jacobeans, in the mind of its writers as in the minds of those for whom it was written.

The curve of greatness reaches its height in the first fifteen years of the century, then wavers and declines, and the interest shifts elsewhere. The public was surfeited and cloyed, ready for diversions which were to be jousts and battles for other ends. But whatever the violence of the political and religious passions that were to absorb England during the twenty-odd years after the closing of the theatres, it would not appear—in spite of a few illustrious examples—that the whole of man was engaged in them.

After 1660 definitely came the age of Literature and Art. The Heroic Drama exploited nostalgia, and middle-class comedy in the baroque splendour of the Restoration needed two essential accessories: the fan to smile behind, the handkerchief for tears. Metaphysical themes gave place to social subjects, chastity was greeted with storms of laughter, debauchery with storms of applause, till the day came when persecuted Virtue, having deluged the stage with tears, reaped the reward of its prudent merit and settled down, like Pamela, in honourable comfort. But it was the novelist, not the dramatist, who, with a firm hand, was to take charge of the new epoch.

PART TWO

TECHNIQUE

L'esprit des formes est un.

ELIE FAURE

ORDER

'THE WHOLE HISTORY of Art', says Elie Faure, 'is dominated and conditioned by . . . the imperishable desire to keep the universal life which at each moment escapes us, in an image that can define it for ever.' The infinite diversity of forms matters little—on the contrary: the only problem they present for the artist, the moment they are created, is how to get the most out of them for his purpose.

The stage is a perpetual illusion or mirage. Whether it be the sacred rite of the earliest religious ceremonies—the cult of Dionysus and, later, of Apollo—in which man offers the gods he fears a representation, fervent and ritualistic, of his way of understanding and fearing them; or whether it be the logical development of a classical tragedy in which he reconstructs for his own aesthetic satisfaction the limited play of a psychological crisis dominated by the passions— the stage is always trying to recreate, by the artifice of language with the help of attitudes and gestures, even of costume, the mysterious life of the universe which is outside man yet to which he belongs, thanks to his intuitions and to his indestructible sense of the Divine.

After action properly so-called, the mind's first requirement is to receive a witness—to see and hear how the world reveals itself to us, what gives us assurance of an identity, of our being integrated into the world. Love of spectacle is inseparable from the very existence of a conscious, percipient being; and the man who prepares or produces the spectacle is primarily concerned to give it that external form by which it will be recognized and thought of as spectacle, and will contrast with the hazardous logic of life with which it could never be confused.

The mistake of the realists has been to suppose that Drama is a mere transcript of life. Possibly the transcript should be understood as moving (insidiously and unconsciously from the moment when the Classical school held and dogmatically laid down that to reach perfection it was sufficient to follow Nature) towards the modern forms of a dramatic production so avid of Truth that it neglects the only truth which should nourish a work of art, the truth which transcends reality. The dramatist, looking round for a form, reserves his right to make reality fit in with his purpose, namely to arouse feelings stronger, more manifold, more rarefied than 'real life' can yield. Or, at any rate, feelings of a different kind. They may stimulate the mind, may indeed involve one's whole being, and yet secretly the mind does not wholly believe in the incidents of the story which it knows to be imaginary. A transparent wall separates dramatist and spectator, and the actors' voices and gestures, the ups and downs of the plot, its *dénouement*, causes, credibility—are, as it were, a trap into which the spectator falls: he remains caught till the last word of the epilogue and, on being released, he remembers only the illusory grave dangers that he has chosen to traverse.

These dangers—of vice, grief, madness, death—assailing the characters from every side and filling the spectator with varied alarms and despondencies, are the plastic substance of Drama which the artist moulds at will, and on which he throws the light best suited to his purpose. He relies on the complicity of imagination and desire, of anguish and hope, of terror and pity—a complicity based on an awareness of the spiritual communion between the spectacle and the spectator.

This means, moreover, that the forms of presentation which the dramatist invents or uses are much oftener, and more effectively, the fruits of experience than of reason. A primitive art is satisfied with what we call unsophisticated productions, but awkwardness and clumsiness are as much the mark of a pathetic stage in man's spiritual evolution as is the most accomplished masterpiece of Reason.

Between the titanic drama of Aeschylus and the dragonfly iridescence of a Giraudoux comedy there is no quantitative difference: one is the product of an epoch when man was painfully freeing himself from the oppressive myth and becoming conscious of the tremendous adventure of his moral grandeur; the other is subtle word-play, delighting a refined sensibility, desperately seeking the height of strangeness to which imagination alone can find the key. But whereas Aeschylus borrows from the necessity of religious ritual the fullness and rigidity which among other things make its greatness, Giraudoux is so supple and presses virtuosity so far in handling the art of dialogue which has centuries behind it, that he loses all consistency and flavour and becomes inorganic and fluid. Yet both, at opposite extremes of theatrical history, obviously expected of their art that it should transcend the reality which nourished it. The great tragic folds of the Aeschylean muse and the shimmering shadows of symbols that make Giraudoux's plays sparkle like watered silk, are divergent forms of the same creative art which in our Western civilization has taken three or four major patterns, determining its evolution perhaps for many centuries.

There was first the Greek Drama, springing from rites that celebrated the gods. Gradually it disengaged from the awful mystery of Olympus the disparate elements of the human personality: to the fate willed by the united gods it opposed man's will to be free by hardship and heroism. Here, the strife of the hero against destiny assumes the simplest form of a straightforward dialogue in which everything is planned in advance, but the muted sorrow of the Chorus represents at the very heart of the drama the lively conscience of dramatist and public alike. The Chorus, a third personage urging, fearing, hoping, begging, lamenting and rejoicing, represents the meeting-point or bridge by which the indispensable collaboration between artist and spectator is effected. Through the Chorus the audience realizes what is at stake, takes part in the struggle, frees itself, on the ideal plane, from an oppression that nothing but the mind can lift.

This is indeed a simple technique, ruling out subtleties: here in mythology, there is no place for the credible, for logical chains of events where everything rushes inevitably towards a known catastrophe, where the only means of expression is poetic language, that is, a manner both ambiguous and rarefied of reaching the deepest truths which words do not yield up without this compulsion.

But this technique was already, in the hands of the Greeks, highly artificial and nothing could more misrepresent it than to describe it as 'close to Nature'. 'The Greeks our masters', says André Gide, 'known well that Aphrodite was not born by natural process.' Euripides, following Aeschylus and Sophocles, for he was anxious to humanize this form of drama, scaled down the size of his heroes. More for the sake of variety than of truth, he began to garnish his spectacle with episodes or anecdotes, the abuse of which later on, even under cover of lyricism, was to break the fine tragic unity of his predecessors' dramas.

When the Romans took up tragedy again, in spite of the powerful lyric inflation of a Seneca, they degraded it and used external elements only to hold the public's attention—sensational incidents, artificial style, purely ornamental treatment of a mythology or a cosmogony in ruins. The grave voice, the pure line, the unity of atmosphere—these were things of the past. The imperishable can be achieved only for a short moment, once only. Perfection cannot be repeated.

Aristotle, no doubt, would have liked to pin down this perfection by borrowing from the old classical models his famous rules which were revived, many centuries later, for quite a different kind of drama. If so-called Classical Tragedy relied on the Unities and, thanks to them, again attained, for a very short time, another imperishable perfection, it was because the need for order, reasonable arrangement, an intellectually satisfying balance became paramount after the boisterous incoherence or the dull grandiloquence of the medieval and Renaissance Drama. It could not justify its survival in France.

The generation of Scaliger and Mairet is, roughly, that of Descartes. The multiple stage and, with it, multiple action was abandoned, after which it seemed an easy matter to conform with the restrictions of Time and Place. Descartes' *cogito* is more than the keystone of a whole system: it is a many-edged weapon, equally apt for driving out the evil spirits of the Dark Ages and of a far-from-penitent imagination, or for giving man, even a man of the theatre, the illusion that everything is ordained and must be arranged with the same strictness in a work of art as in the universe. This exorcising was possible only in France: there alone did it bear fruit, which might have proved barren but for Corneille and Racine (who died, and this was no accident, without followers).

This discipline of coherence and unity which the Cartesian, and therefore the French, mind imposes on the work of art,[1] affected not merely the contrivance of the tragedy, which remained that defined in *The Poetics,* but also the characters, the embellishments, the style itself. But the important fact—so obvious that only the confusion of mind

[1] It is not, of course, a question of direct influence: Racine did not compose *Andromaque* with the *Discours de la Méthode* in mind, and Descartes himself reached maturity after, so to speak, an incubation of centuries, at the exact moment when he was required to lay down and define, once and for all, the paths by which the French mind prefers to reach an understanding of reality.

produced, once more, by the use of the word 'Nature', could cause it to be forgotten—is that thereafter the dramatists thought of their works as works of art. Hence, to return to the first and most imperative of all rules which, thus stated, looks utterly commonplace: the theatre is the theatre, not life nor a reconstruction of life—a simulation (if a concession has to be made to the French realists). But even this word does not convey my meaning. I mean that our concepts of 'realism' and of 'the credible' need to be revised, the prestige of false realism destroyed, and a new lease of life given to the prestige of 'credible'. Only a frank acceptance of poetry's sovereignty can do this.

The substance on which, or with which, the plastic arts work to express beauty can, so to speak, be *objectified* in relation to the executant's conception. The object itself, which serves as a starting-point for sculpture or painting, is merely the pretext of the moment, a happy combination of desire, of feeling, of circumstances. Once the last polish or touch of paint has been given, the form enters into eternity. It bears within itself its own immanence; in its turn, it has become an object, and its immobile beauty, however graceful, can never be more than a memory of the drama of its creation.

The arts of language, on the other hand, never finish with this drama. A certain collocation of words on paper, black on white, remains literally a dead letter till the moment when the reader's eye, the reciter's voice consciously re-creates this drama, with all its train of images, emotions, thoughts. It is the same with music, prisoned in its score, which the conductor's magic wand sets free and which thus recovers for the audience its true life, an infinity of successive lives, every time the sounds rise and fall. Words and sounds are not a mass but a series, perceived as linked together irrevocably, like the events which they purport to relate.

The theatre is the theatre. There is, on the one side, the public—listener-spectator, all eyes and ears, greedy for the spectacle—and, on the other, on the stage, the actors. An imaginary line separates them, sets them face to face, isolates them from each other—a line of resistance, a wall of light which has become footlights but formerly was simply an empty space between spectator and actor, the former lying in wait for the latter, having come to see him suffer, act, die, feigning each action—having come to hear him express by his voice, his cries or his tears the emotions that go with his behaviour on the stage. All this is feigned, is acting. The theatre is a convention set in the very heart of poetry.

For authors, actors, spectators all know well that these gesticulating, declaiming personages are unreal, as are the incidents, the armies that confront each other, the heroes who die a few feet above ground. The secret pact, the connivance of credulity, which binds us to the play, is the essential rule of the game. The reality is no more than an appearance trying to pass for poetic reality. The actor is what he is not, he enters into the personage that the author has created for him. The author asks the spectator to believe what is not and what nevertheless happens, borrowing the form and substance of reality. The character, finally, is distinct from the actor who impersonates him, lives in his own right, accepts the situation that the author imposes on him, is nourished by the substance of reason and feeling implanted in him by the author. All of them are acting, and go on acting to the end.

But the game, in the end, is played against the personages whose destiny is circumscribed by two hours of the clock, and piloted to its end by the author who forbids them to escape from this imaginary universe, beyond the limits of time and space which he has set to their antics. Supreme art consists in making people believe that these personages are free, detached from the author and pursuing their own purposes in complete independence. Thus we have the miracle of theatrical technique, the miracle of poetic language, a means of expression to which all the others are subordinated.

For these personages (just as they are merely illusory by their costumes, their make-up, the subtle or exaggerated feelings which they feign to have or really have, and the situation imposed on them by the plot) speak also a language intended to complete, to sublimate emotion, to give it that real quality, that stuff of a world lost and regained, that thrill which constitutes its virtue and gives the simplest words their strange power to cast a spell over us. Everything in this theatre is illusory, and therefore everything is real. The spectator is simply induced to accept the data of dramatic experience, and a preliminary agreement is established about all the conventions which are, in comparison with these data, occasional conventions of detail, of purely practical convenience, essentially temporary and renewable at the pleasure of each generation.

These propositions are valid also for the French classical

plays with which I wish to conclude. But in the Classical
Drama these conventions of detail were codified by critics
on the authority of the ancient Greeks and Romans. They
were regarded as the only sound method of making plays:
separation of genres, rules of the Three Unities, prestige of
the hero, exceptional character of the incidents to inspire
terror and pity, to instruct and to please; a technique of
execution which simplifies and spaces out the episodes, aims
at stripping the action to its simplest terms; dramatic
rhetoric ordering the reasons for action, clearly classifying
the motives, respecting logic in the sequence of effects, sub-·
jecting even the miraculous to its laws; in a word, obedience
to Nature, harmony of the parts, understatement.

Here is the triumph of reason, of modesty, of balance and
moderation. The most perfect dramatist is the one who
seems most at ease within the bounds; the purest, he who
can be the most moving in the most sober language, applied
to the most banal, that is to say, the most universal themes.
The miracle of Racine was that he reduced tragedy to the
level of a sacred verbal rite, that he made such burning
passion blaze out in a style so plain, by such simple devices, with so few characters. His drama is timeless. It
crosses all the frontiers of reality. It is a supreme art, a rarity
that will not be repeated. His language, above the contami-
nation of life's dubious forms, with a realism that has attained the absolute in the philosophic meaning of the word,
is a dramatic rhetoric without a blemish or flaw, the most
tyrannical but also the most glorious of conventions.

CONVENTIONS AND TRADITIONS

In contrast with this supreme realism, carried to such a
pinnacle by a genius who finds himself at ease even with
the most rigorous austerity, is the apparent disorder of
Elizabethan Drama. It is difficult for the French to realize
that this third form of dramatic art, which they are accustomed to consider undisciplined, had strict rules of its
own. The French have always had their view of the Elizabethan Theatre and of Shakespeare distorted by their habit
of mentally contrasting it either with Classical tragedy or
with modern or contemporary drama—Shakespeare and Racine, Shakespeare and Ibsen, or Bernard Shaw—whereas
Shakespeare and his contemporaries are as different from
the one as from the other. There is nothing profitable to be
learned any longer by setting them side by side or comparing them.

Classical Tragedy, as we have seen, is as outstandingly artificial an essay in the conventional as can possibly be achieved by the devices of a poetical code. Realistic drama, on the other hand, seeks to follow life as closely as possible, and far from seeking poetic escapism does everything to make credible an exact copy of reality. But this reality which it hunts down and brings on to the stage, must be the reality of every day: if the play is to be well written, every-one must recognize its authentic truth. Scenery, costume, language, incidents, action—all must combine to give us the illusion that the plot is an everyday occurrence, taken from life. This is how we live, suffer, dispute, reach serious de-cisions, quarrel, perhaps also kill. The technique of such plays depends on observation and on skilful cutting and linking of the scenes. It cannot be said to serve a really creative art, unless an art be considered creative of which the supreme aim is to make people forget that it is an art, by obstinately wallowing in banality.

This, of course, is not the aim of Renaissance Drama in England. That it sought to be an art admits of no doubt. But the technique of this very special kind of art is so complex and disconcerting that there has never been a body of doc-trine to define it, before or since. For Elizabethan conven-tions, which are far more than customs and much less than rules, did not spring from minds so disciplined as those which laid down laws for Classical Tragedy. These men, indeed, addressed themselves to the performance of plays, not to the drawing-up of codes. In this as elsewhere, and always in England, experience backed up by tradition gave the laws to technique: it was not technique which claimed to make laws before it had any experience and without the help of tradition. But the tradition was old and rich, the experience living and varied.

In the first place, the theatre having originally provided entertainment for the crowd, there was the popular tradition of Mysteries and Morality plays. This had accustomed public and authors to consider that the time and space in which all action took place, far from being a narrow, rigid frame-work, were on the contrary supple and extensible, at the disposal of a plot in which the miraculous element naturally was more important than the realistic. The Bible pageant, legendary or historical, carried its personages to every point of the compass, and in the course of these travels time was telescoped, now quickened, now slackened as the changes in the plot might require.

The Morality play, caring little about verisimilitude in the

painting of character, took for the most part the form of
allegories, bold and exacting abstractions, complicated by
no psychological considerations: from the moment the character appeared on the stage, wearing his motives, as it were,
like armour, he was easy to recognize. To-day allegory is
regarded as synonymous with poor psychology, as dull and
often dry abstraction, but then it was intensely alive in the
popular imagination. It gained in imaginative strength and
sharpness of outline what it lacked in the subtlety which for
us moderns is the very substance of life. Not to mention the
immense place it occupied in the Middle Ages and, long
afterwards, in the plastic arts, the popular ballad and short
verse-tale, allegory reigned supreme and indispensable in
the religious sphere; for it was well fitted to convey in the
simplest, most striking and sometimes the most acid strokes
the elementary ideas that form the eternal basis of man's
mind: the good, the beautiful, vice, virtue, kinship and even
saintliness, evil spirits, sickness and of course death. The
most dramatic conflicts could be evoked in the conscience
of Everyman by the excessive play of abstract passions,
wearing their own mask and speaking the language expected
of them.

When the stage freed itself from strictly religious preoccupations, the custom continued of setting up like allegories a certain number of personages who would thus
make a more instant appeal, of types that hardly varied except as genius gave them marks of its own. The Avenger,
the Villain, the Machiavellian, for example, or the *Miles
gloriosus* derived like other characters from a special psychological conception—those called 'Humours' after Ben
Jonson—owe the modes of their existence to the tenacious
tradition of allegory. It might even be said that a play like
Arden of Feversham develops like an allegory with its repeated episodes—six or seven attempted assassinations which
do not exhaust the reader's patience and which should not
be attributed *prima facie* to poverty of invention. And what
of *Dr. Faustus?*

But there is also a learned tradition which derives directly
from Seneca through the university wits. I have dwelt on
Seneca's influence sufficiently in Part I, and there is no
need to develop the point at length here. Seneca's first gift
to the young dramatists was, without doubt, a high conception of their art. Failing rules which it seems difficult to
define apart from the model that he set them, failing even
the unity of conception—so obvious in Greek Drama, compared with which Seneca appears prolix, sometimes actually

incoherent—it is his grandeur, the nobility of his design which on reflection strike the reader. The sustained lyrical tone sends out sombre waves of feeling, and even the artificial style gives evidence of the height to which the Latin dramatist sought to raise his art.

It has been said of Seneca's tragedies that they were 'salon tragedies', written to be declaimed before an *élite*. I do not deny it, and I find in this criticism an argument in favour of my own view. The long lyrical soliloquies, the impassioned rhetoric, however redundant and declamatory, the piling up of images, the word-play and the shafts of wit, all contribute to assure the triumph of an art which aims at the terrible and the grandiose, and which uses for its effects the most melodramatic means. The Elizabethan dramatists took what was best and what was worst in Seneca, the ghosts and the violent passions, but above all, the extraordinary faith in the magic power of language, thanks to which the drama, whatever its subject, threw off the contradictory shackles of logic, passion and what the public was used to.

For what the public was used to must be reckoned with also. The dramatist obeys partly his instinct, partly the tastes of his audience. His art is directly involved. He never works either altruistically or for the taste of a single individual. His business is to keep in suspense a crowd of people who, once inside the theatre, have a corporate personality which must be mastered, forced to identify itself with the play's characters and their fortunes, and given the intellectual fare it expects. Of course, this crowd is credulous at first and, as the French say nowadays, uncommitted. But it is also exacting, greedy for adventure, for legends and tales of chivalry, for the miraculous; it demands sensation, blood, morality and truth. In other words, it wants poetry.

Strange as it may seem, the legendary and the miraculous must be regarded as true. Shakespeare and many others will be found scrupulously respecting the data of history or legend, following North's *Plutarch* or Holinshed's *Chronicles* step by step, cutting out only such passages as overload the dramatic purpose, adding only what can be included in the general belief accorded to all action: the news-item known to all, the adventure read in a book, which has received the stamp of authenticity by the mere fact of seeing itself in print. One need only look, for example, at the titles: 'The lamentable history of——', 'The tragic history of ——', 'The true history of——', etc. And if the incredible rubs shoulders with the true, is it not a fact that Edward's children were smothered in the Tower, that St. Hugh was hanged and taken down so that his bones might become cobbler's tools, that an apprentice could exchange his leather apron for the richly embroidered robe of Lord Mayor of London, or that Moll Cutpurse lived like a man, on theft and debauchery, at the head of an organized gang?

The bloodthirsty kings, the knights of legend, the enchanters, sorcerers, notorious criminals, all the characters or incidents of history, folklore, thieves' records, travellers' tales—all, as it is to-day, was grist that came to the mill of the masses, the readers of the wonderful medley of the serial story. *Mother and Martyr, The Princess and the Snail, Brothers and Foes, The White Devil* (or the *Black* or the *Green*), *The Revenger's Tragedy, Romeo and Juliet, 'Tis Pity She's a Whore, The Bloody Brother, The Scornful Lady, The Broken Heart*—all these are genuine play-titles, or could be, so small is the difference between the everyday occurrence, legend, history and fairy-tale. At the risk of exhausting the reader's patience, I would repeat (what is the essential theme and *raison d'être* of this book) that everything is true once poetry takes hold of it, once language accomplishes its aesthetic function, which is to create not so much the beautiful as the true. Which of us refuses to believe that Alice, drowsing over her book one hot summer's day, really saw a White Rabbit pull a watch out of his waistcoat pocket?

Moreover, the crowd knows that all human experience and therefore its dramatic counterpart contains a moral. This was the aim of the Morality play; it is also, on a larger scale of edification, the aim of comedy or drama. Dramatic art is not a mere function of entertainment: its example, its advice, its 'message' have to be taken into account. The spectacle of a lamentable destiny incites pity, just as useless cruelty incites disgust or hatred, and courage admiration. Even atrocities carry with them a lesson in humanity, and if Elizabethan speeches were encumbered with sententious moral reflections, sometimes, with boring developments in the form of meditative soliloquies and even with discussions which to our mind unnecessarily hold up the action of the play, it was not so much the memory of the Classics and the desire to appear well-educated that made the author stuff his text with them, as the necessity of meeting his audience's expectations.

Really to know how a man faces death, one must know what he *thinks* rather than what he *feels* in presence of it; one must hear his last counsel, his final confession, his most

significant secret. In the same way, people flocked to hear
the last homily permitted by English Justice to the condemned man when he had one foot on the scaffold before
taking the final plunge. Hence the indigestible, but never
uninteresting mass of reflections, philosophic or moral words;
hence the discussions, the anguished dilemmas and reticences
of Elizabethan plays. The monologue, so often used, served
many purposes to which we shall doubtless have occasion to
revert, but it rarely comes, as in French tragedy, at the
moment of deliberation before the decision. For most of
the time it discloses the essentials of a human experience at
crucial moments of man's destiny.

Elizabethan tragedy—as much as comedy whose rôle it is,
and with a gravity of tone all its own—is a school of morality
to a degree which even propaganda plays have never attained. For it contains no thesis and its appeal to ethical
ends is quite instinctive. When Shakespeare wrote *Measure
for Measure* or *As You Like It* he was not trying to attack
hypocrisy or to prove the blessings of a pastoral life. But
Measure for Measure creates a stifling atmosphere in which
the chief element is a bitter savour of disgust for false voca-
tions (the least one can say in so few words, for the play
is loaded with many other 'messages'); and *As You Like It*
passes a general judgment on life—an ironical condemnation
of the false pastoral, and a lively recognition of love's
sovereignty in the boisterous and healthy personality of
Rosalind.

There is, indeed, no play of Shakespeare or of his contemporaries which does not contain in some degree, under
the discreet veil of allusions, wealth of metaphor or incisive
epigrammatic maxims, essential revelations about the meaning
of life, the moral significance of an attitude or a gesture, so
that the shock to the audience's sensibility is prolonged in
its mind on the ethical plane.

Any human experience, then, seems valid in the eyes of
these dramatists for simultaneously probing the mysteries of
behaviour and is the justification of its gestures. Why should
we be surprised that mind influenced form since the latter
can exist only through the former? Here again, only the regal
detachment of a Racine can depict monsters with such complete indifference that the attention is entirely absorbed by
the incredible beauty of their free movements, and willingly
throws off all moral constraint. It should, perhaps, be said
that if beauty alone is sought, other preoccupations are ruled
out, and that the contemplation of a tiger—as in Blake's

poem—produces those high mystical states in which the soul
melts as in ecstasy, wholly absorbed by the created object,
wholly trusting its creator.

These dizzy moments are rarely free from foreign elements
among Elizabethan dramatists. Shakespeare, however, rises
to them sometimes (as in the death of Cleopatra or Othello's
suicide), and I can find only Ford who lives habitually in
this climate of disinterestedness.

THE STAGE

Were it not for its bearing on the main purpose of this
book, it would be superfluous to dwell at length on the effect
of Elizabethan stage-conditions on dramatic construction, for
by and large they are familiar to the public.

The performance of a Shakespearian play presents a
modern producer with a number of problems which the
Elizabethan author and theatre manager solved very differently. This is due both to the entirely different arrange-
ments of the stage and to the consequent difference in the
conception of production. Everything was governed by the
size and special shape of the theatre, the disposition of
the stage, the hour of the performance, the composition of
the acting companies and the public's habits.

The curious drawing made from memory by the Dutch
traveller, de Witt (1596), of the Swan Theatre is known
to all French schools from Guibillon's *Morceaux Choisis*.
There is no need to describe it, but what strikes one about
it is not so much the bareness of the apron-stage (projecting
into the middle of the building), or its three levels (front,
inner and upper), but rather the absence of a curtain and
footlights, and therefore of mystery. By this I mean that the
pomps and ceremonies proceeded openly, without any attempt at concealment, before the eyes of a public which
pressed close round three sides of the stage. Only the fact
of the stage's being raised enhanced its glamour and allowed, with the minimum of stage properties (each bit of
scenery, each object on the stage assuming a symbolical
meaning) this absence of localization, this neutrality of scene
to be exploited for the most diverse ends.

Not that such an arrangement was rudimentary or, to ex-
cuse its comparative poverty, could be regarded as primitive.
Here again it is true that it came from tradition and experience. The inn-yards where the first popular spectacles
were performed were surrounded on three sides by a gallery,
on to which the guest-chambers looked, and the actors set

up their stage in front of the fourth side which served them as scenic background. Similarly, the big halls of country houses and Oxford and Cambridge colleges, used as refectories or meeting-places, where performances were given, often had a gallery at the back, built in the partition wall between the hall and the offices, with two doors leading to it. Hence the Elizabethan stage, built on the lines of the inn-yards and halls, presented the same characteristics: front, inner and upper stage had each its conventional significance which made realism in scenery unnecessary.

The front stage was the unlocalized spot where the Prologues came and stood, soliloquies were delivered and connecting scenes and interludes were performed which did not need to be identified for the play to be understood. The inner stage under the gallery, isolated by a curtain which was drawn so as to uncover or to divide it from the rest of the stage, had a more definite function. Here, interiors were set (taverns, bedrooms, grottoes, tombs, etc.), and whenever a character came out or went in, the scene of the action was known to lose its locality or to become more localized, as the case might be. Here Antonio in *The Duchess of Malfi* would tell his secrets to the Duchess, or Ferdinand and Miranda would be playing chess when Prospero literally 'discovered' them. Finally, the upper stage could represent rooms above (from which villains, for example, might observe their victims), the ramparts of a town, castle walls (for the scene of the Watch in *Hamlet*), the top of a hill or promontory, sometimes even Heaven.

The play was given without a break, the division into acts and scenes having been introduced at the time of the First Folio and sometimes even later, when editors and commentators felt themselves obliged to conform with the classical convention. Hence the transition from one scene to another was made without any interruption of the action: the characters went off on one side and came on by the other, or left one part of the stage for another, within sight of the audience, each move representing a journey which might be quite a long one and yet occupy only a few seconds. Each new situation was understood by the public either through an allusion in the text (as often in Shakespeare: 'How far is't call'd to Forres?') or by the new locality being identified through some symbolical stage property (throne, dais, bed, coffin, etc.). *Décor* was not completely absent, therefore, but it was not essential.

Thus, two items of scenery at least recur frequently in Elizabethan plays: a wood and the gates of a town. For the former, trees were certainly used, though of what construction is uncertain. They must, however, have been sufficiently strong for people to be hanged on them. As for town-gates, they could be represented the more easily thanks to the balcony at the back, over the side or central doors opening on the inner stage. Thus the besieged could stand over the besiegers, as in the Berkeley Castle scene in *Richard II* where the King addresses Bolingbroke, and from which he comes down shortly afterwards to offer his surrender in the court in front of the castle.

Realistic staging, therefore, was reduced to an indispensable practical minimum, and properties did the rest—properties and costumes. We have a detailed list found among Henslowe's papers,[2] from which it can be seen that they were numerous and varied: weapons or instruments of war, royal insignia, emblems of the gods, dragons, horses, lions' skins or heads, mossy banks, rainbows, coffins and a hundred other different objects, intended to fire the imagination and to complete the illusion of the costumes which, all scholars are agreed, were very rich and elaborate. Costumes and accessories, moreover, had a definite symbolical meaning: the King was recognizable by his crown, Mercury by his wand, Iris by her scarf, the messenger by his boots, the old man by his beard, and so on. Not that there was the slightest concern for historical accuracy or, as we say, 'local colour'; Dido and Cleopatra wore the same farthingales, the doublet was common to Romans and Elizabethans alike.

Nevertheless, the costumes spoke a conventional language, whether they indicated a country of origin (Spanish cape, baggy Turkish trousers, etc.), or were peculiar to a type of character. The enchanter could be known by his mantle, the parasite by his tights, the ghost by the flour which whitened his face. Colour also had its symbolical significance: white and black, for example, represented innocence and mourning, gaiety and melancholy.

Finally, the disguises which were so numerous in Elizabethan drama and of which Shakespeare made such abundant use had no need to be realistic to be effective. I shall return to this point later. Here it is enough to say that they were effected by the simplest means: a false beard, a mask, or a cloak, and the personage was recognized neither by his friends nor even by his nearest relatives. We know, too, that the sexes were constantly mixed, women's parts being played by boys whose voices had not yet broken: the Duke in *As*

[2] Inventory of the properties belonging to the Lord Admiral's Company in 1598.

You Like It fails to recognize his daughter Rosalind, and Viola in *Twelfth Night* can in turn and safely be Viola, the young page and Viola again.

All the dramatic incidents depended on these transparent fictions, which the public accepted without demur, nor did they in any way impair the credibility of the action. What mattered, then, more than any realism was the exact interpretation of the part, which the costume, the attribute or the disguise indicated, whether for the leading rôles or for the servants and walking-on parts. Here, again, the conventional presentation deriving from the Morality plays must be borne in mind: the actor, once clearly identified, was important only by his way of behaving and above all of expressing himself.

Scenic effects also were no less numerous than varied, violent and spectacular; melodramatic we might call them were it not for the powerful poetic effects obtained from most of them. Men-at-arms march past before the battle, or great lords, sumptuously arrayed, before the Council; the crowd throngs the street or the castle precincts or the forum; royal banquets, trial-scenes, solemn processions—all this comes directly from the tradition of the Pageants in which the English crowds first satisfied their passion for spectacles. Then, there were also the effects which catered for the love of the marvellous: apparitions of all kinds, sometimes achieved with the help of machines, ghosts rising from the bowels of the earth (through trap-doors, of course), spirits raised by necromancers or sorcerers mounting from the jaws of hell or from mysterious tombs; angels and demons coming from their appropriate haunts, the gods of Antiquity descending from Olympus and summoning in their turn a motley crew of servitors to provide, at a stroke of the magic wand, an entertainment of dance and music or song, or grotesque revels.

Here, tragedy allies itself with the sumptuous Masque, a lyric pantomime in which poetry rivals music, in the pastoral tradition which was to occupy such a large share of the Jacobean fêtes of Court or castle. It is by no means rare to find, in the middle of the darkest drama, these bright interludes in sylvan settings, adorned by graceful troupes of spirits disguised as harvesters. A funeral dirge suddenly evokes the redbreast or the field-mouse, and the mind is relieved from the horrors of poison and corruption. The pantomime properly so-called, or 'Show', is also included in the drama, not merely to entertain the eye but to avoid the narration of some event that helps the plot forward; it

thus allows of striking short cuts which precipitate instead
of holding up the action of the play. Thus, it can be a
premonitory dream materialized without words; a distant
vision reconstructing a murder down to its smallest details;
or again these Shows may have ghosts, grave and wrathful,
thirsting for blood and revenge as they glide through dream
forests in an unearthly light.

Ghosts without number, doleful and tragic, mute or garrulous, come to threaten the assassin or to exhort the avenger,
and by their piteous miming or their terrifying cries to expose, to the eyes of all, the frightful torment brought upon
them by the supreme injustice of their death. Their hair
clotted with blood, their faces slashed by dagger-wounds,
they adorn the Thyestes banquets, silent and terrible or
stiff and livid, just as they were when death overtook them.
Surrounded by flames and brimstone, themselves invulnerable
in their ghostly armour, they hurl their insults and utter
their prophecies in cavernous tones.

Never ridiculous, ideal vehicles of the tragic, ghosts were
dear to Seneca's admirers; but they were also familiar to the
popular mind which never tired of embodying, under their
bloodless features and their attitudes of despair, its unsub-
duable longing for an after-life—an after-life unthinkable
unless by means of such images as these—and of satisfying
the great thirst for mystery and justice which has haunted
it from the remotest ages. The ghost is thus more than a
stage property. It is an indispensable personage whose expected presence shocks no spectator and whose rôle is often
a major one.

But the ghost is not the only channel of sensation, and
tragic effects are contrived by many other means also. Here,
an aggressive realism is needed to intensify the sensation.
Spectacular horrors are piled up in the Senecan tragedy,
reinforced by a staging obviously intended to produce shud-
ders in the audience. Bloody banquets, ambushes, torments
and executions take place in an atmosphere of the torture
chamber. Decapitated heads are brought upon the stage,
the blood streams (from a concealed bladder), the living
flesh is slashed (as by an illusionist in a fair-booth), executioners pass red-hot irons before their victims' eyes; corpses
and severed limbs (made of wax or represented by dum-
mies), more ghastly than death itself, complete the illusion
of the sensational which the Elizabethan public so much
relished.

Remembering the intolerable scenes in *Titus Andronicus*
or *King Lear*, the reader will not be surprised to find that,

if Shakespeare himself did not eschew these condiments for robust digestions, they formed the basic diet for many of his contemporaries. In this sphere, their imagination reaches the furthest limits of the horrible in the ingenious and also, doubtless, the ingenuous. Tamburlaine harnesses vanquished kings to his chariot, Bajazet breaks his skull against the bars of his cage, the Jew of Malta prepares to hurl his foes into the boiling cauldron into which he falls himself. Webster's Brachiano dies under the beaver of a poisoned helmet, and is made to go through the sinister comedy of Confession, the better to damn him; Duke Ferdinand, before going mad from lycanthropy[3] and digging in cemeteries, shows his sister wax-figures of the corpses of her children; Orgilus catches his rival in the trap of a mechanical chair. And Shakespeare (one can dip anywhere into his plays) like the others piles up duels, executions, beheadings, murders of women and children; he juggles with coffins, makes play with the substitution of one decapitated head for another; brings statues to life, sets the weird sisters dancing in a ring, resorts to oracles, apparitions and ghosts—in short, runs the whole gamut of atrocities like a practised playwright, without compunction or remorse. He appears to have had an inexhaustible power of invention to serve a vigorous appetite, just as in the realm of pure imagination he enjoyed protean supremacy in the use of metaphor.

Such effects, far from enslaving reality for realistic ends, bend it to suit all purposes, indeed go beyond it, manipulating and twisting it for poetic needs, just as a metaphor at the moment when it is perceived, yokes together the poles furthest removed from the object of inward contemplation. Sounds and noises bring to this apparent disorder a contribution of no little value—the war-like trumpet, the oppressive rhythm of the funeral march, the tender modulation of a romance, the comic jollity of a drinking song or the clear notes of a hunting horn; cannonade, drum and thunder join in, and the very bells strike the death-blow when the deluded assassin, dagger in hand, throws himself forward into the shadows where the owl has already sounded his knell. Similarly, at Newgate, the fatal bell rings in the final hour of the doomed man.

It must not be forgotten that the Elizabethan theatre was very small. According to the specifications for the Fortune Theatre built by Henslowe and Alleyn in 1600, on the lines of the Globe, the 'yard' or pit must have been 55 feet wide (not counting the galleries), and the stage, 43 feet wide,

[3] *Duchess of Malfi*, V, ii.

came forward into the middle of the building far enough to allow for processions, grouping and movement of the players. Performances always took place in the afternoon, which precluded the elaborate lighting effects of our modern producers, though there was some use of candles and torches for interiors (such as prisons and tombs), and even for heaths and forests, or for processions and Retreats. Though the theatres were not always completely roofed in (the stage alone— sometimes merely a part of it—and the balcony were protected), it would not be correct to compare them with our open-air theatres.

Since the stage, as we have just seen, came forward to the middle of the pit, the actor was surrounded on three sides by the spectators who could hear him without difficulty. His asides and soliloquies could be spoken without raising his voice, in a confidential tone, direct to the audience, with whatever shades of intonation the subject required. But otherwise Elizabethan delivery was probably declamatory and the acting conventional. Shakespeare frequently refers to the bombastic tone and arrogant gait of the player who 'struts and frets' upon the stage[4] and whose 'action' was to be as violent and unrestrained as the speech and the circumstances required.

The powerful rhetoric of a Marlowe or a Kyd, the paroxysms of terror or passion in the great Senecan dramas, the grandiloquent fury of the Revenge tragedies, the harrowing cries of the ghosts and madmen, called for a robust voice and lungs, which accounts for the celebrity of a Burbage and an Alleyn. 'I will play it in Ercles' vein', Shakespeare makes Bottom say in the admirable parody of a tragedy which he gives in *A Midsummer Night's Dream*: 'in Ercles' vein', that is, the tone adopted by the braggart, the *miles gloriosus*, in delivering his set-piece which the mechanical 'lift' of a blank verse not yet tamed into suppleness carried from one level up to another, until it ended in a roar. The violence of the action, the length of the soliloquies (*Tamburlaine* is one long series of monologues) the dramatic rhetoric of the earlier authors, the love of excess in anger, hatred and defiance—everything, obviously, must have contributed to inflate the tone of voice, to exaggerate the gesture and to fire the glance of the actor.

This was the player's tribute to the passion expressed in the text, his complete self-surrender to the dramatic fiction, which won even that difficult character Hamlet who re-

---

[4] *Macbeth*, V, v. See also *Troilus and Cressida*, I, iii, 153, and in *Hamlet* the scene with the Players contains valuable hints about the actor's technique.

proaches himself that he 'can say nothing' though he is
burning with a hate which should

> drown the stage with tears, . . .
> Make mad the guilty and appal the free,
> Confound the ignorant, and amaze indeed
> The very faculties of eyes and ears.
>
> *Hamlet*, II, ii., 596 *et seq.*

The irony in this passage is full of bitterness. Hamlet is
amazed by the player's delivery of a speech intentionally
composed in the turgid style of the bad melodramas of the
day (though without the buffoonery in which Shakespeare
indulged in the *Dream*): he does it with so much passion
that he forgets the wise advice given him a little later.[5] But
the roaring matters little: such lines, after all, were written
as if they were to be roared, and if they make us smile, as
they irritated Hamlet, they afford indisputable evidence of a
zeal to entrust to speech the sacred mission of delivering man
from the nightmare of his suffering.

Moreover, there is no doubt that the famous banquet scene
in *Macbeth*—the drama to which Shakespeare brought all
his powers of playing upon the *senses* of the audience—
could only be played with cries and grimaces ('Why do you
make such faces?'), so complete is the terror that the words
convey. And, all told, it is a triumph of poetic language,
even if the desire for the grand manner sometimes takes
paths where we hesitate to consider it supreme.

SPACE, TIME

Let us now leave the stage, or rather, let us penetrate to
the heart of the plays, and see inside the playwright's mind,
if we can, while he is constructing them. Let us arbitrarily
isolate the problems and clear the ground by treating them
as pure concepts: space, time, action, character, theme, and
finally language. We shall thus complete the circle of questions involved, whether the playwright had them clearly in
mind or not. Let us regard as errors of judgment on our part
those which cannot be reduced to the terms of our own age.
Let us not prospect space like a geometer, or measure time
like a chronometer.

The Elizabethan dramatist, as we have seen, did not bother

---

[5] 'Speak the speech I pray you as I pronounced it to you, trippingly on the
tongue; but if you mouth it as many of your players do, I had as lief the
towncrier spoke my lines.'—*Hamlet,* III, ii. Here one almost hears Molière
speaking!

about space and time. Dr. Johnson, in whom the first signs of modern critical thought can be detected, strives ponderously (as his manner was, and he sometimes strove superbly) to justify Shakespeare against the reproaches levelled at him by those whose minds are haunted by the belief that dramatic credibility requires conformity with the unities of time and space. But what need is there for this? The scene of the action is as imaginary as it can be since the stage is neutral and, thanks to its arrangement in depth and height, as well as to its *décor* and its symbolical stage properties, it can represent everything.

Why should the fabulous world of Tamburlaine and Titania, of Antony and Cleopatra, of Dr. Faustus or Rosalind, allow itself to be 'cribb'd, cabin'd and confined' in a single desert, a single balcony, a single forest? At once more abstract and more concrete than the scene of a classical tragedy, the Lebensraum of the Elizabethan is multiform and capable of any degree of localization: it coexists with the peripeteia; it is, in the philosophical sense, immediate, not like a rational phenomenon foreseen and unexposed to contingencies, but given as a series of necessary supports, open to any event and capable, therefore, of becoming this, that or the other.

'The truth is', says Dr. Johnson, 'that the spectators are always in their senses and know, from the first act to the last, that the stage is only a stage . . . and where is the absurdity of allowing that space to represent first Athens, and then Sicily, which was always known to be neither Sicily nor Athens but a modern theatre?' There is, indeed, nothing simpler than to accept a fiction which presents itself as such. This theatre contains the whole universe, a stage more magical than the devil's cloak offered to Dr. Faustus, which can combine ubiquity with immobility. Everything is possible to the 'willing suspension of disbelief'.

As regards time, the problem is more complex. Initially, nevertheless, it is of the same kind. Any narrative, since it may take place at different points in space, has at least two speeds which are superimposed one on the other: the time taken in the telling and the time taken by the action described. A life can be told in a few phrases; an instant may last five hours. Our idea of time depends on our consciousness of it. We are accustomed to say that happy hours fly whereas suffering or annoyance lasts interminably. This is wrong, for completeness may touch eternity and boredom be forgotten as soon as its cause has disappeared, boredom being simply the waiting for the unpleasant to cease, whereas happiness distends time without stint.

At all events, the drama of duration—the most perceptible to the human mind—can be reduced to nothing only if a man is willing to recognize this characteristic of variability which makes its mystery and its grandeur. Time is necessary for man to vanquish space and for life to develop in it. But since we talk of Zero Hour, we should also talk of Zero Instant. In any life, as in any play, there are instants of incredible richness, so completely satisfying that they sweep away all the dull, featureless moments between.

The classical dramatist contrived to seize these rare moments when a life's graph touches dangerous heights that give it its full meaning. This is what is called the crisis, when the storm breaks, the thunderbolt falls and destinies are determined. The two phases of time can then closely coincide. In a couple of hours destiny is consummated, and the tragedy closes. The mind apparently derives therefrom an increased satisfaction—but only on reflection, for during the play time does not in truth elapse. The tension is too great for thoughts to stray. The mind is entirely absorbed by this concentration and emerges exhausted from the strain put upon it. I have always wondered whether the running champion *lives* the ten seconds of his sprint. I cannot think so. He merely runs, that is, throws all the resources of his body forward.

These critical moments, these painful seconds are really a succession of Zero Instants. Time starts up again at the end of the race as soon as the time-keeper declares what his stopwatch recorded while the sense of duration was suspended. But over a long course, an obstacle race, time and duration come into their own again. There are monotonous stages, and stages full of difficulties and exaltations, when the anguish of mortal time by turns grips and leaves the athlete who feels himself time's prey:

> But at my back I always hear
> Time's winged chariot hurrying near.
> —Andrew Marvell, 'To His Coy Mistress'.

The hero whom the Elizabethan playwright takes to the end of his career resembles the steeplechase runner who climbs hillsides, plunges through marshes, crosses different kinds of country and finally reaches the borders of the forbidden land to which only victory or death gives access. The diversity of his trials, his energy, his endurance bring into play the sliding scale of his own perception of time, just as—if we followed them with our eyes—they would fix for us the stages he has passed. The dramatist chooses

the trials, rears the obstacles, settles the resistance and con-
trols the impetus. Hence, for him, time can be expanded
or compressed at will, just as, for us, the feeling of time is
bound up with the credence we attach to the story. It may
give time seven-league boots, make it skip over colourless
hollows or slow it down to the pace of the tortoise, thus ob-
taining strange and striking effects of slowness or speed,
which range from the telescoping of time to its almost total
negation. Sometimes incidents, turns, stumbling-blocks play a
delaying part; at others, events come thick and fast like
messengers arriving on each other's heels from all points of
the compass, whose messages there is no time to read; or
again, simultaneous actions proceed in succession like the
turning of a many-sided mirror containing the images which
will shortly make up the whole picture.

Hardly a thought is given to analysing the part played
by time in a classical tragedy unless to measure it by the
severe standard of Unity. If he exceeds the limits that Unity
assigns him, Corneille is accused of being unskilful. This
supposed lack of skill consists in his wanting to deny time
while feigning to respect the abstract concept of it imposed
on him. Time thus conceived is an embarrassment. But freedom from it is possible only to those who frankly enter into
the spirit of time's game, as one does with an idiot who has
to be induced to behave with comparative sense. Or better
still, it is possible if one forgets it like an over-zealous servant
whose reminders and hints and remonstrances go unheeded
when one has too much of importance to do. When the
house is on fire, it signifies nothing if one forgets a social
engagement: the matter can be put right afterwards. The
dramatist deals with first things first, and this is sometimes
a long business if the road travelled has to be measured.

Take *Richard II* or *Macbeth,* for example. First of all,
Richard has to be brought as soon as possible face to face
with Bolingbroke after the latter's return from exile; in
Macbeth the King's murder must be secured. But, *Richard
II* is set in motion with majestic slowness, full of emphasis
on the ritual of challenge and tourney. Throughout the early
scenes we have an impressive display of the pomp of chivalry,
with its processions, speeches, provocations, throwing down
of gauntlets, appeals to the King for justice, and finally the
sentence which cuts short the spectacle. Then Richard starts
for his Irish war and Bolingbroke goes into exile. But neither
war nor exile occupies the stage or our attention. The play
is the dethronement of Richard by Bolingbroke. So, hardly
has Richard time to reach Ireland and Bolingbroke France,

before we learn that both of them have returned to England
—Bolingbroke first, so as to give him the advantage, and
this takes place (it is scarcely credible) in the very scene
where we heard of his departure.

Weeks and months have thus been telescoped so as to
reach without further delay the burning topic—the tragic
story of a usurpation. Now the scenes go very rapidly till
the moment when the whole time-drama takes place within
the King's conscience. We have the feeling that the King
is *losing his time*, that he is always straggling after the
march of events and is left behind. It is this immobility in a
world where everything is rushing on, that kills him where
he stands. When Richard in prison, conscious at last that he
has been defeated by time, bethinks him of his immobility,
it is too late. He becomes acutely conscious of his inaction,
of his repeated failures to keep his rendezvous with Destiny,
of the terrible opposition between yesterday and to-day—
such is the pathos on which he feeds, this proud and prolix
spirit who ignored the traps laid for him by time.

To make matters quite clear: there are two years of history
narrated by Shakespeare in two hours, and the audience
never quarrels with this freedom taken by the playwright.
There is the variable speed with which he presents the facts
selected as the fittest for his purpose, and this speed varies
with the dramatic urgency of these facts: as each event
gathers speed, there is a corresponding or opposite delay in
the action which is required of the menaced King by his
wild imagination. It is here that the game is played with a
Crown as stake. Finally, there is the psychological drama
of the clear-thinking Richard who relishes his powerlessness
and reigns over his sorrows. Here the stake is no longer a
Crown, nor even his life, but self-possession in face of man's
mortal enemy, time—a self-possession which only knowledge
can give. The problem in *Richard II* is not which of the
two rivals is worthier to reign, but which, in spite of appearances, is the more conscious of the relativity of Fate.
The dramatic tension is merged in metaphysical tension, and
it is Richard's frenzied metaphors which make him an intellectual hero, a precursor of Hamlet, whereas Bolingbroke
appears to us a narrow-minded realist.

Then, take *Macbeth*. Look at the terrifying rapidity with
which Act I rushes towards the crime. Battles and break-
neck rides on the heath follow each other thick and fast
till Inverness Castle is reached. It is a race of messengers, of
the King, of Macbeth towards the abyss. Who will arrive
first? 'Where's the Thane of Cawdor?' asks the King.

> We cours'd him at the heels and had a purpose
> To be his purveyor: but he rides well;
> And his great love, sharp as his spur, hath holp him
> To his home before us.
>   *Macbeth,* I, vi, 21-4

Macbeth himself, stopping to breathe his horse, sends two messengers to his wife: the first brings the strange news of the Witches' prediction, and when Lady Macbeth comes on the stage reading the letter, Fate is already on the move, already the second messenger collapses exhausted at her feet. There is just time for an evil invocation, bearing crime and death in it—'The raven itself is hoarse'—and Macbeth arrives. A few words ambiguously threatening, and the King reaches the castle-site where the air 'nimbly and sweetly recommends itself unto our gentle senses'.

Then, suddenly, night seizes upon the castle. Time is abolished, merged in the night. Nothing remains but spells, and owls' cries, the dagger sweating blood, the ring of reddening torches fitfully stabbing the inspissated gloom. A long, long nightmare, which lasts some seconds or some centuries, in the midst of which a bell strikes, always the same, the bell that summons man to meet his fate. Shakespeare now has no more need of time, or rather he can take his time. Justice is on the move, can move slowly. Macbeth thought he could read in the Witches' eyes the ambiguous message of Fate, but the message was blurred with blood and the ravens' wings. Time, which he thought to pass through, was full of dread secrets which he would gradually unfold.

Some eighteen years, according to History, remained to fill the last three acts and to reach the terrifying penetration of:

> To-morrow, and to-morrow, and to-morrow,
> Creeps in this petty pace from day to day,
> To the last syllable of recorded time.
>   *Macbeth,* V, v, 19-21

Macbeth has lived all these days, one after the other, in the intoxication of power and fear, in the anguish of the next crime to be committed, but the more salient days in this monotonous series are sufficient for us. The rhythm may slacken but the fatality of the crime is ineluctable, as is the inevitable recovery of the powers of good. Time cowers like a wild beast which watches the movements of its prey and has only to stretch forth its claws at its own appointed hour.

Macbeth narrowly triumphs over himself, and his triumph

is again clear-sightedness: it sustains his final heroism, which it might have deserted in the desperation of cowardice—an ultimate 'what's the use?'—were it not that its function is at this point to throw down to appearances the final challenge of a soul escaping at last from Time's ambushes.

Hamlet, on the other hand, is the Tragedy of Delays. Here the dramatist continually retards the progress of the action. The lust for vengeance once aroused might be frenzied, as it is in most of the plays which have revenge as their subject; the play is then prolonged by the raising of repeated obstacles, replaced as soon as they are overcome. This is not true of *Hamlet.* We do not know exactly how many months the tragedy covers. Some of the episodes might be very long, such as Laertes's journey, Hamlet's exile, or Fortinbras's campaign. Hamlet rejects certainties, retreats two steps for every one he takes forward. No play, doubtless, is so ill constructed, allowing for the revisions, the additions to the first, incomplete, text, for it is true that it existed in different versions, at different stages. But this was not the reason for the procrastination.

The drama was extraordinarily difficult to set in motion, for on what could it be focused? Hamlet's love for Ophelia is an inglorious episode. The apparent subject is Hamlet's revenge against the criminal usurper who had killed his father and defiled his mother. But the real subject is the disintegration of Hamlet's moral being as a result of the Ghost's revelations. His world totters and falls apart; an odour of corruption rises from the ruins. The bewildered Hamlet must recognize that 'there's something rotten in the state of Denmark'. The rottenness is a woman, his own mother, so tender, so soft, so foolish. He is revolted. He throws overboard love, reason, and time. None of the familiar landmarks is left. He is face to face with the eternal evil which torments him in his most sensitive flesh and sacrifices his inmost heart. He cares nothing for time since he cannot remedy the ill. To kill Claudius would no doubt appease the uneasy soul of the Ghost, but how would it wash away the defilement of Gertrude? 'What's done', as Lady Macbeth said in another context, 'cannot be undone.'

Hamlet keeps his passion for understanding, his acute intelligence, which nourish his anger while deepening his disgust. Hence his clear-mindedness takes so many detours, delves into so many dark corners, turns over so many stones —and under each there is vermin crawling—that 'conscience doth make cowards of us all. . . . And enterprises of great pith and moment . . . their currents turn awry, And lose

the name of action'.[6] There should, therefore, be no surprise
at the slowness of an action which is no action. It is not
Hamlet who says: 'But at my back I always hear . . . ,' for
he neither listens to nor hears Time's winged chariot. He
piles up unnecessary words and superfluous gestures; he
leaves it to chance, to the King himself, to bring about the
accident which will put an end to his lamentable choppings
and changings. He degrades love, he kills right and left, he
debases even revenge. He muddles through.

It would be instructive to study in any other play of
Shakespeare's the part—active or passive—played by Time,
and to see how he lengthens or shortens it, compresses or
expands it, for his dramatic purpose; how he jumps[7] over
long years, to allow his heroes to grow up (*The Winter's
Tale*), how he immobilizes it (the storm in *King Lear*), how
he encloses the comedy or the tragedy within a single night
or day (*A Midsummer Night's Dream; The Tempest*), or
how he deploys it over vast perspectives of the greatness
and fall of an empire (*Antony and Cleopatra*). His messengers may fly with Ariel's invisible wings or arrive too late.
His action may be swift as lightning or slow as legal process.
In plays with a subsidiary as well as a main plot, two series
of happenings, different but subtly mingled, may proceed
at two different speeds and give the impression that they
also coincide.

And what is true of Shakespeare is true of others: Time for
the Elizabethans is a servant not a tyrant. It is a dramatic
convention and must be regarded as such, but a pliable,
supple convention which the dramatist breaks-in to do every
kind of service; closely linked not only (as is logical) with
space but with the very nature of the play, its object, its
chief personage, its message.

Finally, it often happens that the poets' Time, so familiar

---

[6] *Hamlet*, III, i, 83-8.
[7] See, among many other possible examples, the Prologue to *Henry V*:

> . . . For 'tis your thoughts that now must deck our Kings,
> Carry them here and there, jumping o'er times,
> Turning the accomplishment of many years
> Into an hour-glass.

Or again, in *The Winter's Tale* (Act IV):

> . . . Impute it not a crime
> To me or my swift passage, that I slide
> O'er sixteen years, and leave the growth untried
> Of that wide gap; since it is in my power
> To o'erthrow law . . .
>   . . . your patience this allowing
> I turn my glass and give my scene such growing
> As you had slept between. . . .

to the crowd, comes on like an old allegory with his scythe
and hour-glass, his hoary locks or his astrolabe, as the case
may be. Or it may be a monster, such as Ulysses describes in
his famous remonstrance to Achilles: 'Time hath, my lord, a
wallet at his back' [8]—which devours reputations, swallows
up famous names, makes armour rusty; a grinning monster,
protean and fantastic, which goes its own way and never
forgives. Or again, the dilatory hero, feeling the approach
of decay and death, offers as a final jest to identify himself
with it, in a series of forced metaphors, loaded with bitter
irony, which do not convince even him, but which, all told,
clearly remind the audience that every tragedy is written in
time.[9]

ACTION

This extreme suppleness in the use of space and time that
we have noted is required also in the play's construction, in
what is called the *action* of a comedy or a tragedy. The action
consists of a series of successive events leading to the solution of the problem or problems posed in the opening scene
or scenes. The interdependence of events and personages is,
of course, obvious. Faced with a given problem, or with
some obstacle, the personage reacts according to his own
character. He may bend the sequence of events in this or
that direction by the force of his will, the violence of his
passions, his desire to vanquish, or his disgust with life. He
may forge his own fate or let himself be guided by it. An
event may strengthen his will to resist or, on the contrary,
break it down, and lead him to defeat, from one incoherence
to another, from surrender to surrender. Failure, death, madness—these are the supreme refuges where safety is found
in escapism if the conflict exhausts his strength, if the obstacles are too much for him. Thus the tragedy closes.

But, tragedy or comedy, there is always a conflict, whether
the character oppose other characters or events take an accidental or compulsive form, whether it be Chance or Fate
that plagues him or strikes him down. The play is the story
of this conflict. The dramatist has his own way of telling it,
of arranging its presentation, the elements and the mystery,
to bring it to its solution. This is what constitutes his technique and what interests us at this point.

Despite the claims of the Classical school to dictate theat-

[8] *Troilus and Cressida*, III, iii, 145.
[9] *Richard II*, V, v, 50 *et seq*.:

   For now hath Time made me his numb-ring clock.

rical fashion, and despite the apparent diversity of techniques and conventions used in different centuries, there are only two ways of offering the spectator entertainment in the theatre: either directly to accept the general convention that is implied by the fact of presenting on a stage, with the help of actors, a dramatic action which has its special requirements, or to feign to refuse it.

Most discussions on this point have dealt with the wrong problems. Great play has perpetually been made with abstract concepts ('Nature', the 'Credible', the 'Real', etc.), whereas these words were obviously being distorted in advance by the meaning given to them, by the use to which they were put, by applying them arbitrarily to other epochs or different schools in regard to which they had neither the same validity nor contained the same implications. To say that a cry of Sophocles is 'natural', that Corneille parts company with the 'credible', or that Shakespeare works in the 'real', does not mean very much: it certainly does not mean that Sophocles was closer than Shakespeare to Nature, or that Shakespeare was further than the author of *Rodogune* from the 'credible'. People forget that for both dramatists a play is a work of art and must be regarded from this angle; they overlook the fact that it is only in the modern age, and more particularly since Ibsen, that dramatists have devoted all their efforts, in constructing their plays, to pretending that they were not plays.

The so-called drama of 'Realism' which flourished at the end of the nineteenth century and the beginning of the twentieth, no doubt for other than dramatic reasons, wanted the spectator to forget, on entering the theatre, that he was going to see a play *acted*. Everything contributed to take away dramatic illusion or, it might be said, everything contributed to strengthen it. A 'slice of life in the raw' was offered in its most objective details; the characters were 'real', the story was 'true', the incidents 'authentic', the language appropriate in the mouths of the characters. The effort of belief asked of the spectator would be reduced to nothing in a play of this kind if the author could achieve perfection in the contriving of sequences of events, the matching of the characters with the general design of the work, and the scrupulous logic of the detail.

This concern for 'truth' was even carried so far that an American author[10] put into the mouths of his personages two lines in succession, the first emanating from the social self, the other reflecting the real thought, stripped of the

[10] Eugene O'Neill, *Strange Interlude*.

mask of falsehood required by convention or cleverness. This
is an admission of failure since a new (and how clumsy!)
convention has to be introduced to inform the spectator of
that intimate reality of the personage which dramatists in
the past had no need to express in such explicit terms.

The logic of life, of reasoning, of emotions—that sovereign
law governing and linking cause and effect—has now only a
relative value in the sphere of art. There its hold is fragmentary and disconnected. The reality of experience and the
reality of art are superimposed but do not mingle. This self-
evident truth, which is not disputed in the plastic arts or
painting, by a false analogy loses its force in the literary arts.
Yet we know that every art is a transposition of the real.
Accumulated experience, knowledge of the human heart, of
historic fact—this is the starting-point, the substance to be
transformed.

Until the realists took pains to hide this transformation, the
dramatists of the past, according to the conventions ruling in
different ages, never claimed to do more than dispose, for a
work of art, of all the possibilities of transformation offered
by their imagination, their epoch, their public's taste, and
that mysterious form of instinct known as genius, which
raises to the dignity of art the illogical and even the absurd,
because it confers on everything that air of supreme reality
which distorts and transcends the real.

For the dramatists of the English Renaissance the problem
did not even arise. Their logic defied all logic, alike in the
presentation of facts and in the depiction of characters. Yet
they succeeded in imposing an illusion of reality much
greater (and more paradoxical even) than could the most
punctilious realists. On a close examination of any play of
that period, not excluding Shakespeare's, the logic is found
to be shaky down to its very roots, and credibility is flouted.

To take an example, one of the greatest: the tragedy of
King Lear, which oscillates between the sublime and the
mad, between the absurd and the blinding perspicuity of
despair. Here we have an aged King who suddenly decides
to throw off the burden of power. He calls before him his
three daughters in order to divide his kingdom between them
according to their merits, the shares being allotted in proportion to their filial love. Here is a first absurdity: has so grave
a political decision ever been taken so frivolously, has a
father ever subjected his daughters to such a ridiculous and
useless test? Could the old man have remained all his life
ignorant of the qualities and feelings of his daughters,
brought up by him, married off by him and designated his

heiresses? A second absurdity arising from the first and without which the drama would not be possible: how, unless suffering from senile imbecility, can Lear be so mistaken about the real meaning of his three daughters' speeches that he deprives the one who obviously loves him best, in favour of those deceitful and cruel creatures, Regan and Goneril? What psychological explanation is there of this blindness, this obstinacy (in face of the protests of Kent who for his pains receives sentence of banishment), this incredible slowness of Lear to realize his fatal mistake, and finally this basic unreality in which the whole play is lapped?

How can it be believed that Edmund would dupe Edgar and Gloucester so easily, and is not the letter which he so ostentatiously conceals (II, ii) in the convention of comedy? How is one to accept all the surprises, all the improbabilities, all the sensational incidents with which the tragedy teems? Madness, disguises, battles, thunderclaps and lightning, strokes of fate and ironic events overdrawn, and, to crown all, the abortive suicide attempt of the blind Gloucester, led by his son, whose voice he fails to recognize, to the edge of an imaginary cliff,[11] from which we see the old man fall in despair? Finally, there is the most serious objection: how can we term the madness of Lear sublime, and claim this as among all Shakespeare's plays the most magnificent monument of his genius, if we confine ourselves to ordinary common-sense judgments on the psychology of the characters and the development of the incidents?

It would mean a complete loss of critical sense to approach the tragedy from this angle. All the plays of the Elizabethan Age, Shakespeare's included, could be made to look ridiculous in this way. Thomas Rymer, towards the end of the seventeenth century, had no difficulty in making fun of Othello.[12] Examining the incidents of the plot, point by point, he drew from the tragedy the following moral:

> The moral, sure, of this Fable is very instructive.
> First, This may be a caution to all Maidens of Quality, how, without their Parents consent, they run away with Blackamoors.
> Secondly, This may be a warning to all good Wives that they look well to their Linnen.
> Thirdly, This may be a lesson to Husbands that before their Jealousie be Tragical the proofs may be Mathematical.

I shall doubtless return to Rymer in a later chapter. Here

[11] King Lear, IV, vi.
[12] In A Short View of Tragedy, 1693, quoted by L. C. Knights in 'How many children had Lady Macbeth?'.

I merely quote one more phrase, the conclusion of his essay: 'The tragical part is plainly none other than a Bloody Farce, without salt or savour.' What, then, is to be said of romantic plays like *Cymbeline, Pericles* or *The Winter's Tale*?

Clearly, therefore, all the objections levelled at this technique of the Action, on the score of its not observing 'credibility', are based on false premises. The action, properly so-called, may be very simple and eventful (as in Marlowe's *Tamburlaine*) or very complex, occasionally even complicated (as in Tourneur's *Revenger's Tragedy*, or in *Cymbeline*). Not only is Unity of Action a dead letter—that is common enough—but it happens that two, three or even four plots (no fewer than seven in Ben Jonson's *Alchemist*) sometimes lack the obvious, indispensable links of dramatic logic.

Of all the Classical requirements, the one whose absence surprises us most—the law of causality, so dear to reasonable minds, and, since the nineteenth century, so tyrannical—was treated without any respect and enjoyed no prestige. It had to yield—as we have seen Time and Space yielded—to the dramatist's purposes. He proceeded not from cause to effect, sometimes not even from the possible to the real, but directly from the impossible to the real, from the improbable to the possible, and from the supernatural to the natural. The most modest of realistic playwrights takes more care to avoid the arbitrary than did the Elizabethan.

In this respect a comedy of Labiche is better constructed than a comedy of Shakespeare. In the latter, the same causes do not produce the same effects; there are effects without a cause (whence came the jealousy of Leontes in *The Winter's Tale*?) and causes which remain without effects (provocations which provoke no reaction). The story develops in a way that upsets all the calculations of good dramatic arithmetic. What became of Lady Macbeth's children? [13] How many children had the Duchess of Malfi and how old were they? How did Thaisa[14] reach Ephesus safely, after being thrown into the sea during a violent storm, in a 'caulk'd and bitumed' coffin? Innumerable questions of this kind would remain unanswered.

The Elizabethan Drama swarmed with *dei ex machina*. Surprises, unexpected, impossible, absurd incidents, complete reversals of situation abound. So do anachronisms, prophecies and marvels. At one moment events rush for-

[13] 'I have given suck,' she says.
[14] *Pericles*, III, i.

ward, as it were, in serried ranks, with overpowering speed and relentless continuity: the hero is hustled and crushed by the fatality of accumulated effects. At other times, everything is limp, jumbled, slack as an unresilient spring; and we do not know whether the author is communing with himself or forgets what he is about, nor whether it is he or the hero who has lost in the maze of tangled incidents and plots the impetus that seemed to direct the play.

What is this personage's motive? Why the repentance and conversion of Bosola? [15] Why Ferdinand's hatred of his sister, the Duchess? [16] Why this death and this feigned madness? A chaste love leads to crime; crime is a purification. The will is stiffened, then relaxed, in the stronger man; the coward ends the play a hero, or the hero a criminal. Cruelty puts on a mild front, revenge mistakes its object, anger suddenly subsides, pride is humiliated without a defeat, lust defiles everything around it, but chastity is doomed to an ignominious death. Everything seems to be steeped in an atmosphere of unreality, and not only in the so-called romantic plays or the tragi-comedies of Beaumont and Fletcher. We seem to be in a new universe, that of the work of art destined for the theatre, where the principles of identity and causality—so tyrannical to the modern mind —are replaced by extraordinary relations and interactions.

Thus, for example, there is no relation of cause and effect apparently between the terrible scene of Duncan's murder and Lady Macbeth's sleep-walking scene, which comes years later, at the end of the Play (V, i). Yet, just as the spectator immediately realizes the contrasted characters of the two criminals from the way they each react to the sight of blood on their hands ('A little water clears us of this deed', says Lady Macbeth; 'Will all great Neptune's ocean wash this blood Clean from my hand?' groans Macbeth); so the obsession of the spot of blood which 'all the perfumes of Arabia' will not wash from 'this little hand' is a tragically ironic reminder, which assumes its full significance only if we remember Lady Mabeth's behaviour on the fatal night.

Again, the symbolic dream of Vittoria in Webster's *The White Devil*,[17] implicitly in close relation with the sequel in the action, starts Brachiano upon his career of crime which, however essential, will be shown to us only through the veil of a magic pantomime.[18] But it is the interpretation of

[15] *Duchess of Malfi*, IV, ii.
[16] ibid.
[17] I, ii.
[18] ibid., II, iii.

the nightmare itself which gives the action its drive,
whereas, for anyone unaware of this mysterious logic, the
dream may seem a useless prelude.

This play of implication is met with everywhere, and tends
to give Elizabethan tragedies that inner unity which simple
logic denies them. We shall see later how poetry gains by
it and how it brings about the close fusion of lyric and
dramatic of which modern authors seem to have lost the
secret.

Often also the play is encumbered with a host of strange
tangled elements and incidents—soliloquies, speeches, moral
or political dissertations, maxims, songs and ballads, funeral
liturgies, ghosts, sword-play and combats, presages, panto-
mimes, masques and disguisings, buffoonery—which follow
each other or are juxtaposed in a disorder more apparent
than real but likely, none the less, to irritate the reader.
For the unity of movement and tone seems to be broken on
this brilliant, and at the same time tiresome, method of
continually creating new focuses of interest, irrespective of
whether they can be harmonized with the central problem
or not. Some of these dramas, indeed, are more like revues
than authentic tragedies, and the least gifted authors are
occasionally incapable of imposing on their play that poetic unity which alone can save it from incoherence. From
the absolute point of view, the value of the play is the
value of the author. In other words, this multiplicity of
effects is made homogeneous only when the author's personality is strong enough to fuse the disparate elements.

But the Elizabethans had to take account of the miscel-
laneous impacts of daily life upon their artistic design much
more than have modern authors: allusions, clowning, arguments, what the public recognized as topical, what its
taste wanted, what threw light on its aspirations—the
latest scandal, the sensational murder, the plot that failed,
the schemes of ambitious politicians, the double-dealing
of diplomats, the moral of this or that event; even the
jokes which some actor had made popular, the lyrical
themes or the puns that had become the talk of the town.

Webster, it will be remembered, protested with some
reason against the tyranny of the public. 'If it be objected', he writes ironically in the Preface to *The White
Devil*, 'that this is no true dramatic poem, I shall easily
confess it', and he goes on to explain that he has 'faulted'
not ignorantly but intentionally, for even if his tragedy
conformed in all points with the taste and habits of the
crowd, it would still be open to objections. Webster is not

sparing in his strictures on the mob which he, like Martial
and Horace, calls 'ignorant asses'. This does not prevent
him from himself making the same mistake as the others
in *The Devil's Law-case*, though it is easy enough to
recognize his hand in the few really great, inspired scenes
of that play. But Webster, with that critical clear-sightedness which is possessed by most of the major English poets,
is deceived neither by the tyrannies to which this *genre*
is subject nor by his own technical skill in freeing himself from them: 'A great part of the grace of this (I con-
fesse) lay in Action; yet can no Action ever be gracious,
where the decency of the Language and Ingenious structure of the Scene, arrive not to make up a perfect Harmony.' This 'perfect Harmony', the unique glory of Elizabethan technique, is achieved by the great dramatists despite the innumerable conventions to which their genius is
forced to bow.

It breaks out in many plays, as anyone can see who
takes into consideration the conventions and the genius.
Ben Jonson, Webster, Shakespeare, Ford—to mention only
the greatest—were not dupes of their twofold debt: what
they owed to their age and what to their instinct. They
might snap their fingers at chronological sequence, causality, credibility; they might juxtapose irreconcilables, pile
up climaxes, drive the action forward in sudden bounds
instead of developing with a steady uniform pace; they
might use extraordinary coincidences, employ substitution
and disguise, pass from the pantomime to the pageant,
place a play within a play, invite the audience to take
part in the action under various pretexts, pursue simultaneously two parallel or divergent and even contrary plots,
and yet be working with the most precious substance of
their thought and experience.

There is, on the one hand, the external appearance of
the play—the palpable, the material, which shocks our
habits, outrages our common sense, offends our taste. But
these are mere surface tricks, only the superficial garb,
and what right have we to quarrel with an artist's choice
of his medium? On the other hand, there is the underlying significance of the play, the human experience inform-
ing it, the poetic vision of the world emanating from it,
the meaning it gives to life, the metaphysical drama which
is its spiritual framework—in short, all that is implicit in
it.

Every playwright, moreover, has his own way of solving difficulties. I mean that a thorough study of technique

would show the diversity of their particular methods, at the very heart of the apparently persistent disorder which modern criticism has so pitilessly analysed and condemned. A strong personality emerges alike from the structure of a play and from the poetic halo surrounding it, and the intimate coherence of composition and poetry takes on, according to circumstances, a different tonality. If Webster brushes aside objections about the logical linking of events, because the virtue of his means of expression and the whole aim of his work lie elsewhere, Ben Jonson on the other hand is all for the art of strict construction; he even takes delight in the difficulties presented by the manipulation of several lines aimed at the same goal by contradictory movements. Violently opposed to all sentimentality (we might say 'all romanticism') Ben Jonson's poetry has a harshness, a violence, perhaps even a sour, dry quality which distinguish him among all his rivals.

Construction and poetry, what the English call 'plotting' and lyricism, are not set side by side but are interdependent; are not parallel but complete each other, proceeding together with the same pace, slowed down or speeded up, towards the same end. Every twist and turn in the plot, every purple passage contributes to give the work its aesthetic quality in a perfect harmony. The Jonsonian construction is immediately recognizable by this cold balance of the parts, by this tension in the interest, of which he is a master, which he tightens or loosens at will; by this acceleration of the movement which suddenly precipitates the play forward, brings it to an abrupt stop, and sends it on again towards its conclusion. This rather crabbed mastery, ordering a world the unreality of which fascinates rather than enchants, congeals the imagination rather than sets it free and carries it away, is of the same nature as that which makes up and sets in motion before our astonished eyes the saturnine types and the joyous revellers, the cruel or greedy characters, sordid or stupid personages, thrown up from the melting-pot of the Humours by some leering, ferocious Alchemist.

Marlowe's *Faustus* derives from the Miracle Play and the Allegory; Peele's *Old Wives Tale* is a fairy-tale intermingled with peasant farce, in which folklore is allied with the supernatural; *Arden of Feversham*, attributed to Kyd, has the innocence of an everyday occurrence described by some unskilful artisan, who has little idea of varying his effects. And as one goes on to the Decadents, their anxiety to rejuvenate their method of presentation, to renovate out-

worn conventions, to enlarge the field of dramatic experience, leads the authors to essay more and more complex
constructions, effects of contrast, parallels, entanglements
of themes and plots which by their over-violence or over-
subtlety may give us the impression of a slackening of the
technique, akin to organic disorder and far exceeding the
object they had in mind.

As a whole, then, each author, and often for each play,
had his own technique, answering to his temperament and
his subject. Each in his own way hacks out a slice of reality
and, with fragments often heterogeneous, reconstructs a
universe that owes nothing to the logic of the reality from
which these fragments came. For the Aristotelian mind,
progression, the order of events, their mutual relativity,
presents a stumbling-block. But we know that the plays were
not arbitrarily cut up into Acts, but into scenes which followed each other without interruption, as one car follows
another in a pageant. If too big a gap separated two series
of events, it was filled by some contrivance such as the
Chorus, who came on to justify the passage or enlighten the
audience; or a song, a pantomime or clowning. Shakespeare
resorts to this device and from the point of view of modern
criticism, the construction of his plays is as open to objection
as that of any other Elizabethan dramatist.

The most direct technique is naturally that of the historical drama, which was originally merely a chopping up—
clumsy at first, then more skilful—of events, with some regard for chronological order. But gradually, as the chronicle
play merged into the study of character and—like any other
drama—received its share of contemporary thought and emotion, it changed its tune, became more varied, was given a
conscious organic construction, and shared in the general
complexity of the age. Between Marlowe's *Tamburlaine*,
which can be regarded as a Chronicle—a series of scenes
modelled on the amazing career of the Tartar conqueror—
and the same author's *Edward II*, in which there are hints
of an attempt to follow the evolution of a character and to
indicate the reasons that drove him to his ruin, there is all
the difference between a lyrical outpouring, carried irresisti-
bly downhill like lava, and a careful composition picking
its steps and determining its stages.

But even in the Chronicle it was difficult for the author
not to succumb to the temptation of the Interlude, of the
overloaded spectacle, the irrelevant episode, the superfluous
allusion—all the diffuse, elaborate encumbrances which a
modern writer pitilessly rejects in favour of other elements

indispensable for logical coherence. For what strikes us is the extreme conciseness, entailing sometimes the complete absence of what I might call the link. In order to illustrate a favourite theme or to speed up a character's career, the Elizabethan author had no compunction in ignoring psychological difficulties or physical obstacles. It is not only the extreme rapidity of the scene in which Lady Anne glides from hatred to indulgence towards Richard, the murderer of her father-in-law and of her husband, standing actually beside the King's corpse,[19] which shocks us, but that this transition should be possible. Yet in this decisive scene Gloucester's qualities of audacity and duplicity break out better, perhaps, than in any other, and it is the passing triumph of these qualities which Shakespeare has to assure for the moment. Elsewhere, the historic truth on which the tragedy as a whole rests is sufficient argument for its credibility. The improbable is as true as the reality, and artistic success justifies the wildest impossibility.

The historic data, the realistic or sentimental story transmitted from mouth to mouth, the romantic or legendary adventure repeated in innumerable works, the ordinary contemporary incident, the fine fable from remote ages or from the ends of the earth (*maior e longinquo reverentia*)—all is grist for the dramatist's mill. But his constant care is to make his story ring true. What happens in a tragedy is fact—what actually happened: books, travellers, the Ancients, the audience in the pit, say so, know it, believe it. There is no doubt about their believing the core of the matter. Whether the incidents conform or not with absolute truth is of little importance. It is enough to know that there is this basis of faith on which the whole structure rests. Similarly, in our day, there is for simple folk the prestige of what they read in print. So, between the author and his audience there is a tacit understanding which facilitates their relations, and Coleridge, to the objection I made above regarding *King Lear*, replies: 'Improbable as the conduct of Lear is, in the first scene, yet it was an old story, rooted in the popular faith—a thing taken for granted already, and consequently without any of the *effects* of improbability.'

The playwright's desire always to keep in touch with his audience underlines and strengthens this patent complicity. What end do the prologues serve but to establish it once and for all? Why do modern authors contemptuously relegate the Prologue to the storehouse of outmoded theatrical prop-

---

[19] *Richard III*, I, ii.

erties? [20] So the Elizabethan establishes contact and blazes his trail. Now, it is the victim's ghost which comes to ingeminate revenge; now, a secondary personage, inviting you to witness the tragedy; or, it may be, an allegorical figure, with symbolical attributes making clear from the outset the underlying meaning of the play: an old man, Time, a politician, witches or a warrior. The key for the symphony is given, a friendly sign prefiguring the theme, commenting on the event, creating the atmosphere, sometimes even unveiling the action and opening the characters' hearts.

The interest, in fact, does not lie in the unforeseeableness of the outcome, since this is often known beforehand: it turns on the behaviour of the characters confronted with the situation invented for them, and on the human experience to be derived from it. The Prologue sometimes brings out the implicit content of the play. With Ben Jonson it is ironical and even satirical: Machiavelli presents Barabbas,[21] and apologizes for his intrusion. Andrea's Ghost, accompanied by Revenge, opens Kyd's *Spanish Tragedy*. On the threshold of *David and Bethsabe*[22] the Prologue strikes the epic and lyric note (*arma virumque cano*). Time invites the imagination to leap over the centuries, and, returning in the course of the action, allays alarm and justifies the caprices of Destiny.[23]

Failing a Prologue, an introductory scene or scenes, of very great diversity, fulfil this complex function of presenting the personages in their respective relationships, of setting the action in motion, and of establishing the connivance— which can be ironical—between author and audience. What English critics call the Induction or preamble, lends itself to this twofold or threefold play, explicitly, or implicitly by way of allusion, and it forms one of the most original features of this technique, which is rich in surprises.

Here again the authors, while respecting the usual conventions, display a most varied gift for innovation. It may be a soliloquy in which the chief personage shows himself as he is and will remain until the end of the play. The first forty lines of *Richard III* throw a crude light upon the character of Gloucester:

I am determined to prove a villain. . . .[24]

[20] This was written before Sir Laurence Olivier's film version of *Henry V* which very effectively retained the Chorus.
[21] Marlowe, *Jew of Malta*.
[22] By George Peele.
[23] *Henry V*, Choruses; *Winter's Tale*, Act IV.
[24] I, i.

while they open the series of plots and crimes hatched by this sinister King. Or it may be a dialogue, in which the less important speakers, as often happened in Classical tragedies, present the leading characters indirectly, telling us what we ought to know so that the play may be intelligible, and, most often, giving by the tone, style, images, or themes they broach, the atmosphere of the play. It may also be the principal characters who come on first, in attitudes apparently static but already shedding upon each other the particular shafts of light that place them in dramatic perspective.

Such, for example, is the very fine introductory scene of *The Duchess of Malfi*, in which the mortal conflict between brother and sister is already sensed in the subtle stage-setting, just because the groups of characters come on one after the other, in echelons as it were: nothing essential seems to pass their lips, yet already the worm is in the fruit; danger seeps out of the formal speeches, the perfidious questions, the whispered confidences. The action, slow to be set in motion, is moreover fraught with peril and, before we know which way it will turn, we are aware of the relative position of the characters, and of the peril that threatens the frail and radiant figure of the Duchess, surrounded by the dark shadows of Ferdinand and the Cardinal.

But the most remarkable Inductions—and Shakespeare has used them freely—are those in which the tone, atmosphere and theme of the play are accented. Here, there is no dramatic realism but an episode, very variable in length, in which the author shows little concern about starting the action. There is a prelude, swift as lightning on the heath, in *Macbeth* where the witches are glimpsed in the flashes amid the noise, uttering their hallucinatory shrieks and imposing the obsessive theme of evil and confusion—a theme immediately repeated by the wounded Serjeant in the following scene and developed from one end of the play to the other, in the thickening murk of equivocation and blood. In these scenes there is no reserve, no irony but the metaphysical irony precariously balanced between the double meaning of the words and the disquieting discords of contrasts in the moral world. Compared with such a powerful poetic driving force, the ferments of character seem of minor importance.

Another Prelude is the opening scene on the storm-tossed ship in *The Tempest*: it tells us nothing that is not set out at length in Scene ii, but it offers a surprising mixture of colour, energy and humour, in the supernatural commotion of sea and sky which prepares us for the magic—complicated, genial and vigorous—of which Prospero is the ruler, as well as for the truculent realism of the comic interludes.

Shakespeare lingers more than appears necessary over these introductory scenes, as if he were sorry to leave the atmosphere that so soon afterwards would give the play its underlying meaning. There is, for example, the slow start of *Hamlet* in which we are first seized by the 'bitter cold' of the guard-night, and gradually our flesh is made to creep by the presence, so much feared, of the Ghost; and when at last it appears we ask ourselves the passionate questions that Horatio hurls at the spectre, hoping with the same feverish anxiety for the arrival of the hero who alone is worthy to meet the mystery and able to dispel our foreboding. But the forebodings persist and increase, and Francisco's 'I am sick at heart' assumes a deeper significance in Hamlet's first soliloquy, some 250 lines later. It might even be said that the whole of Act I is required for presenting the characters, posing the subject, setting the tone and making the tragedy start.

This complicated task, then, has been achieved, sometimes, as in *Macbeth*, with a great economy of means, sometimes with supreme elegance as in *A Midsummer Night's Dream*, or again, as in *Hamlet* or *Timon of Athens*, without regard for brevity or even perhaps, as in *Measure for Measure*, for relevance, and sometimes, finally, with that inimitable vigour of imagery which in a few lines sets before our eyes the character wrapped in his destiny:

> . . . you shall see in him
> The triple pillar of the world transform'd
> Into a strumpet's fool.[25]

Now the action can begin, that is, the characters can come to grips with the situation invented for them.

Here again it is not so much a question that is raised as a line of conduct to be put to the test of facts. Will Macbeth assassinate Duncan to gain the throne? Yes, but how will he bring himself to the point, how will he set about it and what will be the sequel? There is Hamlet's behaviour in face of his duty of revenge, Antony's between political power and love, Coriolanus's between patriotism and pride. At any moment some new fact may break in and change the course of things. Obstacles arise which the hero has

25 *Antony and Cleopatra*, I, i, 12-14.

not foreseen, to which he is often blind, and then we are
given the dramatic story of his blindness.

It would be interesting to examine the part played by
Error in all these plays, a part no less immense and fatal
than in life. There is fighting against shadows, restlessness
in the fog of uncertainty where true proportions are distorted and the sense of reality blunted, the moral sense
warped; where the consequences escape the limited pur-
view of passion and folly, until the hero, hunted by the
very shadows he has so obstinately been pursuing, awakens
terror-stricken at last to the intolerable, blinding truth.

It is on Error and its potent auxiliaries—falsehood,
hypocrisy, paroxysms of madness—that tragedy and comedy
alike are hinged. Deceptive appearances precipitate criminal
jealousy; a false sense of security disarms the victim doomed
to ruin; pride often, credulity, thoughtlessness—these make
men the playthings of calculating minds or of Fortune's
accidents. But it is precisely in so far as he escapes from
the twilight and the darkness that the hero rises to the
full height of tragedy. His march to the stars, his rising
towards the sun, are fraught with pain. His clearness of
vision is dearly won at the cost of sufferings innumerable,
where all activity is denied him and the only reward is to
relate the vanquished hero to the family of the gods.

One may say that the whole economy of Shakespeare's
dramas rests on this discovery of a reality unknown, deformed, almost caricatured. His clear-sightedness, full of
bitterness and steeped in regrets or tears, makes the hero
adopt an attitude that is sometimes melodramatic (e.g. the
theatrical importance attached by Othello to his suicide;
Richard II's metaphysical chatter, etc.) or steels him in the
stoicism of despair after progressive revelations have hardened his nerves (e.g. Macbeth and Coriolanus), or even
burns him up, to the roots of his reason and his being
(e.g. Lear and Timon). The sole exception to this rule,
perhaps, is Hamlet because vision is given him *before* he
has reasons for acting. But I shall return to Hamlet later.

Before this release is reached, Fate has to strike repeatedly. Hence, often, the technique of accumulated effects,
of the simplest and most impressive kind. In this case there
is no complexity: the action follows straight lines, the same
incident being repeated, if not with increased speed, at
least with each time a greater weight, a more redoubtable
impulsion. Tamburlaine flies from victory to victory till he
meets an enemy whom neither his fame nor his power can

intimidate—Death. Richard III strikes down victim after
victim, always with the same ritual. Macbeth goes his way
in blood; nausea may slow down his pace, but crime calls
for crime, and after Duncan it is Banquo's turn, then
Lady Macduff and her children's, until the supernatural
intervenes to crush the monster it has aroused. In *Arden of
Feversham* the attempted murders foiled by chance are
numbered by the half-dozen, till the taut spring of the
action is successfully unwound. There is less of the straight
line in Antony's career or the Duchess of Malfi's death-
march; but Fate strikes its repeated blows, from downfall
to defeat, from torment to despair.

The dramatists, however, are far from being content with
such elementary moves. Their technique, indeed, is much
more varied, supple and complicated. The ups and downs of
a story may follow a winding path where acceleration of
movement and symmetry of design play only a subordinate
part. The action is diversified by incidents quite unforeseen,
mistakes, misunderstandings, surprises, coincidences cunningly devised to sidetrack or delay it, sometimes to obscure
and make it difficult to follow.

Above all, there is at the side of the principal action almost always a secondary plot—sometimes several—which
give the Elizabethan Drama its special character. For often
two parallel plots proceed at the same pace or a broken
pace, cross each other's path, lose themselves, catch up, and
end by being solved together. In some plays, such as *Much
Ado* or even *As You Like It*, where, towards the end, the
couples file past the Duke to receive his blessing, we have
a ballet-movement. In others, the secondary plot either imi-
tates the principal plot as an ironic reflection of it—thus,
Caliban's conspiracy in *The Tempest* is a comic parody of
the real conspiracy against the King—or, as in Thomas
Heywood's *A Woman Killed with Kindness*, in spite of the
situations being reversed, serves as an implicit commentary
on the theme of the principal plot, without being merged
in it.

Or again, three worlds, strangers to each other, act as the
dramatist's auxiliaries in weaving a pattern of many threads,
a rainbow-hued web, where mythology, dream, history and
reality harmonize their contrasted and complementary tones:
of this, *A Midsummer Night's Dream* and, in a more primitive stage, Peele's *Old Wives Tale* are examples. Even in
Ben Jonson—the supreme artist, as I said, in strict construction (the more numerous and complex the plots, the
more difficult the task)—you find a thousand plots at work

simultaneously, catastrophe brushing closely past the characters who should remain unscathed, and finally, by a succession of miraculous balancing feats, striking down the
character who threatened the others. Volpone, for instance,
is the duper duped by his accomplice; or *The Alchemist*
an even rarer triumph of a clever technique, a wild obstacle-
race against the clock, on a moving staircase the steps of
which slip away from under the feet (reminding one of
Chaplin when, with a trayful of valuable glasses, he was
hurrying to prevent himself from falling); but every time
the character recovers his balance and his aplomb, another
trip-up threatens, and all his skill, audacity and speed cannot save him from being brought down in the end.

Then, sometimes also, the fiction abruptly changes course.
A new play, with new actors, comes on suddenly, taking
up the principal theme as in *Hamlet*, the *Murder of Gon-
zago*, a machination aimed at confounding the criminal,
reconstructing the murder in the presence of the assassin
we should say nowadays; or, as in Kyd's *Spanish Tragedy*,
the new play, performed by the same actors, prolongs the
theme and solves the plot under cover of a violent fiction,
thus adding to the bloody climax the strong condiment of
melodramatic irony. In another play, it is the Prologue itself
which introduces the new play—whether the characters of
the Prologue impose their own choice of action on the
players (e.g. Beaumont and Fletcher's *Knight of the Burning Pestle*) or follow the action, punctuating it with their
comments (e.g. *The Taming of the Shrew*) or, using the
magic power of words, produce, like Madge in *The Old
Wives Tale*, a fairy-like action, real or fantastic, under their
very eyes. Finally, the Masque was introduced into the
play to underline its moral significance, to comment on the
theme, or to help in solving the plot. It added the spectacular element of the unfamiliar, the charm of music and of
sumptuous costumes, the entertainment of the dance and
often the piquancy of parody.

It is in comedy, or the romantic piece, that the interlacing
of strong lines, the multiplicity of movements, the subtlety
of stratagems are the most complicated. But Drama does not
exclude involved constructions in which different planes
crash, each group of personages seems to move in its own
world, whereas all of them, from the lower plane to the
higher, end by rejoining each other in a single picture—as
in a modern painting, the lines, the cut corners, the masses
of light and shade compose a surprisingly harmonious whole.

This analogy with the plastic arts, remote though it may

be, has some significance. For example, the eye can take in only one side of a cathedral at a time, yet all, distributed on different planes of space, exist simultaneously and in relation to each other. The balanced volume of this mass can be perceived only by the application of thought which produces order among things ill assorted and re-establishes fragments in their proper relative proportions. And thick masonry justifies the elegance of flying buttresses, just as the bold thrust of walls necessitates the pointed arch, the darkness of the nave calls for the light of foliated rose-windows, and the glory of saints for the grotesquely contrasting devils.

We are far from the regular architecture preferred by classical art. A work of art is like life: perfection of detail is required of it, and the luxuriance of undisciplined foliage, which makes an instinctive harmony out of apparent disorder: here subjected to conventions of climate, ground, or season; there, in cool exultation pursuing poetry and beauty.

'We should not look for perfect verisimilitude to life', writes Mr. Wilson Knight,[26] 'but rather see each play as an expanded metaphor, by means of which the original vision has been projected into forms roughly correspondent with actuality, conforming thereto with greater or less exactitude according to the demands of its nature', and, he adds, 'the persons, ultimately, are not human at all, but purely symbols of a poetic vision.' It remains to be seen, in the following chapter, how far this observation is justified and what pawns the dramatist advances on his chess-board.

THE CHARACTERS

Tranio, at once
Uncase thee; take my coloured hat and cloak.
The Taming of the Shrew

In the foregoing pages the reader has been sufficiently prepared for a new critical approach: he will not be surprised if the rules of traditional psychology applied to the study of characters are similarly called in question. It is advisable to do so both from the point of view of their rôle, or of their relative importance in the economy of the play, and of the criteria by which their absolute human and aesthetic values are to be judged—if it be true that human and aesthetic are identical, which not everyone will accept.

T. S. Eliot posed this problem on its true ground, in an

[26] *The Wheel of Fire*, p. 16, quoted by L. C. Knights: 'How many children had Lady Macbeth?', p. 8.

article that he wrote more than thirty years ago. Most critics of *Hamlet*, he said, have failed to notice that the play is the crucial problem and Hamlet, the character, the secondary problem.[27]

The trouble goes a long way back: at the end of the seventeenth century Thomas Rymer (1641-1713), already mentioned, took up a resolute stand in 1694 against *Julius Caesar* and *Othello*,[28] in the name of common sense. In the eighteenth century it was the fault of the actors, who wanted big parts, as much as of the critics. As for the Romantics, they (Lamb and Hazlitt) were chiefly concerned to extract from Shakespeare's plays a gallery of idealized portraits.[29]

There have been innumerable studies of Shakespeare's heroes and heroines from Thomas Rymer down to our day. Even the actors have dwelt lovingly on their meeting, their passing identification with the Shakespearian character whom they tried to play, and have discovered in studying it some 'rich novelty', some trait worthy of admiration and tenderness; including, of course, the blackest and bloodiest heroes, but not the unpleasant ones.

[27] T. S. Eliot, *The Sacred Wood* (1920)—'Hamlet and his problems', p. 95. There is much talk to-day of Mr. Eliot, but the excellence of his critical teaching, which has had a decisive influence on the younger generation of English critics, has not in France so far gone beyond the narrow circle of English scholars. His lucid analysis, his pertinent observations, the detachment of his mind from pure academic and anecdotal considerations, have opened the way to a fundamental renovation of literary criticism. The present writer owes to him, as well as to F. R. Leavis and his Cambridge followers, both admiration and discoveries.

[28] And with so much appearance of reason that T. S. Eliot himself says that he has never seen a convincing refutation of Rymer's objections. This greatly shocked L. C. Knights (op. cit.).

[29] Here, from L. C. Knights's little book, already quoted, is a short list of works which have as their theme 'the characters of Shakespeare': *A Philosophical Analysis and Illustration of some of Shakespeare's Remarkable Characters*, by Richardson, 1774; *An Essay on the Character of Hamlet*, by Pilon, 1777; *Essays on Shakespeare's Dramatic Characters*, by Richardson, 1784; *Shakespeare's Imitation of Female Characters*, by Richardson, 1789; not to mention the important *Essay on the Dramatic Character of Falstaff*, by Maurice Morgann, 1777, of which Dr. Bradley—the most eminent modern critic to adopt this attitude—said in 1904 that 'there is no finer bit of Shakespearian criticism in the world' (*The Scottish Historical Review*, Vol. I, p. 291). To these may be added, in the nineteenth century, books like Mrs. Jameson's *Shakespeare's Heroines* and Mary Cowden Clarke's *Girlhood of Shakespeare's Heroines*. Actors and actresses have also written about the characters, describing with feeling their encounter with the hero or heroine as if it were a question not merely of a theatrical personage but of someone that might be met with in the street or a drawing-room, with whom relations of friendship, of sympathy, of antipathy, etc., could be established. Again may be cited the patronizing, half-amused, half-contemptuous heartiness with which that symbol of blustering, Falstaff, has been treated; the heart-broken pity for Ophelia, the reprobation, coupled with admiration, of Othello, etc. But little is said of the unpleasant heroes and heroines—Bertram and Helena, Claudio and Isabella, Bassanio, Gratiano, Nerissa.

Most commentators, though anxious to establish Shakespeare's pre-eminence, make some reservation about the ruggedness of his style, the obscurity or the preciosity of his poetry, the extravagance of his metaphors, the disorder of his method, his cavalier treatment of the rules, of propriety, his anachronisms and his puns[30]—in short, all the clumsy defects of a primitive art destined for an age still rude. Such reserves made by rule-bound Classical critics from the end of the seventeenth century have repeatedly been echoed, though in a milder form, even by Shakespeare's most ardent admirers. On the other hand, there has been unanimity in praising the art with which he creates and depicts characters. From Dryden to Dowden, from Addison in *The Spectator* to Dr. Bradley and to John Palmer's last book,[31] there has been the same eulogy in which the accent has been put on the natural, the credible, richness, diversity, the 'unique and inimitable' figure of the personages. 'No one', wrote Dryden, 'has drawn so many characters.' 'His characters', said Pope, 'are so much Nature herself that 'tis a sort of injury to call them by so distant a name as copies of her'; and 'Every single character in Shakespeare is as much an individual as those in life itself; it is as impossible to find any two alike.' [32]

Addison even goes into ecstasies over the ghosts and im-

---

[30] Thus Dryden, adapting *Troilus and Cressida* to the taste of his day (1679), justified himself as follows: 'Yet it must be allowed to the present age, that the tongue in general is so much refined since Shakespeare's time, that many of his words, and more of his phrases, are scarce intelligible. And of those we understand some are ungrammatical, others coarse; and his whole style is so pestered with figurative expressions, that it is as affected as it is obscure.' The style of Dryden's Age had, in fact, lost the incomparable vitality of the Shakespearian period, familiarity with mystery, dramatic rhetoric and the common touch.

[31] John Palmer, *Political Characters of Shakespeare* (London, 1945)—the latest, so far as I know, of the gallery of Shakespearian portraits. Though the author was concerned with the political content of the history plays, and emphasized the political behaviour of the characters, his critical attitude did not differ from that of his predecessors. Thus, he writes in his Preface (p. 7): 'Almost every kind of man to be met with in public life, great or mean, wise or foolish, wicked or virtuous, simple or subtle, calculating or generous, is to be found in these plays. Some are sketched with a few apparently negligent strokes; others are drawn with elaborate care. All can be recognized as political characters who have their counterparts in every generation.' Or again: 'It is true that, Shakespeare being Shakespeare, his political characters interest us also as private persons and have an interior life of their own; but they are essentially political characters.' *Mutatis mutandis*, it is the same attitude that prompts some critics to ask, as a prelude to study of the characters, such questions as 'Was Caesar really superstitious? Did Brutus believe in premonitions? Did Richard III in fact have a withered arm? Did Lady Macbeth really have children, and how many?'—the kind of question that gives its ironical title to L. C. Knights's essay.

[32] Quoted by L. C. Knights, op. cit., pp. 18 *et seq.*

aginary personages, for the same reason: 'There is something so wild and yet so solemn in the speeches of his ghosts, fairies, witches and the like imaginary persons, that we cannot forbear to think them natural, though we have no rule by which to judge of them, and must confess, if there are such beings in the world, it looks highly probable they should talk and act as he represented them.' [33] A century later Hazlitt makes the same remark in almost identical terms: 'The world of spirits lay open to him, like the world of real men and women: and there is the same truth in his delineation of the one as of the other; for if the preternatural characters he describes could be supposed to exist, they would speak, and feel, and act, as he makes them.' [34] It is partly to this notion of 'nature', of 'natural', a touchstone common to so many critics, partly to an inadequate literary sense (refusal or inability to recognize the poetic value of a text), and partly to a vague romantic aspiration (desire for sympathy and communion with the personages created) that this critical attitude towards Shakespeare and, *a fortiori*, towards his contemporaries is to be attributed.

The notion of 'natural' is at once too vague and too tyrannical not to confuse our ideas. In reality it is too summary (people forget that the word has had several meanings since the Renaissance), for it tends precisely to throw into obscurity the other fundamental notion—of a difference in kind between 'Nature' and Art, between objective reality and aesthetic creation. To the classical mind the term 'natural' conveys no doubt a certain cohesion between behaviour and language, an easy elegance in this cohesion in a certain social class. It is 'natural' for a given personage to behave thus or thus in view of his age, his breeding, his station and situation. A mother who did not utter a cry of horror determining the judgment of Solomon, would be inhuman. A Hermione who received Orestes with open arms after Pyrrhus's murder would be improbable. A Harpagon suddenly become generous, an Alceste genial and cured of his misanthropy in the fifth act, would be incredible.

Thus a strict psychological determinism, the laws of which should perhaps be sought much more in the preferences of feeling and reason than in the observations of scientific character-study, rules the conduct of life even when dominated by the passions; and it is the satisfaction afforded by foreseeable behaviour which makes us conclude that it is natural. Once in possession of the basic elements of the

[33] *The Spectator*, No. 419, July 1712.
[34] William Hazlitt, *On Shakespeare and Milton*.

personality, it would be surprising and therefore a violation of the laws of nature, were our forecasts not to be fulfilled.[35] To the requirements of psychological logic must be added those of good taste and style, of balance and an extreme mistrust of any sort of eccentricity, irregular instinct, conduct or thought, arising from a secret caprice or wild idea, even a tendency to philosophize or to dream, or an ill-explained preference for some particular form of poetic expression.

Hence this 'natural', however large the part left to intuitive sympathy for disclosing it (in the creator, I mean), to methodical observation for enriching it, to the technique of imitation for setting it in motion, clogs the creative imagination with its fetters. It intimidates inspiration, stranges fancy, enslaves all youth and desiccates all freshness. Style loses its pace and dash, poetry its mystery, the personages themselves their easy 'naturalness'. And so life is ossified in a rigid framework. It is at this point that the critic comes along and declares that such works are 'pseudo-classical' or decadent.

But the paradox with Shakespeare is that the characters cannot lie down on this Procrustes bed, yet they are granted the supreme title to naturalness at all points. Here lyricism is taking control and sympathetic attachment replaces critical detachment: the sympathy aroused by this or that feature of the character—simple, spontaneous, passionate—is extended to the whole personality, and the extraordinary liberties that the dramatist allows himself are left unnoticed. A word, a gesture, a rhythm, an image, like a sudden lightning-flash, lights up the surface of a commonplace or obscure mind, whose importance is merely fleeting, and confers upon it the authentic lustre of life. In the same way as the recollection of an intonation lingers in the memory and the brightness of a glance or the curve of a smile brings suddenly to mind a long-forgotten face; so the mind, thrown into confusion by this sudden appearance, which strips the deceptive veil covering reality like a film of dust, leaps to identify this surprise with its own unexpressed perceptions.

It is true that with Shakespeare one runs the risk of this experience every moment, and that it is easy to fall into the trap of being carried away by the emotion of joy. And how easy then to glide from sympathy to familiarity, from familiarity to lyric expansiveness, and to allow oneself

---

[35] The Russian novel, Dostoievsky in particular, and psycho-analysis have, however, upset this notion of the natural, with results sometimes just as amusing for the study of Shakespeare's characters.

to be possessed by the personage so exclusively that any contemplation or critical reflection becomes impossible. Is not that what happens with Hamlet, Cordelia, Othello? I really believe it. Yes, one would like to be in love with Rosalind, to spar with Beatrice, to be sentimental with Viola, and no doubt, during a visit to the Chamber of Horrors, to hear Macbeth donning his armour and hurling desperate challenges in Time's teeth, and Lady Macbeth, rigidly walking in her sleep, breathing her three-fold sigh as she rubs the ineffaceable spot that stains her hand.

But is that, I ask, an attitude worthy of a critic? Rather, it is that of Margot at the melodrama: I do not blame her for tears there, but too many susceptible hearts are easy-going about the validity of reasons for those tears. A simple, indeed over-simple, state of mind. For that matter, the sentimental ask nothing else than the chance to make friends with the hero or heroine, to identify themselves with him or her for the duration of the performance or the reading of the play. The eighteenth century was already contaminated by the orthodox sentimentality of Richardson, then by the more artistic and therefore more dangerous sentimentality of Sterne. The nineteenth, even more romantic, raising sentiment to the height of the transcendental and poetry to the dignity of an ethic, was prone to take the shadow for the substance, to delude itself with words, and in spite of the fruitful revival which enriched its capacity for wonder, to evade real problems and be content with illusory realities.

As Dryden's attempts to refine Shakespeare show, it was already difficult in 1693 to appreciate Elizabethan and Jacobean Drama for the right reasons. The meaning of the language had been lost, just as the dramatic conventions, on which the Elizabethan stage had established its greatness, had been forgotten. The Classics no less than the Puritans had dealt it the fatal blow. People could no longer conceive that an author, so careless of rules, so cavalier in his treatment of a refined taste, might, by genius alone, produce immortal masterpieces. They forgot that other ages had other rules and other tastes. They forgot also, and above all, that the contemporaries of Elizabeth and James looked to the English language to do more than did those of Charles II or Queen Anne. And as their characters, despite their lack of discipline, compelled that energy, that gaiety, that ardour for good or for evil which was no longer to be found in Addison's *Cato* or Lillo's *London Merchant*, obviously they must have possessed some magical superiority, rules or no rules. The most permanent was clearly the superiority in treatment of human nature since the other aspects were a matter of taste, of fashion, of conventions.

The nineteenth century gave the mistake a still more personal twist, and falsified the perspective still more. Concentration on the characters distracted attention from the other elements of interest in the play, or imposed upon it an unnatural division into parts which made any view of it as a whole almost impossible. The characters were isolated for study, given prominence, put up on show. Men and women, great and small, wise and foolish, the libertine and the chaste, the mad and the jealous, the kings, the people, Sir Andrew Aguecheek and Coriolanus, Caliban and Prince Henry—what a procession!—from the princess to the cobbler, the bellows-mender to the drunkard, not to mention the fabulous creatures or the fairies, elves, ghosts, witches, monsters. They were torn from their context, out of their natural setting and surroundings and companions. They were to be analysed, caressed like rare hot-house blooms, petted with smooth words, cries of admiration, collectors' gestures.

Then, on reflection, Victorian critics wondered whether these Shakespearian creations were *types,* as Dr. Johnson insinuated, or *individuals,* as it was more romantic to believe. The individual became a symbol, an allegory even; and, rationalism gaining the upper hand, the personal traits exalted to the rank of symbols were transformed into abstract qualities: Macbeth or ambition, Othello or jealousy, Lear or madness and the sublime, Ophelia or pathetic purity, Shylock or rapacious cruelty, Desdemona or innocence, the victim of a tragic mistake.

Then, again, since the play (apart from its hero) presented a few other problems, Shakespeare's political and social ideas called for discussion: was he a democrat or did he favour a dictatorship? In religion, was he a Catholic, an Anglican, or an atheist like Marlowe and his disciples in the School of Night? In his moral, philosophical and metaphysical ideas, had he faith in reason or did he prefer instinct? Was he divided between hope in an explicable world and the sense of an irrational Absolute? Was he an optimist or a pessimist? Did he see order, method and hierarchy, or confusion, despair, nothingness? The nineteenth century did not doubt that he was a poet, but forgot it, acted as if it went without saying, as if it were superfluous to mention—as if, on the contrary indeed, everything should be discussed independently of this essential fact without which no satisfactory explanation of Shakespeare's immense, unequal and disconcerting output can be given.

Only a partial and imperfect understanding[36] can result if we relegate to the background the obvious fact that each play presents itself as a *dramatic poem,* the component parts of which all contribute to the general impression and total effect: they cannot be isolated from each other any more than they can be objectively judged if removed from the poetic ideas, conceptions and taste of the age. The verse, the prose, the rhythms, the vocabulary, the metaphors; the characters, themes, allusions, plot; even the division of the play into acts and scenes—all this has to be taken into consideration.

Now I have not the slightest wish to deny Shakespeare's incomparable superiority in the depiction of characters, which comes from his supreme artistry in the use of his medium—Elizabethan English—which moulds the fundamental themes of his day. But it is equally undeniable that, allowing for his own peculiar genius, he conforms with the accepted conventions of character-drawing as with other conventions. In this matter the Elizabethans obeyed the strict, traditional rules which often make the characters unsuited to the test that modern psychology would apply to them.

In the first place, the characters are situated *outside* all realism, that is to say beyond the psychological determination governed by the chain of normal cause and effect. What motivates the action, as we like it motivated so as to be intelligible, is, first, an immediate, fundamental idea. The character generally comes on cast in a simple mould, and we are not allowed to dispute or assess the motives of his behaviour. Thus the whole of Lodovico in *The White Devil* is contained in the opening word of the play—'Banished'. It was the sentence of banishment, rightly or wrongly given, which decides the rôle of hateful avenger that is allotted to him—I say the rôle, not the character. Once committed, the tragic hero hardly evolves from one scene to another, unless it be so surprisingly that no explanation is possible. There is no psychological crisis in Tamburlaine or in Hier-

---

[36] For example, when *Love's Labour's Lost* was performed at the Odéon Theatre in Paris the critics—either because the production displeased them or because the translation failed to do justice to Shakespeare's intentions—questioned the interest of the play. Yet this comedy cannot leave any admirer of Shakespeare indifferent. The variety in the style, the rich word-play, the massive brilliance of the poetic experience—all contribute to give it a high rank. But it contains no lovable character, and hence the charge of flatness and aridity.

onimo or in Richard III, and the debate in *Doctor Faustus*
is the same from the opening scene, in which he is seeking a reasonable justification for his decision, to the last in
which he succumbs.

External events have no effect on the mind of the hero
who, moreover, can make a sudden *volte-face* and radically
alter his attitude so as to adapt himself to the author's
dramatic purpose. Of course, if Lear did not realize the
ingratitude and cruelty of his daughters, there would be no
tragedy; but the important fact is not that he should open
his eyes but that, on opening them, he should react as he
does. A character may pass from cruelty to pity, like Bosola
in *The Duchess of Malfi*[37]—a wonderful effect of repentance
which fits in with the general scheme of the play and
owes nothing to concern for psychological probability—from
loyalty to treason, from love to hate and hate to love, under
the power of a sudden and inexplicable grace, as gratuitously
as when Lear suddenly realizes the gulf he has thrown himself into—too horified to believe in it—then rushes into
madness.

Proteus in *The Two Gentlemen of Verona* abandons Julia
for Silvia, betrays his friend and tries to steal his mistress,
and then returns to his own first love; and all ends in a
general reconciliation which the baseness of his treacherous
conduct makes very improbable.[38] Love is really swift as
the thunderbolt and repentance rapid as lightning. Chastity
is changed to corruption, avarice to generosity; the wicked
may make themselves gentle and full of pity, yet remain
wicked. The fact is that both attitudes are equally valid,
and such changes, however incredible, leave the character
as much of a piece as he was before, and just as dramatically
effective.

It is rare, therefore, to find the words or action of one
character helping to bring about a change of attitude or
feeling in another, in the sense that we can say that
Pyrrhus's behaviour entails Hermione's decision, or Androm-
ache's the attitude of Pyrrhus. Only Shakespeare can be,
here and there, more flexible and subtle than his contemporaries in this matter. There is no doubt that Iago does in
fact produce the jealousy in Othello (who is predisposed

[37] Bosola, moreover, changes his personality at the moment of the Duchess's
murder and appears as an old man.
[38] The two gentlemen belong to the most marked of romantic conventions:
Valentine in the noble, Proteus in the villain type. No psychological study
of either is possible. Seen from this angle, they are mere puppets of romantic
comedy, like the false brigands, the perfect lover Eglamour and the stupid
rival Thurio.

to it),[39] just as the Ghost's revelation upsets the balance of Hamlet's mind, and Hamlet's behaviour and insults overthrow Ophelia's reason. But if Othello has *apparent* grounds for jealousy—grounds insinuated by Iago—he is at once more and less than a jealous man, just as Leontes in *The Winter's Tale* (in whom the same passion is equally fierce though Shakespeare does not trouble to justify the origin of it) expresses in a different way a suffering and the rage it liberates in terms denoting a different poetic experience and producing a different ending.

If Lady Anne yields in the famous Act I, sc. ii of *Richard III* to the repeated advances of Gloucester whom she detests and despises as much as she hates him, it is not the evolution of feeling that attracts the dramatist and gives the scene its exceptional interest, but the ritual verbal fencing, as brilliant as the sets of wit in *Love's Labour's Lost*—the rhetoric of hatred, of invective and cynicism. There are frequent wooing scenes, moreover, in which the man goes over to the attack, with the added tension of the presence of death, of hatred, and contempt. The villain's insolent victory is only the more effective.

Finally, what are we to say of the extravagant excesses of emotion indulged in by a Timon or a Lear for reasons quite disproportionate to the effects they produce? Motives and reasons are of merely secondary interest. The exigencies of the conduct of the plot, or the moral purpose, of the poetry, even of the verbal rhetoric are more imperative than those of the characters, and the Elizabethan audience would find nothing surprising in this. Thus in Macbeth ambition is but a minor aspect of the character which we should willingly forget without our admiration for the play being thereby affected, if the commentators would cease telling us about Lady Macbeth's ambition. For it is the tragic hero's behaviour in the crisis produced by Duncan's murder, and still more its expression in personal terms, that makes the grandeur and beauty of the tragedy. If ambition is the mainspring of the action, the postulate from which the play starts, it ceases to have the slightest human and poetic interest even before the murder is done, and psychological interest it has never had.

Further, these initial motives are simple and few. In the

[39] Though Shakespeare seems anxious to draw attention to the artificial character of the change in the Moor's attitude towards Desdemona:

> Now do I see 'tis true. Look here, Iago,
> All my fond love thus do I blow to heaven:
> 'Tis gone.
>
> *Othello,* III, iii, **445.**

Elizabethan Age properly so-called, they are almost exclusively ambition—in different forms: the thirst for power,
appetite for conquest, desire for the possession of earthly
goods, the powerful instinct of pleasure—and revenge, in
the service of the noblest as well as of the most ignoble
causes. Revenge and ambition are potent levers of human
tragedy. They were redoubtable passions in the days of
barbarous conquerors, when the sentiment of honour and
the desire to surpass oneself continually made men engage
in violent and dangerous action, and relegated to the background even the passion of love, an appanage of more civilized times. Ambition and revenge give the drama its irre-
sistible power to soar with the *Tamburlaine* of Marlowe and
the *Spanish Tragedy* of Kyd. The Avenger and the Conqueror, leaders of men of action, fill the stage with their
shouts, their menaces, their invective, their paeans of triumph.

The echo of them reverberated down to the decadent
period, with a fertility of invention in the choice of formulas
and situations and a surprising diversity in the composition
of the character which succeeds in making us forget how
monotonous he is. Pride, ferocity, imposture, cynicism, an
extreme tautness of will and passion combined, characterize
him as a rule. The range of psychological states extends
from cold and calculating premeditation to the most frantic
exasperation. The heroes, highly strung and stubborn, are
steeped in a tragic atmosphere in which they often rise to
a paroxysm of hatred and cruelty, rage or madness. They
go forward from scene to scene with the terrible stiffness of
the automaton deaf to all objurgations, knowing nothing
of reason, pity or forgiveness, carried away by the finality
of their rôle. Thus they put themselves upon an almost
supernatural or, rather, superhuman plane.

Seneca, of course, overtops the Elizabethans with his lofty,
admired heroes, fabled figures of unchallenged prestige,
whose sentiments, desires and passions are simply bombastic
appeals for violence and frenzy. The tragic buskin and the
declamatory style increase their stature. The heroes of
tragedy derived from legend or history or everyday life form
an imposing family, but whatever their origin they always
have a family resemblance. For it is the rule of this kind
of play to give it to them. History and legend contribute to
it, but also the class vision of the age which sees kings,
princes and high personages of state surrounded by a sacred,
almost a divine, light: by it all their strange passions, inflexible wills, terrible explosions of wrath and colossal vices

are seen. So much so that Shakespeare, wanting to humanize those of his kings for whom he seems to have felt most tenderness or admiration, is forced either to palliate their wickedness by an extravagant preciosity (Richard II), or to make them express for themselves the consciousness of their common humanity with other men (Henry V), just as he does for the Jew Shylock.

The world of common humanity that revolves round them, the swarm of little people dazzled by the sun's rays but receiving from it the golden reflection that rescues them from their sombre obscurity, is satisfied objectively with ritual and instinctively reverences with wonder the traditional symbolism of the Crown: the outward forms of pomp, authority and fealty. The kings really are tragedy-kings, and the people, who often speak in prose (unless their rôle is merely that of Chorus), are as stylized in language as in attitude and feelings. Remember the importance of the Sun theme and the Crown theme in *Richard II, Henry IV* or *Macbeth,* the royal function in the whole series of Shakespeare's Histories, and the reactions of the humble or unimportant people in the natural hierarchy of social or political functions, whenever they have to comment on events affecting the whole body politic.

'A God is not so glorious as a King', says Tamburlaine,[40] and he dreams of reaching 'the ripest fruit of all, that perfect bliss and sole felicity, the sweet fruition of an earthly crown'.[41] The scenes of the deposition of Edward II or of Richard II, like the one in which Prince Henry puts on the kingly crown before his father is dead, are significant in this connection, and it may well be that the two Shakespearian historical tetralogies, from Richard II to Richard III, though written at different periods, had for their major theme the search for a perfect unity between the royal office and the men who filled it.[42] The pathos of the fall, the

[40] *Tamburlaine,* II, v, 57.
[41] ibid., II, vii, 27.
[42] *Richard II,* the two parts of *Henry IV,* and *Henry V;* the three parts of *Henry VI* and *Richard III.* Shakespeare did not follow the chronological order in writing these plays: *Henry IV,* Parts I and II and *Henry V* came after *Henry VI,* Parts I, II and III, and *Richard III.* It was perhaps for this reason that Richmond, the future Henry VII, of whom there is a glimpse in *Henry VI* and who at the end of *Richard III* restores the national unity and order broken by the bloody Wars of the Roses, was merely a conventional and almost allegorical figure of the perfect king, the anointed vice-gerent of God on earth, destined to restore the material and spiritual harmony disrupted by Bolingbroke's crime in *Richard II.* The portrait of Henry V, Falstaff's companion, more elaborate and more human, is nevertheless in certain respects highly idealized, conforming with the traditional conception of the King which is further strengthened on the stage by his dramatic function. Hence his cruelty, his inflexible contempt: he causes the

deposition or the murder of more than one King seems to lie, for Edward II as for Richard II, Henry VI or Duncan, in this inadequacy of the man for his sacred mission. Macbeth's murder of Duncan is more baleful and horrible since King Duncan is in every respect (except clear-sightedness) a model king. All Nature that night associated itself with the *supernatural* upheaval which provoked Macbeth to give himself to the forces of Evil. And Richard II's lyrical and precious eloquence is the more harrowing since it separates the King the more from the action, so clearly defined by the gardener under the transparent cover of a symbol—the action which alone could save him.[43]

Sin, crime, blasphemy, death assume then in the audience's mind a much more fruitful meaning, and the implied moral lesson that every tragedy necessarily contains harks back—by the behaviour of the characters as much as by the finality of the action—beyond Seneca's gigantic ghosts, to the tenacious tradition of the Moralities. The disturbing allegories of the Moralities, all wrapped up in abstractions, however awkward and stiff they may be, had not ended their moving story in the Elizabethan Age.

It would be absurd to maintain that the personages of the Elizabethan Drama resembled the Morality figures, feature by feature. But the dramatic tradition they represented was perpetuated by successors more varied and complex who borrowed the old mould of the Morality and filled it with flesh and blood. Above all, they inherited from the Moralities the prestige conferred by the poeticized figure of an idea. The frontiers between allegory, type and individual are movable, for the type and the allegory may be individualized without losing their general character.

The analogy I wish to underline strikes us on the first appearance of the character—no mistake is possible about his fundamental identity with a known type, or therefore about the sentiments or passions which animate him, or about the part he has to play in the action. What distinguishes him and what—apart from any realistic purpose

---

French prisoners, taken after Agincourt, to be murdered; he repudiates Falstaff the old man whom as a Prince he had tolerated. On the other hand he appears as a symbol connoting the body politic, torn between divers tendencies, a battlefield between right and wrong, between instincts (good or bad) and reason—the eternal conflict of the natural order with the disorder that always threatens to destroy it.

[48] *Richard II*, III, iv: the scene between the Duke of York's gardener and one of his servants. There is a clear symbol in the analogy between the head gardener's business and that of the king: both must maintain, in garden as in kingdom, the order necessary for prosperity. 'O! what pity is it That he hath not so trimm'd and dress'd his land As we in this garden!'

—gives him a semblance of life, of a life of his own, is his behaviour and speech in the situation where the dramatist places him. The old men *are* old men, the villains villains and the mad mad. But within his own category each character, according to the talent or genius of each dramatist, according to his environment and to the adventures on which he embarks, is particularized more or less clearly, picturesquely, profoundly, while each preserves his own idiom and function.

One cannot imagine Rosalind exchanging her Fool for Olivia's or Lear's, so full of personal traits is each, so suited to the situation, to the atmosphere of the play, and so well does each fit in with the general scheme of the work. Similarly, the villain—the commonest type, indispensable in every tragedy, and ranging from the blackest to the motley of comedy, often a symbolical incarnation of Machiavelli—may in his function be tainted in different ways. Often a bastard (Edmund, Don John), he is also misshapen by nature (Richard III), a Jew (Barabbas), or he may have been reduced to hatred, ferocity and deceit by some major injustice at the hands of Society, some accident of fortune or some harsh discomfiture in love. His physical blemishes (Richard III is deformed, with a withered arm), his bitter experience, sometimes even an evil spell cast upon him, sufficiently justify his moral defects, his greed and his cynicism. As a rule, his superior intelligence gives him the right to despise his dupes, to prepare his approach to evil courses with skill; his audacity and stubbornness authorize him to brave all dangers, to defy all laws, including the laws of character.

The villain's personality, compelled by the game he is playing to adopt various and sometimes contradictory attitudes is astonishingly agile, incredibly versatile. So much so, that the dramatist, fearing lest the spectator also be deceived by the villain if the acting carries him away and his willingness to believe passes over into credulity, warns us from time to time by some soliloquy or aside which sets him in his true light once more and leaves no doubt as to his real intentions. The tawdry finery, grimaces and sarcasms of the Vices are always perceptible in some way or other, from the

I am determined to prove a villain

of Richard III's first soliloquy to Iago's

I hate the Moor,

not to mention the demons who haunt the mind and speech

of Edgar, disguised as Tom o' Bedlam on the heath where
Lear's reason deserts him.

Each personage is thus clearly classified and in all his
infinite variety easily recognizable. The boastful soldier, the
coward, the revenger, the prodigal, the shrew, the high-
minded prostitute, the clown, the tyrant, the pathetic child,
the murderer, and so on—taken thus in any order all have
a family likeness. They act up to the conventional idea
people have of them, and even if there is a temporary
lapse, it entails no mistrust in the spectator's mind. For
it is another convention that the personage sometimes steps
out of his character either to become the mouthpiece of the
author or to give concrete form to the reactions of homely
common sense, or to draw the conclusions from a particular
situation (which the public always appreciates), or simply
because the play's ending requires it. Hence the confusion
noted by the critics in the drawing of certain baffling characters, taken to all appearances seriously, who present a
double aspect, are equivocal like a two-faced personage
and hard to define: such as Isabella in *Measure for Measure*
or Helena in *All's Well that Ends Well*.[44]

The difficulty is further increased by the sovereign convention of the disguise and its impenetrability. The costume
is sufficient to ensure the authenticity of the character's new
incarnation. A hat, a beard, a cloak, the face made-up white
or darkened—and the father does not recognize his own
son (or daughter), the brother his brother (or sister), or
subjects their King. In the simplest cases the new personage,
thus supposed to be unrecognizable, retains for a time none
of the traits of his former character. But there is still the
underlying community of aims, the dramatist's concern to
make the disguise serve to advance the action while relying
on the twofold advantage of complex character and complex
situation to increase the dramatic tension and therefore the
interest of the play.

It even happens that the incredible paradox of an impossible situation may be a powerful attraction and may reinforce the pathos, the charm, the irony and the satire. Thus
Rosalind under cover of the transparent disguise of her
Ganymede continues to have Rosalind's feelings, while giving
the play (and feigning to be caught at her own game) an

---

[44] Isabella, destined for the convent, and despite her protestations of chastity
when Angelo proposes his bargain, despite also the horror that her brother's
pathetic plea causes her, marries at the end of the play; Helena, to get a
husband who hates her and flees her, employs tactics unworthy of a well-
bred heroine, even in comedy. Shakespeare continually uses disguises, substitution of persons, etc.

equivocal turn at once perilous and delicious: this weaves
more surely the subtle strands of love and was for the
Elizabethan spectator the more piquant since women's parts
were played by boys. Thus we have a girl disguised as a
boy for the purpose of her part, and in changing sex she
resumes her actual sex while pretending that it is not hers,
and she reverts to the sex of the borrowed personage. And
on these variations is played the comedy of love.

Malevole, in Marston's *Malcontent*, disguised till the end
of the play, lends piquancy to the incidents of the plot,
which his false identity makes frankly improbable, if only
in the scene where he urges his own wife to play him
false.[45] Vendice in Tourneur's *Revenger's Tragedy* is similarly a virtuoso of disguises and double rôles. He makes
himself the docile tool of the man on whom he wishes to
take revenge, accepts the mission of inciting his sister to
debauchery, urges his mother to assist him in this task,[46]
and plays his successive and incompatible parts with incomparable mastery, on a note of extreme realism which the very
absurdity of the situations further accentuates. The personages thus depersonalized seem to have a double and even
a triple function: they carry forward the play, of which they
are the king-pin; they have a satirical function which links
them, in another respect, with the Morality convention; and
finally, on a still more impersonal plane, they release the
violent passions which supply the lyric framework of the
play.

Such variety is, indeed, calculated to disconcert the modern reader who sees only clumsiness in this subtle art. At
one moment the personage talks in his proper rôle in the
cast to his fellow-actors on the stage; then addresses himself
to the audience, confiding to them his intentions, his feelings towards the other characters, or for ironical ends against
himself or against the others; at other times, he speaks in
the name of the play's idea, its general theme, moral or
political, and then he is no longer this or that personage but
the voice of the general conscience; then he changes, sees

45 *The Malcontent,* V, ii.
46 *The Revenger's Tragedy,* II, i. The contrast between the improbability of
the situations and the violent realism with which they are treated raises the
dramatic interest much more than the episodes themselves do, and helps
to place the drama on the poetic plane. It is almost the 'poetry of the
absurd' already. We are far from the romantic conception of characters
and of idealized poetry. Vendice, becoming himself again, is ordered to kill
the personage he was representing, by the same master, whom he thus
twice betrays. The doubling is so complete that Vendice disguised as Piato
in the scene with Castiza plays his part under the coldly ironic eye of
the original Vendice—Himself and the Other.

himself in a dramatic light and talks about himself, his own part, like someone who knows quite well that he is merely acting, that he is only a comedy-character. 'Farewell, my dear friends, expect nothing more of me. Thus ends my part in this comedy of love', says a personage in Marston's *Antonio and Mellida*. And Shakespeare by way of parody, makes Thisbe say after stabbing herself:

> And farewell, friends,
> Thus Thisbe ends
> Adieu, adieu, adieu!

(T. S. Eliot, reverting to this convention in *Murder in the Cathedral*, makes Thomas say at the very height of his ascetic aspiration:

> What yet remains to show you of my history
> Will seem to most of you at best futility,
> Senseless self-slaughter of a lunatic. . . .)

Vendice in the admirable *Revenger's Tragedy* schemes, jeers, declaims, carries the play from melodrama to satire, from satire to the most intense lyricism—and Vendice is not a *human* character. It is the same with Iago, in a tragedy on the purest lines (the most psychological, no doubt, of all Shakespeare's tragedies), in which his conventional duty is both to further the drama (as Oenone furthers that of *Phèdre*) and to allow the experiment of jealousy—which he creates from the very first and watches gloatingly and hatefully—to develop on the lyrical plane, of which he remains to the end the aggressive and ironical counterpart. This function is, I believe, much more important than the interest of his character, however diabolically intelligent this may be supposed to be.

Side by side with these types, sketched above in broad outline, there develops, for similar reasons and for similar purposes, the convention known as that of the Jonsonian Humours, of which the Melancholic is the most marked and also the commonest type. It is not a question of the classical abstractions, catalogued as the Miser, the Jealous Man, etc., but of peculiarities which end by absorbing the whole personality. We know the theory of the four Humours (Sanguine, Phlegmatic, Choleric and Melancholy), the proportions of which in a man's body determined his temperament: too much of this or that humour destroyed the balance, inclined to this or that disposition, favoured this or that passion which it whipped up to a frenzy. The whole character was impregnated with it.

The effects of the predominance of each humour were well

known and, though numerous, could be immediately as-
cribed. But the proportions varied infinitely, and the un-
balancing could be brought about by a hundred fortuitous
influences, hereditary, physiological, astrological which governed the individual's behaviour and dominated his life in
the most tyrannical manner. Burton wrote a massive and
documented book on the causes, effects and remedies for
melancholy, in which he reviewed all the varieties of the
malady. To read *The Anatomy of Melancholy* (1621: its
composition dates it in the mid-Jacobean period; it went
through a dozen editions in the course of the century) is
to watch a procession of all human follies, from the oddest
to the wildest.

In a volume bristling with quotations, under a shower of
anecdotes, the Christ Church solitary, a melancholic of
melancholics, hunts down his fellow-sufferers from the remotest antiquity to modern times, diagnoses their trouble,
studies the symptoms and effects, and prescribes cures. Admirers of the Elizabethan Drama can find in Burton, dogmatically, almost scientifically analysed, the most outstanding of the types found on the stage: the *inamorato*, the
hypochondriac, the solitary, the faddist, the superstitious,
the lycanthrope, the jealous man, the frenzied, the ecstatic
—all who, in one way or another, need to be treated with
hellbore and borage (then regarded as potent remedies
against madness).

These personages, however psychologically justifiable they
may appear, however firmly anchored their character, come
even less than the traditional types within the normal range
of classical psychology. More marked, more artificial, more
on the fringe of humanity, they often achieve an halluci-
nating reality. Their very names, symbolizing their condition
and function, put them immediately beyond the pale of
ordinary human beings and into the fabulous province of
monstrous creations. Let us merely recall the rapacious,
grimacing trio: Corbaccio, Corvino, and Voltore, three birds
of prey who lie in wait for the carcase, with sensual, shifty
faces: they gravitate round Volpone, while Mosca buzzes
about his canopied bed, slyer than the Fox, more rascally
than even the dehumanized, predatory trio.

The animal resemblances, of course, are symbolical: they
go no farther than allusions, there is no actual metamorphosis. But analogies are common enough. Among innumerable
examples we might point to the quartet of disreputable
sons whom Tourneur sets beside Vendice: Spurio the
bastard, Lussurioso the debauchee, Ambitioso and Super-

vacuo; whereas Castiza, the incarnation of purity, a life-
size doll, her face white as wax, moves about in an uncertain light, in which the green of the corpses melts into
the red of the bloodshed and lights up the dazzling radiance
of her icy, inhuman virginity.

All these personages wear their characters, so to speak,
on labels and the mention of their name guarantees us the
colour of their liver. The Malcontent, immortally pilloried
in Marston's comedy that bears his name, at once Altofronte
and Malevole, has become almost as indispensable as the
Revenger with whom he is often confused. He has brothers
and cousins everywhere, in tragedy or comedy, suffering
from recurrent or chronic melancholy, impulsive or reflective,
victims of the world or of their own passions, servants drawn
with satirical intent or, it may be, noble nonentities in the
blackest of tragedies. Sardonic and mocking, this snarling
misanthrope is ready for any kind of imposture and crime,
insults foaming on his lips, like Timon of Athens, or a
skull in his hands, like Vendice or Hamlet, or his hat pulled
down over his eyes, like Webster's Lodovico or like Bosola:
by turns he storms and grins, meditates and menaces. He
is the moralist's and the satirist's tool, whose invective, while
it lashes the vices and corruption in the toils of which
humanity is caught, presupposes a positive moral code, a
far-off redemption to which even the most hardened blas-
phemer aspires.

What a strange gallery of abnormal characters, with their
stiff movements, their unfinished thoughts, their powerful,
primitive emotions! What a disconcerting tribe, grimacing
amid the motley throng of uncompleted figures that gesticu-
late in the immense Elizabethan Drama! Whether the touch
be light, as in the melancholy Jaques of *As You Like It*,
so ill treated in his scenes; or whether the traits be harsh
and hard, as in Ben Jonson's characters, or crude, bold
woodcuts (Webster's villains), or sharply incised (Tourneur's), or explored to the point of disquieting ambiguity
as—if I may be forgiven the heresy—in Hamlet: all are so
many partial masks upon man's face, and the art of this
sensitive, intelligent age, haunted by a moral sense, sought
to pin them down for the drama's service. They are so
many pieces, puppets or living portraits of which modern
art, in its humbler moments, would not be ashamed.

Evoking them in this way, watching their traits with
fascination, one is tempted to think of those paintings in
which the smile becomes a grimace when looked at from a
different angle. If in spite of myself I revert to the analogy

—arbitrary and imperfect though I know it to be—of an art gallery, it is because the shifting crowd of picturesque personages forms, in the vast perspective of memory, an abstract, perhaps moral, poetic order that is greater than reality. Here, it may be, is a hateful lip suddenly transfigured by the vision of death; there, a bovine image calls up a legendary Minotaur—nothing exists save on canvas or on the stage or in our imagination. Ecstasy is to be perceived only in a face deformed by grief or by laughter. The strange denizens of this elusive world of ours create out of themselves a sort of fantastic, measured ballet in which each finds his place, serves for contrast or harmony, joins the troupe of his fellows, dreams or observes; acts aggressively or cunningly, humbly or arrogantly; then night falls upon them, the dead mingled with the living, in attitudes tender or base, while the shadows determine for ever which are the victims and which the executioners. And the colloquy goes on, without beginning or end, the more real for being unreal, in a language as strange, as full of light and shade, as outrageous as possible—a supreme convention giving coherence to the dream and body to the insubstantial, making perceptible the ideal order of life by its capacity for expression and its power of creation.

In this universe Shakespeare no doubt claims room for his own creations who always seem to have some feature marking them as his rather than as conventional figures. Even his most restricted portraits, the most extravagant, or incredible or most colourless, give proof of an experience that cannot be reduced to their prototypes. And it is about them that there are most questions to be asked. Yet in his plays there are 'flat' characters as impersonal and vague in outline as those of other playwrights. There are all the walking-on parts, lacking in finish; there are the types and 'humours', monsters and giants. It is useless for the psychologist to try to analyse them so as to discover their nature and satisfy our passion for logic. But the impenitent critic, despite all his discomfiture, still has the illusion that they have a more concrete life, more intense and full of light and shade; he finds them nearer reality, and disconcerting features in them are unhesitatingly put down—after all attempts to explain them fail —to the fact that 'life is like that'.

The automatic reflex of the class or kind the character belongs to seems suddenly to be broken by some wonderful cry or gesture; it is destroyed by an unexpected emotion produced by the dramatic incident, and at once the eyes light up, the cheek flushes, the blood courses through the veins. Freedom has broken in upon the determinism and makes credible a world about which we had our doubts, and where everything is possible, creates and re-creates itself because the creature evades the law of its creation. The depressing rigidity of an unchangeable finality that checks movement, freezes attitudes and dictates language, is tempered in the Shakespearian character by the unexpected: he is a chartered libertine. There is an abrupt change of tone, a word fraught with familiar sound, an image that throws a new light on the scene, a certain way Shakespeare has of being aggressive, or ironic or full of grief; and then the sky clears, there is electricity in the air, and a new world is born. 'O brave new world that has such people in 't!'

But let us never forget that it is with words that this miracle is produced and that the miracle is possible only because of the potency of language.

LANGUAGE

Few things that can happen to a nation are more important than the invention of a new form of verse.
T. S. ELIOT

Those who read French translations of Shakespeare cannot fail to be struck by the uniformity of their language and style. Yet everyone knows that *Richard II* and *The Winter's Tale* show all the difference of conception and treatment that exists between an imperfect work and one written fifteen years later by an experienced artist. It is rare, even, to find in the course of a single play no variations of tone and style, calling the reader's attention to the fact that the author is changing his attitude, his intention or his conception regarding his characters or the world they represent. Thus in *Love's Labour's Lost* there are several styles and tones, which Shakespeare is at no pains to combine and harmonize: it is an experimental play.

The translation generally reduces everything to the same dead level. Often, while seeking to preserve the metaphors and mannerisms, it fails to follow the variations of mood, or the breaks in the rhythm, to keep the connotations and associations of words which the translator's language blunts or simply omits. In the original there is always something that cannot be rendered in a foreign tongue and it is precisely the essential thing: what constitutes style. Yet it is natural to say that a play, like any other written work, attains its own particular form of greatness or beauty only because it has style, its own style.

The best introduction that I know to the study of problems of style is Middleton Murry's book comprising the six Lectures that he delivered at Oxford in 1921.[47] In trying to make the tour of his subject before coming to grips with it, and rejecting the famous but deceptive formula of Buffon, Middleton Murry quotes Stendhal: 'Le style, c'est ajouter à une pensée donnée toutes les circonstances propres à produire tout l'effet que doit produire cette pensée.'[48] Here is a fairly abstract analytical definition which has the advantage of being free from all romantic associations. For style does not mean only the presence of a particular writer's characteristics by which he can be differentiated from all others (the style of Sterne or of Saint Simon, for example). Nor is it merely that consummate art possessed by a Flaubert or a Gide, of describing, exposing or setting an idea or emotion in its right place. Style is also, and above all, a quality that 'transcends all individual characteristics', though it needs these in order to display itself; it is 'a complete fusion of the personal and the universal'. And if Stendhal's definition, as Middleton Murry complains, 'carries us instantly into the ether of metaphysics', it none the less covers exactly the ground which criticism must explore when it seeks the reasons for this complete fusion of the personal and the universal.

For Stendhal clearly saw the *function* of style, if not its precise nature, and how style can best fulfil this function. He realized that a thought is never expressed in the absolute but in relation to an effect to be produced. And style, he implies, is the most perfect, the least questionable co-ordination between the expression of the thought and the purpose for which it is expressed in that particular form. It is this idea of function, of the goal to be reached, which marks the writer's intention to produce such and such an effect, and which in consequence must be borne in mind. All style, therefore, is directed towards achieving a certain effect (defining, describing, demonstrating, refuting, catechizing, moving, causing laughter or fear, etc.), and no style more than that of the dramatist.

Once this idea has been granted, we shall have no objection to recognizing that the Elizabethan dramatist's style is one of impassioned poetic rhetoric, the two commonest functions of which are to persuade and to touch the emotions. This twofold object is at once inside and outside the

[47] John Middleton Murry, *The Problem of Style* (O.U.P.). This is the best Murry and is of capital importance for anyone interested in the problem. [48] 'Style is the addition to a given thought of all the circumstances calculated to produce the whole effect of which the thought is capable.'

play. The character—any character—addresses himself to his fellow actors but he also addresses himself to the audience. He strives by words, alike for himself and for his author, to achieve his destiny and to make a success of the play as a work of art. His language is literally rhetorical, and I use the term in no derogatory sense, for it must be admitted that rhetoric may be good or bad, and that it is not uniformly bad. The word is unfairly decried. The Elizabethan Drama alone should have saved it from contempt.

Racine explicitly recognizes the double function 'of instructing and of pleasing' which he assigns to Tragedy, and the choice of these two words is significant. It commands a harmonious vision of the world and implies an acknowledgment of the good taste both of dramatist and audience. It is a more limited but more refined function of art than that assigned to it by Corneille, for Racine belongs to a less boisterous, more civilized age. His rhetoric also differs from Corneille's, which tries to follow the evolution of taste rather than of subjects and to catch up with the new fashion. But it was a fruitless attempt for, as he grew older, Corneille's experience of life did not become richer: he could not change his personal vision and integrate it in the universal. The universal is not the eternal but the reflection of one community's characteristic modes of thought and feeling at a given moment of its history. Shakespeare's achievement was to make his art express his own experience, and by his treatment, plots, characters and style faithfully to record the mind and movement of his age. A study of his rhetoric would show in brief not merely his individual qualities but the evolution of rhetoric in Elizabethan Drama.

This rhetoric is a very special art—the art of one epoch and of one kind, pursued for definite ends, working with and upon a certain form of sensibility. Gathering experience as it proceeds, this art as always happens grows richer and more various: it evolves from the simple to the complex, from the stiff to the flowing, passing from one mode of expression to another until it wears so thin, so unmindful of its own conventions or so anxious to innovate that it loses itself in a fatal formlessness by which even Shakespeare's last plays are threatened.

We must remember that the theatre cannot neglect ethical purposes (taking the word in the widest sense), and the Elizabethan dramatist was constantly reminded of this by Seneca, the Middle Ages and the last of the Moralities. Vices and Virtues, variously disguised, fill the stage and remain—whatever changes they may undergo—the antinomies that

constitute the moral world. Man's destiny is a strife, continually renewed, between Good and Evil, and without
trying to make of the theatre a kind of misbegotten, misapplied pulpit, Drama takes up man's cause, incessantly
opposing a moral order to the forces unleashed against him
even when hope is at its lowest ebb. By direct or roundabout
channels, according as the author's intention is deliberate
(which the author of Moralities was), or instinctive (as any
playwright's generally was), the essential aim remains the
same: to persuade by argument and by emotion, so as to
induce man to give a positive meaning to life. The two
functions of argument and emotion are inseparable, and the
exercise of them calls for the use of rhetoric.

The consideration of this rhetoric raises many difficulties.
It is in the first place *dramatic,* which implies a technique
of dialogue, soliloquy and aside. It is also *poetic,* which implies the use of a certain logic of poetry, not excluding but
completing the narrative, exposition, demonstration or refutation which is addressed solely to the intelligence; poetic
imagery, vocabulary, rhythm, sound effects also penetrate to
the very roots of sensibility. Thus the appeal is, by turns
or simultaneously, to the mind and the heart, in proportions
that may be varied *ad infinitum,* until that closest fusion is
experienced in which they are indistinguishable. Then occurs
the miracle which is always the dramatist's aim: the transposition on to the aesthetic plane of a human experience,
imagined or real, that is worthy of belief and admiration.

Only the very greatest can succeed here, yet all attempt
it assiduously, whether seeking with rudimentary means to
get the easiest effects, or, as their mastery of means of expression grows in extent and complexity, to stir the deepest
feelings and the subtlest apprehension of the most harrowing
problems. An infinite range of devices is thus brought into
play, some of them transparent, others exhausting the resources of the most experienced commentator.

The language, then, like the construction and the characters, will not be in any way 'realistic': I mean, it will be far
removed from the everyday speech which the modern stage
tends to employ. This is true even of realistic comedy, so
called (as opposed to romantic comedy or tragi-comedy), in
which it is commonly supposed that the characters talk the
language of every day under pretext that it is familiar, racy
or aggressive. The fact that it is, indeed, idiomatic and
borrows its rhythms, its vocabulary, its turns of speech from
the spoken language does not in any way contradict this
statement. For it is obvious that the language of the theatre

(which was, or was to become, a written language) derived
from the rhythms and phrases of the spoken tongue its most
effective power of expression, while taking its stand on a
higher and very different plane.

This is true also of non-dramatic poetry. The great poems
of Donne, for example, are composed with the idioms, the
syntax and the rhythms of the English spoken in his day,
and yet were never 'realistic'. Similarly, T. S. Eliot, through
love of contrasts as much as through his own poetic inevitability, will suddenly (and ironically) introduce whole
passages that seem to be transcribed from current language,
and are none the less great art.

In the Renaissance Theatre these remarks apply to the
pages of prose that are found in the comedies as in the
tragedies and are governed in the same way by the laws of
a rhetoric less formal, indeed, but as carefully planned as that
of verse. Here the use of prose is more than an attempt to be
true to reality. It is an effort to make supple, not to degrade,
a style which is comparatively free to resort to violence,
irony and satire, less formally, more at ease than in the
rigorous rhythm of verse. Thus we pass from one plane to
the other, or sometimes the same themes are given higher
value by a change of tone, by the play of fancy, by a clever
imitation of local idiom, of the people's way of speaking, of
trade terms, even of foreign languages, in which occasionally
whole passages are met with, both in the comedies and the
tragedies.

But it is verse that the playwright most often employs in
order to give his work the prestige of poetry. Not that he is
invariably bound by the convention that noble heroes must
talk nobly (some humble characters like the gardener in
Richard II are given poetry as stylized as that of kings and
great lords). But verse has for more than two thousand years
been a device for ennobling and dignifying language. It
immediately seizes the attention, instantly raises tragedy to
a higher plane than that of life. Verse is a form of expression
with solid rhythmical foundations, well articulated, with
visible structure, capable of bearing the image, the aphorism,
the emotion more strongly, crisply, brilliantly. It strikes
peremptorily upon the ear; it dwells in the memory; its
repetitions fall thick and fast, and it lends itself to the full
and well-planned period. It calls for embellishment, it can
be graced by music and the magic of rhythm—in a word,
it affects the senses and captures the mind; it is the hand-
maid of drama and poetry. To attain perfection it has but
to abate its rigorous formality, that it may follow every shade

of feeling, every twist and turn of thought. It is the dramatic
fortune of every form of art to pass from stilted, mechanical
awkwardness of the early stage to the harmonious mastery
of the great ages.

It is hardly necessary to call attention to the great variety
of the dramatists' versification, from the abandonment of the
'fourteener' [49] up to the general adoption (which did not
exclude other forms occasionally) of the unrhymed iambic
pentameter. Marlowe, though not its inventor,[50] made it
the great metre of the theatre and it became the dramatic
vehicle of expression *par excellence*. The fourteener and the
alexandrine were far from easy to handle. The pentameter
(own brother to the French decasyllabic metre) had proved
its value in Chaucer's hands: its divisions are less monotonous, the rhythm can be made more supple by the introduction of Latin polysyllables, and the absence of rhyme gives
it an unlimited freedom of enjambment. It can be varied,
also, by reversing the metrical pattern (passing from the
iambic to the trochaic), and with occasional anapaests it
readily adapts itself to the fluctuations of emotion without
any loss of vigour or speed.

It is equally suited for exposition and narrative, epigram
and maxim, long flights of oratory or the rapid give-and-take
of dialogue, for the movements of passion or the calm unfolding of ideas. Its history from Kyd and Marlowe to Webster or Massinger would serve as a sufficient guiding thread
for a study of Elizabethan Drama. This would in point of
fact be a study of the progressive liberation of form, parallel
to the evolution of sensibility, and would show the gliding
of one rhetoric into another, like a mirror reflecting the
originality and genius of each artist.

For it was to the handling of blank verse that all applied
themselves. Each writer stamped it with his own personality,
much more than was possible for the French classical drama-

[49] Line of seven stresses (or fourteen syllables) with two well-defined
caesuras, iambic in rhythm, alliterative and rhyming. Monotonously rising
and falling, it is not capable of much variety. It is the ballad metre (cf.
The Nutbrown Maid) revived with a typographical arrangement dividing
it into one line of 4 and one of 3 stresses by Coleridge in *The Ancient
Mariner*. Chapman used it for his translation of *The Iliad*, and Thomas
Preston in his *Lamentable Tragedy of Cambyses, King of Persia* (1569),
the turgid style of which was parodied by Falstaff. Traces of it are found
in *Love's Labour's Lost* (1593), though here, it is true, Shakespeare uses
it ironically. An example of a 'fourteener' from Cambyses is:

Do not entreat my grace no more for he shall die the death.

[50] The credit for having been the first to use blank verse is due to Henry
Howard, Earl of Surrey, in his translation of the second and fourth books
of the *Aeneid* (1557).

tists who were wedded to the regal grandeur of the statuesque
alexandrine. Of course the poetry of these great writers also
had its individual characteristics: Racine's, a suave purity,
grace and clearness, with sometimes a dream-like quality that
prolongs the spell in ever-expanding ripples; Corneille's, a
majestic eloquence, often packed with sober, proverbial wisdom; and Molière's, an elegant ease and facility in repartee.
But, considered as a whole, the French mould does not vary,
the metal poured into it is free from debasing alloys, doubtful adjuncts or foreign elements. French rhyme gives the
verse its regularity, prefigures the pattern of its curve, and
imposes the divisions which occur but rarely and unevenly.
The vocabulary is conventional, and the playwright seldom
gets his effects merely by combinations of words or by undisciplined metaphors: his discipline tends to make his work
of art perfect, with a formal, harmonious perfection, and to
lift it to a higher intellectual plane.

In Elizabethan Drama, on the contrary, each writer can
give blank verse the 'bite' and forthrightness, the ingenuity
and suppleness that will make it the willing tool of his own
sensibility and experience. Hence an incomparable diversity
not to be found, I believe, in the poetry of any other age
or perhaps in any other literature. And hence, consequently,
all critical opinion must be supported by a careful examination of Elizabethan verse. The reader cannot really appreciate
the text of a play if he knows it only through the flat, colourless medium of a French prose translation.

Originally, associated as it was with the rhymed verse of
an erudite, mannered tradition and with various regular forms
(distichs, stanzas, sonnets, octosyllabic or other shorter verse,
lyric interludes or songs, even doggerel [51] introduced into
its fixed pattern for reasons almost always dramatically valid),
blank verse was no more supple, and hardly less monotonous, than any other verse-form. Indeed its constitutional
stiffness and the automatic beat of its rhythms no longer
adorned by rhyme (though rhyme, too, could be monotonous), made it the ideal vehicle for robust ideas and strong,
simple passions, driving straight forward without heed for
light and shade. It began as the awkward instrument of a
rhetorical mode of speech with an ascending rhythm; it was
not afraid to be turgid or repetitive—on the contrary, it
forged ahead tirelessly, like a piston-rod, to achieve its full

[51] Doggerel covers any verse of careless form and rhythm, essentially popular and often burlesque, misusing the classical metres which even the most
respectable authors sometimes employed for broad farce and satire. It often
appears in comedy.

effect without regard to the means. It almost attained greatness by sheer force of intimidating the reader.

In this declamatory and lyrical phase, facts, ideas and
passions were juxtaposed, piled up or linked together in
succession cumulatively, with a simple, pitiless logic that
must carry conviction: as a battering-ram burst open the
gateways of a town, so did the verse storm its way into the
emotions. Demonstration and association of ideas were un-
answerable, the invective or vituperation superb, the lament
or the lyrical outburst moving in the extreme. Such was the
blank verse of Kyd or Marlowe or of Shakespeare's early
plays.

Here one may speak of bombast, inflated style and terrible
monotony. The trouble is that the characters and the passions that motivate them are larger than those of the common
run of humanity, alike in their violence and in the simplicity
with which they rush into speech and action. But this rhetoric
which employs the most striking devices of oratory—the
earliest—is adequate for its purpose and always fulfils its
function. The extraordinary vitality of this dramatic style
is supplied from a great variety of sources—figures of rhetoric of all kinds, anaphora, antithesis, repetition, parallelism,
apostrophe, exclamation, simile, hyperbole, metaphor, sen-
tentia, hackneyed expression and mannerisms innumerable.
They give the paragraph and the dialogue the bony structure
which bears the flesh of idea and emotion.

The Elizabethans considered the two major arts of eloquence and poetry to be inseparable from each other. They
attributed a prophetic function to the poet (*vates*)—the
Oracles of Delphi and the utterances of the Sibyl, as Sir
Philip Sidney observes, were given in verse; they regarded
the dramatist's function as similar to that of the orator: to
persuade a large number of people simultaneously by an
appeal to the emotions; and the rhythmical movement of
the poetry itself required the breath-control and delivery of
speech. For some or all of these reasons a dramatist combined the powers of poet and orator.

In his famous treatise, *The Art of English Poesy* (1589),
George Puttenham devotes his third book to 'ornament' and
studies in detail with the aid of numerous examples all the
figures of rhetoric, to which he tries to give in English the
learned names. 'There is nothing', he says, 'so fitte for
the poet as to be furnished with all the figures that be
Rhetoricall and such as do most beautifie the language with
eloquence and sententiousness.' The dramatists did not stint
themselves! Sir Philip Sidney similarly said of *Gorboduc*,

'the first English tragedy' (1561) that it 'is full of majestic speeches and phrases which sound well, rising to the height of Seneca's style'.

And here we find Seneca again, the cynosure of the Elizabethan generation, whose influence in forming this dramatic rhetoric was so great that T. S. Eliot has no hesitation in asserting that 'Not only the evolution of the dramatic structure, but the evolution of the blank verse cadence, took place under the shadow of Seneca; it is hardly too much to say that Shakespeare could not have formed the verse instrument which he left to his successors, Webster, Massinger, Tourneur, Ford and Fletcher, unless he had received an instrument already highly developed by the genius of Marlowe and the influence of Seneca.' [52]

Here some quotations may perhaps be useful, for a conclusion that will be reached below must be amply justified at this point. It is a thoughtful style, direct and clear in syntax, logically articulated; the images discreet, the monosyllables plentiful, each verse with its conjunction, adverb or relative pronoun:

> A day will come when York shall claim his own;
> *And therefore* I will take the Nevils' parts
> *And* make a show of love to proud Duke Humphrey,
> *And*, when I spy advantage, claim the crown,
> *For* that's the golden mark I seek to hit.
> *Nor* shall proud Lancaster usurp my right.
> *Nor* hold the sceptre in his childish fist,
> *Nor* wear the diadem upon his head,
> *Whose* church-like humours fit not for a crown.
> *Then*, York, be still awhile. . . .
>   2 *Henry VI*, I, i, 240-9.

This style is frequently met with in the soliloquy, spoken in front of the stage to the spectators so as to establish between hero and public that almost impersonal link required for the full understanding of motives. Elsewhere the methods are more obvious. Here Lorenzo in *The Spanish Tragedy* wants to make Balthazar woo his sister Belimperia. He piles up comparisons, all applied in the same pattern:

> My lord, though Belimperia seems thus coy,
> Let reason hold you in your wonted joy.
> *In time* the savage bull sustains the yoke,
> *In time* all haggard hawks will stoop to lure,
> *In time* small wedges cleave the hardest oak,
> *In time* the flint is pierc'd with softest shower,
> *And* she in time will fall from her disdain.
>   *The Spanish Tragedy*, II, i, 1-7.

[52] T. S. Eliot in 'Seneca in Elizabethan Translation', page 85 of *Selected Essays*.

Or again, the well-known lament of Henry VI on the battlefield of Towton, in which the monotonous repetition produces an effect of hypnotism, of indescribable weariness:

> O God! methinks it were a happy life . . .
> To sit upon a hill, as I do now,
> To carve out dials quaintly, point by point,
> Thereby to see the minutes how they run,
> *How many* make the hour full complete;
> *How many* hours bring about the day;
> *How many* days will finish up the year;
> *How many* years a mortal man may live.
> When this is known, then to divide the times:
> *So many hours* must I tend my flock;
> *So many hours* must I take my rest;
> *So many hours* must I contemplate;
> *So many hours* must I sport myself;
> *So many days* my ewes have been with young;
> *So many weeks* ere the poor fools will yean;
> *So many years* ere I shall shear the fleece:
> So minutes, hours, days, months and years . . .
> Would bring white hairs unto a quiet grave.
>   3 *Henry VI*, II, v, 21-40.

Here the rhythm is that of a whispered confidence, of a prayer almost; the censer-like swinging, that of a ritual. In other passages the same rhythmical movement is repeated for an exhaustive enumeration, as when Richard II renounces his royal privileges, one after the other:

> I'll give my jewels for a set of beads,
> My gorgeous palace for a hermitage,
> My gay apparel for an almsman's gown,
> My figur'd goblets for a dish of wood,
> My sceptre for a palmer's walking-staff,
> My subjects for a pair of carved saints,
> And my large kingdom for a little grave,
> A little little grave, an obscure grave. . . .
>   *Richard II*, III, iii, 147-54.

The speech full of repetitions rises at times to the 'Ercles' vein' (a reminiscence of Seneca's *Hercules Furens*), at which Shakespeare mocks through the mouth of the naïve Bottom, or in that extraordinary passage in *The True Tragedie of Richard III* (which preceded Shakespeare's *Richard III*) where the word 'Revenge' sounds at the end of every line like a prophetic knell in the terrified mind of Richard:

> Thus sleep I, wake I, whatso'er I do
> Methinks their ghosts come gaping for revenge . . .
> My nephew's blood Revenge, Revenge doth cry,
> The headless peers come pressing for revenge
> And everyone cries, Let the tyrant die!

> The sun by day shines hotly for revenge,
> The moon by night eclipseth for revenge,
> The stars are turned to comets for revenge,
> The planets change their courses for revenge,
> The birds sing not but sorrow for revenge,
> The shrieking raven sits croaking for revenge,
> The silly lambs sit bleating for revenge,
> Whole herds of beasts come bellowing for revenge,
> And all, yea, all the world I think
> Cries for revenge and nothing but revenge.
> But to conclude, I have deserved revenge.
>   *The True Tragedie of Richard III.*

One can imagine the effect on the stage of this verbal hammering by the actor's delivery. The declamation aims at raising to a cosmic scale the revenge that is about to fall upon the tyrant. This impassioned rhetoric leaves all similar passages far behind—even Hieronimo's verbal extravagance in *The Spanish Tragedy.*

But there is another figure of rhetoric, even more formal if that were possible, and known by English critics as 'tracers'. This word-play consists in starting the line off again with the keyword of the preceding line. Kyd is fond of this trick. In *The Spanish Tragedy* the Viceroy says:

> My late ambition hath distain'd my faith,
> My breach of faith occasion'd bloody wars,
> Those bloody wars have spent my treasure;
> And with my treasure my people's blood;
> And with their blood, my joy and best belov'd,
> My best belov'd, my sweet and only son.
>
>   I, iii.

Or again:

> First, in his hand he brandished a sword,
> And with that sword, he fiercely waged war,
> And in that war he gave me dang'rous wounds,
> And by those wounds he forced me to yield,
> And by my yielding I became his slave. . . .
>
>   II, i.

Here the word is made the rigorous link in a chain of statements mounting to a conclusion which is simply a sharper, inevitable realization of a fact, generally tragic; this in turn will determine an attitude or action. The thought progresses slowly, like children counting on their fingers and finally adding up their sum. The emotion is slowly elaborated, the resolution built up, and the tragic hero then reaches a perfectly clear mind. Sometimes the reasoning assumes the form of antithesis and line is opposed to line in the hero's inmost consciousness, as if he were conducting a debate. Thus Balthazar, in love with Belimperia, meditates:

> Yet might she love me for my valiancy:
> Ay, but that's slander'd by captivity.
> Yet might she love me to content her sire;
> Ay, but her reason masters his desire.
> Yet might she love me as her brother's friend;
> Ay, but her hopes aim at some other end.
> Yet might she love me to uprear her state;
> Ay, but perhaps she hopes some nobler mate.
> Yet might she love me as her beauty's thrall;
> Ay, but I fear she cannot love at all.
>   II.

This is nothing but the pattern of stichomythia, reserved for dialogue, in which each of the two speakers is given a line or hemistich in turn. It can produce excellent verbal fencing, as in the two scenes where Richard III courts Anne (Act I, sc. ii) and later, Queen Elizabeth for the hand of her daughter (Act IV, sc. iv). The repetition of a word or part of a phrase—either using the word in a different sense or adding a kindred idea or making the word contradict itself—may, at pathetic moments, achieve a veritable antiphonic style akin to that of liturgical ritual. Thus, in 3 *Henry VI* on the very field where Henry VI had indulged in his sad pastoral meditation, and to underline still further the horrors of war which this 'too human' king detests, Shakespeare brings on successively a son who has killed his father and a father who has killed his son. The king and the two men echo each other in a formal lament:

> *Son:* How will my mother for a father's death
> Take on with me and ne'er be satisfied!
> *Father:* How will my wife for slaughter of my son
> Shed seas of tears and ne'er be satisfied!
> *K. Henry:* How will the country for these woeful chances
> Misthink the King and not be satisfied!
> *Son:* Was ever son so ru'd a father's death?
> *Father:* Was ever father so bemoan'd a son?
> *K. Henry:* Was ever King so griev'd for subjects' woe?
>   3 *Henry VI*, II, v, 103-11

In laments this rhetoric rises to a kind of incantation, as in the famous scene from *Richard III* (Act IV, sc. iv) already mentioned. There, led by Queen Margaret (a grand, motionless figure, bent upon revenge, who, whenever she speaks, prophesies, threatens and curses in measured beat), the unhappy, dispossessed queens, mothers and widows of kings, indulge in a veritable conspiracy of grief, a sacred rite of sorrow, in which sighs and sobs alternate with piercing cries.

Q. Margaret: If sorrow can admit society
                Tell o'er your woes again by viewing mine;
                I had an Edward, till a Richard kill'd him;
                I had a Harry, till a Richard kill'd him:
                Thou hadst an Edward, till a Richard kill'd him;
                Thou hadst a Richard, till a Richard kill'd him.
Duchess of York: I had a Richard too, and thou didst kill him;
                I had a Rutland too, thou holp'st to kill him.
Q. Margaret: Thou hadst a Clarence too, and Richard kill'd
                him . . .

Richard III, IV, iv, 38-45

In this great static scene, until Margaret leaves the stage, we have as it were an orchestration of grandeur which only a rhetoric so formal could achieve. It is brought about by the repetition of *motifs*, the alternation of reproaches, the similarity of the complaints, the parallelism of the situations and the depth of the personal feelings, which are first opposed to each other and then join forces. The grand speech of Queen Margaret—'expert in curses', as Queen Elizabeth calls her—is the perfection of this proud, haughty, nostalgic and strictly balanced style in which, under the almost impersonal character of the traditional themes (the theme, for example, of 'mais où sont les neiges d'antan?'), a personality is expressed beyond that of Queen Margaret herself, the personality of Shakespeare.

Already in her sorrowful speech to Queen Margaret, the Duchess of York, within the framework of rhetorical forms (enumeration, repetition, balance of epithets, antithesis pressed to the point of punning), succeeds in that condensation of verbal effects which is the royal characteristic of Shakespeare's own style:

Dead life, blind sight, poor mortal living ghost,
Woe's scene, world's shame, grave's due by life usurp'd,
Brief abstract and record of tedious days,
Rest thy unrest on England's lawful earth,
Unlawfully made drunk with innocent blood!

ibid., IV, iv, 26-30

Here the effects are more subtle and complex. The rhetorical forms are coupled with a particular use of language: the violent metaphorical handling of the abstract gives poetic force to allegory, and by piling up images tends to exhaust the very substance of the object to be described and seized. The portrait that the Duchess of York tries to give of Queen Margaret is, as it were, a white funereal symbol of man's unspeakable misery, composed of mourning, shame and bloodshed; of the crumbling of past grandeur—a symbol in which life and death, the world and the tomb, survival and nothingness, human laws and crime all interpenetrate till they become identified in that pathetic ruin, Queen Margaret.

From simple tautology to the striking effects produced by reiteration of words, images and themes, the gamut is inexhaustible. Rhetoric takes control of eloquence and gives a solid basis to lyricism while introducing infinitely varied shades of expression. It may be the ecstasy of exclamation produced by the sight of beauty:

> Zenocrate, the lovliest maid alive
> Fairer than rocks of pearl and precious stone,
> Whose eyes are brighter than the lamps of heaven,
> And speech more pleasant than sweet harmony. . . .
> > 1. *Tamburlaine*, III, iii

where the preciosity of hyperbole in images, the images of pomp and circumstance, ennobles the naïvety of the enjoyment of beauty. Or it may be the indignant protest:

> Accurst be he that first invented war,
> They knew not, ah they knew not simple men
> How those were hit by pelting cannon shot,
> Stand staggering like a quivering Aspen leafe,
> Fearing the force of Boreas' boistrous blasts.
> > ibid., II, iv

where the sigh in the repetition of the second line lends full force to the vigorous alliteration of the last three. Or again it may be the affecting sorrow of:

> Ah! my poor princes! ah, my tender babes
> My unblown flowers, new-appearing sweets. . . .
> > *Richard III*, IV, iv, 9-10

or supplication:

> Pitie our plightes, O pitie poor Damascus:
> Pitie olde age. . . .
> > 1. *Tamburlaine*, V, ii

or invective:

> Foul devil, for God's sake hence, and trouble us not . . .
> > *Richard III*, I, ii, 50

or sorrowful questioning:

> Have I a tongue to doom my brother's death,
> And shall that tongue give pardon to a slave? . . .
> Who su'd to me for him? Who, in my wrath,
> Kneel'd at my feet, and bade me be advis'd?
> Who spoke of brotherhood? Who spoke of love?
> > ibid., II, i, 103-9

or even irony:

> York cannot speak, unless he wear a crown.
> A crown for York! and, lords, bow low to him!
> Hold you his hands, while I do set it on.
>   (*putting a paper crown on his head*)
> Ay, marry, sir, now looks he like a king!
>   3 *Henry VI*, I, iv, 93-6

These lines, all belonging to the first period, are not re-markable for the diversity of their workmanship. The beats are regular, the graces of style simple, the enjambments few. Yet upon this solid bony structure, the movement, tone and choice of words can express very different emotions with shades of meaning already subtle. In the quotations from Marlowe, Kyd and Shakespeare quite distinct personalities can be detected, and no confusion between them is possible. Nevertheless, they are using the same instrument and identical methods. The difference between them is perceptible in the quivering beneath the rush of syllables, in the rhythms of attack and liaison, and in the images peculiar to each.

A study of images alone would provide material for a whole book. It is by his choice and use of images that Shakespeare is the most remarkable of all the writers of his age. This is a quality which all critics have long ago recognized. 'Every word in him', said Gray, 'is a picture.' 'This unparalleled wealth of imagery shows itself, above all', wrote Logan Pearsall Smith, 'in that royal use of metaphor, which is the most distinguishing quality of his style.' Nothing could be more just. Yet here again it must be remembered that image and metaphor are figures of rhetoric and that they were first used for decoration. The recognition of this fact will give full weight to the following remarks.

No strict rule allows us to say at what point we pass from the plane of pure rhetoric to the plane of psychology, and even the metaphysical plane, in the use of imagery. For that, we should require to know how the artist's mind worked at the moment when he was writing. All we can do is to give the relative judgment of literary criticism, the object of which is to appreciate why and how a literary form of expression fulfils its emotional function. To pose the problem of imagery is to pose that of all poetic expression; it is also to go beyond expression and touch on the function of poetry itself. Consequently we should be leaving rhetoric for poetry.

Imagery may be shortly defined as a concrete illustration drawn upon by the poet to clarify or embellish the object that he seeks to describe. In its primitive state it is a comparison. The mind looks for a visual analogy that will make something seen and understood more clearly. The quality of the imagery depends on the nature of the relations contained in the analogy that presents itself. This may be near or remote, obvious or hidden, broad or acute, rational or strange, natural or forced. The gamut of these relationships, in short, is infinite. It ranges from the comparison time-honoured by tradition ('Achilles charged like a lion') to the most far-fetched conceit.

At first the playwrights used the comparisons best calculated to illustrate their point, and they were the most traditional. They had a decorative function and were employed to enhance the effect. Derived much oftener from the Classics or from the Italian poets than from personal experience, they were designed to raise the object to the poetical plane by assimilating it to something rarer or nobler. It was essentially the laudatory image, the basis of all poetry, which naïvely tried to express itself: the illumination on a text still dull or clumsy, exalting the qualities—abstract or concrete—of the woman or the warrior, of love or courage, of the Creation, etc. Its aim was to awaken the feeling of beauty, to provoke admiration and even adoration. Breasts were described as of ivory or alabaster, lips of coral, eyes were stars. Goddesses, heavenly bodies, the seasons, birds and flowers, precious stones and metals formed charming symbolical teams, harnessed to the objects to be illustrated, and made to assume an emblematic value.

How often we meet with gold, swans and roses, Flora and Phoebus, suns and moons, Venus's white breasts! 'Zenocrate', exclaims Tamburlaine (and we remember Shakespeare's sonnet: 'Shall I compare thee to a summer's day?'),

> Zenocrate, the loveliest maid alive,
> Fairer than rocks of pearl and precious stone.

One might quote innumerable examples of this strictly Elizabethan imagery which asserts the lyric temperament of the age and gives dramatic poetry itself the indisputable prestige that all poetry should enjoy. Here, Spenser is the great master and the great purveyor, and in the 1590's Marlowe and Shakespeare were writing in his manner. Too literary, such profusion risks running dry by repetition, which produces monotony (though the wish to refine is a valuable quality); confined to these comparisons and parallels, conjunctions and analogies, the mind cannot be satisfied. Affec-

tation is the only result of pressing comparisons to the point
of Euphuistic conceits and ranging the whole vegetable and
mineral world for likenesses.

Nor is there any use in placating the logical, inductive
type of mind by employing the acutest resources of analogies
and reasoning, turning comparisons inside out and unfolding
the poem like a theorem. Such a method is doomed to be
bizarre, and even absurd, so long as it refuses to draw upon
living experience. There the poet acquires an unequalled
virtuosity; he exploits the sonorous resources of his native
tongue, and even discovers new rhythms, but he cannot
claim to be writing poetic drama. Sensibility exhausts itself
by being a slave to conventions of elegance and preciosity.
And those poets—like Sidney, clever, frequently exquisite,
or, even more, like Spenser—who do not evolve beyond these
conventions, are brilliant but immobile stars; and immobility
for a poet as for a heavenly body is synonymous with
sterility.

The dramatist cannot, on pain of death, be content to remain static. Shakespeare, a particularly fortunate rival of his
poetic contemporaries or his predecessors who supplied him
with models and created a poetic language and established
powerful conventions, followed in their wake for a time
only. His first plays show him at ease among Classical
imagery as well as traditional rhetoric. It is hard to distinguish between him and Spenser, sometimes between him
and Marlowe, their styles resemble each other so closely,
their concern for smoothness is so identical, their images so
interchangeable. George Rylands gives a remarkable example
of this.[53] Here is Spenser:

> At last the golden Orientall gate,
> Of greatest heaven gan to open faire,
> And *Phoebus* fresh, as bridegroome to his mate,
> Came dauncing forth, shaking his deawie hair:
>> Spenser, *Faerie Queene*, Book I, v, ii

and Shakespeare:

> See how the morning opes her golden gates,
> And takes her farewell of the glorious sun;
> How well resembles it the prime of youth,
> Trimm'd like a younker prancing to his love.
>> 3 *Henry VI*, II, i, 21-4

At most, Shakespeare can be conceded more polish, suppleness and delicacy. He was never to lose this eminence

---

[53] *A Companion to Shakespeare Studies*, p. 94 (article by George Rylands on
'Shakespeare the Poet').

which he was already displaying and for which he was en-
vied, this wonderful faculty for making poetry something
rich and rare within the framework of a convention, with
the ordinary resources that the English language offered to
him as to others. From *Romeo and Juliet* to *The Tempest*
these qualities will be found again and again, this ear sensitive to even quarter-tones, this sense of inner movement
accompanying the development of an image or an emotion.
But very soon he acquired additional powers. Musical poetry,
decorative imagery, conceits, puns (verbal images, abortive
metaphors), the unilinear process of the analogy which subjects syntax to no violence—in all these arts Shakespeare
was a master. He practised them like a virtuoso, but they
are mere externals compared with the real dramatic expression to which he was hastening with more internal urgency
than any other dramatist.

It was to personal experience that he turned and consequently achieved a personal expression. This is no play upon
words. I do not mean that Shakespeare expressed *his* thought,
his emotion, that of the *man* Shakespeare, although in one
sense this might be arguable. What I mean is that his personal
experience passes into the consciousness of the character
and that the man Shakespeare disappears behind the man
Macbeth, for example. First the poet enlarges his field of
perception: there are still lilies and roses but all the other
flowers are also within reach of his hand. The fauna and
flora, the palette of the seasons, natural phenomena, the
panoply of colours, a multitude of objects which man's ingenuity invents from century to century, the exact or abstract
sciences, Elizabethan demonology, alchemy—all that the
human mind perceives and conceives constitutes for him
the immense reservoir upon which he freely draws. He makes
no distinction between the poetic image and the non-poetic
image. In great poets all images may become poetic.

Beside the conventional image, in the perfumed boudoir,
the fair stranger enters, a surprising newcomer who upsets
people's habits, alarms the conceited women and the *pré-
cieuses* (who were soon to feel themselves *ridicules*), crushes
the smooth folds of the rose-petals and settles down with
assurance. She comes from outside—from everywhere in the
vast universe, vigorous, mud-bespattered, learned, arrogant;
she smells of the stable, the tavern, the open fields; she rises
from the depths of the sea or from the still more disturbing
mysteries of the subconscious. She brings with her a train
of reminiscences, of superstitions, of ritual, in which the
most diverse sensations come into play in continuous dis-

order. She dances with her own rhythm, powerful and supple, to the often discordant music of her own invention, hitherto unheard, and by the glittering light of her own fires.

This is the first revolution wrought by the intrusion in the poetic field of elements drawn from a personal experience which takes all creation for its province. Donne, at the same time as Shakespeare, is an adept of it, with a preference, however, for the scientific, more esoteric and more tortuous, with one dominating passion (which Shakespeare does not share) for discovering the fundamental unity of creation under the contradictory appearances of the diverse elements, Matter and Thought.

But Shakespeare's great novelty does not lie in this. It is his progressive advance from the purely decorative to the functional image: there is a complete change in the destination of the image. It is no longer merely for show—the placing of one concrete object side by side with another so as to bring about, for poetic purposes, the substitution of one object for the other, or the application of one quality for another so as to provoke this or that emotion as a result of perceiving the image. Nor is it a case of substitution through the *rapprochement* of a passing identification. It is a perfect substitution. Thought and emotion express themselves in terms of images in a simultaneous mental operation. That would be 'thinking in images' if this expression had not suffered a kind of degradation owing to certain rather rash applications of it.

But let us be quite clear about it. The idea to be expressed needs the help of imagery to arouse an emotion more directly, for the pure idea is devoid of emotional content when expressed in the abstract. It may also present itself directly in the form of an image, and this image is charged by the poet with assuring the unfolding and development of the idea. Think, for example, of Ulysses's speech to Achilles in *Troilus and Cressida*. The idea is that men forget the inactive hero, and hence the ingratitude theme. Ulysses does not philosophize in the void. The aim of his speech on ingratitude is to press Achilles to act. With the theme of ingratitude, therefore, must be associated a certain number of emotions calculated to bring Achilles out of his legendary tent. And so we have the unexpected presentation of Time (the abstract idea) in the form of a pilgrim receiving alms for oblivion (another abstract idea), which in its turn appears in the form of a monster that feeds on ingratitude (a third abstract idea). But, to quote:

> Time hath, my lord, a wallet at his back
> Wherein he puts alms for oblivion,
> A great-sized monster of ingratitudes:
> Those scraps are good deeds past; which are devour'd
> As fast as they are made, forgot as soon
> As done. . . .
>
> *Troilus and Cressida*, III, iii, 145-50

Here we have, not the simple allegory, the essential idea-image, an abstraction frozen in the stiff folds of traditional garb, but a metaphor in action which springs up suddenly and makes the idea spring up with it. Time and his wallet, a cave where oblivion gorges itself with 'ingratitudes', good deeds past that have been forgotten. The logical coherence of the idea wins acceptance by the very illogicality of the succession of images. For this wallet suddenly assumes gigantic proportions: it is a 'great sized monster'—oblivion which crouches there and gluttonously devours 'ingratitudes'. And these 'ingratitudes'—alms thrown to oblivion—are themselves assimilated to the 'scraps' of 'good deeds past' (this is in itself illogical, for the action is not ingratitude, which is an ungrateful attitude towards a good action). But this telescoping of images, compressed into three or four lines, is not a description of ingratitude but the personal experience of an emotion which, in expressing itself, arouses the same emotion, and hence the baroque vision of a pitiless, devouring chaos. The only thing that could touch Achilles was the wound inflicted on his pride. The whole magnificent speech of Ulysses is in this tone and style. Metaphor is piled upon metaphor; and Ulysses is a reasoner, often, let us not forget, cold and calculating, but in any case completely master of himself.

If we read on a few lines, we find perseverance making honour shine, like the armour that is being polished. Hardly have the words 'keeps honour bright' been uttered before we get the image of 'rusty armour', which illustrates 'have done'. Then honour (and a whole series of military metaphors, the likeliest to be understood by Achilles, follows) 'travels in a strait so narrow Where one but goes abreast'. But 'emulation hath a thousand sons That one by one pursue', and 'if you give way, Or hedge aside from the direct forthright . . . they all rush by And leave you hindmost'. Or 'like a gallant horse fall'n in first rank' (the image of the rising tide calls up that of the cavalry charge), you are 'o'errun and trampled on'. And, finally, Time once again makes his appearance: it is no longer Time the devourer, but (here Ulysses becomes once more the society man, the

courtier) Time 'the fashionable host That slightly shakes
his parting guest by the hand', in order to welcome the newcomer with open arms.

I have intentionally not chosen a passage in which the
great passions are involved—one of those passages in which
the whole man is engaged, at that moment of his Fate when
he realizes his failure, such as, for example, the famous
'tomorrow and tomorrow and tomorrow' of Macbeth. Rather
I have taken a speech where the emotional tension lies behind the humour, since Ulysses's serious words conceal a
provocative intention towards a character (Achilles) to whom
Ulysses feels himself superior. Nevertheless, we have seen
that a train of apparently illogical images can take the place
of a strict logic. The initial metaphor is not developed here
as that of the ship is, carefully in accordance with the sound
rules of rhetoric, in Queen Margaret's speech.[54]

The rhetoric of the three parts of *Henry VI* is still a formal
rhetoric which employs tropes appropriate to the purpose of
the speech. These images have not passed through the
dramatist's sensibility or formed part of the character's experience. Margaret, a woman of courage, full of hatred and
quick-tempered, wants to stimulate her followers before the
battle of Tewkesbury. She exhorts them with a controlled
verbal passion, developing the theme of the ship in a storm,
its sails carried away, its anchor (Warwick) gone, its main-
mast (Montague) brought down; and it is she herself and
her son Edward who are going to take the helm, brave the
rocks and the waves, and bring the ship safely to harbour.
Substantives are all strictly in keeping with the central point
of the metaphor (mast, anchor, cables, sailors, pilot, helm,
tide, shipwreck), as are the verbs ('blown overboard', 'swal-
lowed in the flood', 'splits on the rock', 'wash you off', etc.)
and the adjectives. It is the very model of a coherent metaphor, developed in forty lines. It would satisfy even French
rhetoricians, and Shakespeare cannot be charged here with
incoherence. What is lacking is the fire of conviction. Carried
away by her own eloquence, Margaret is yet moved coldly.
An image occurs to her; her vehement mind seizes upon it
but does not do it violence. The image comes to her from
without and remains outside her. It is not the passion itself
which calls it up, breaks it and pulverizes it at the risk of
incoherence but greatly to poetry's gain.

Margaret is a Lady Macbeth before Lady Macbeth's creation, as vigorous in temperament, of greater stature perhaps,
but with a sensibility and faculty of expression not yet

awakened. Lady Macbeth also has someone to convince, and courage to infuse in him, but it is upon herself in the first place that the incantation is exerted. The metaphor is no longer a mere emblematic decoration nor a traditional allegory nor even an occasional symbol. It is a living operation of the mind which digs out of the surrounding material universe the substance on which sensibility is nourished. Night, evil, cruelty—I am thinking of the succession of addresses in the form of incantations (Act I, sc. v) which begins with the raven's croaking:

> . . . The raven himself is hoarse
> That croaks the fatal entrance of Duncan
> Under my battlements,

and which ends in the famous image, so often discussed:

> Nor heaven peep through the blanket of the dark.

Lady Macbeth, one might say, sublimates herself—exchanges her woman's nature for a rarefied essence of the powers of evil. The invocation works like magic—*black* magic if ever there was!—and now she can talk this direct language, abrupt and sharp, now realistic and ordinary, at one moment toying with metaphor with a refined sophistry (. . . 'memory, the warder of the brain, Shall be a fume and the receipt of reason A limbeck only'), at another, brutal again as steel, more inhuman than Clytemnestra herself ('I have given suck, and know How tender 'tis to love the babe that milks me'), yet there is not a superfluous syllable, not a word or rhythm which is not the one exactly required, in complete harmony with the emotion, and best calculated to cast upon her husband the spell that will enslave him body and soul to the accomplishment of her purpose.

All critical comment on this passage seems vain, so perfect is its coherence (yet of a kind very different from Queen Margaret's speech), so imperceptible are the tricks of its style, so discreet its use of metaphor, and yet so powerful is the balance between passion and its expression. For images, however numerous they be, serve only to express a sensibility, in perfect unison with the situation and with the speaker. Such is the supreme aim of dramatic expression.

It is towards this point that the development of Shakespeare's dramatic style tends. The image, once incidental, now becomes indispensable, while admitting of infinite variety in quality, discretion, intensity and symbolical function. Critics have noticed in recent years (and this has led to various studies on the function of imagery by Miss C. Spurgeon, Mr. Wilson Knight and Mr. E. A. Armstrong) how the image sets the general tone of the passage and even of the whole play: how images of the same family group themselves together, evoking similar ideas; how one family of images produces similarity of themes between one play and another; and finally how the study of a play could even be considered as that of an expanded metaphor (as Wilson Knight calls it).

All these points are true, and the only mistake would be a too-rigid systematization. It is true that metaphors about disease abound in *Hamlet*, that mythology does much to give another play its vaguely unreal character, that certain images of birds and insects have strange symbolical connotations— often unexpectedly contrasted, which gives added force to the tragic effect—and that the two opposite poles round which Shakespeare's world revolves are the antithetical themes of Life and Death, Good and Evil, Order and Chaos, implicitly colouring the whole play or explicitly stated; and that they are revealed to us dramatically by this poetic function of the image which is like a metaphorical key that with difficulty unlocks the mystery of man's fate between two infinities.

But it is not so much the philosophical import of the image that concerns us here—that is, the response which the image and its use give to questions about Shakespeare's conception of the moral and spiritual universe—but rather its poetic function properly so-called: how the image animates the world of the senses apprehended through it, and how it is produced and coloured by the sensibility of the character, so that it similarly moves and colours our own sensibility. In other words, how the poetic function of the image and its dramatic function coincide so closely that they cannot be seen apart. Here, it will suffice to take one or two out of innumerable examples to illustrate the point.

Act V of *Antony and Cleopatra* is one of the summits of Shakespeare's art because every moment we find in it that intimate fusion of dramatic emotion and poetic vision which lifts us on to a plane of ecstasy where the dead Antony assumes gigantic proportions, a blinding radiance. Cleopatra's imagination, borne along by the intensity of her feelings, burning with a passion purified at last by death, is bathed in the supernatural clarity of the starry universe where the hero now dwells. Yet her love for him does not make her lose touch with the immediate reality. After her lie—a cruel ruse of love, following so many other caprices—Antony dies. His death, an error tragic but inevitable, sets Cleopatra free from the bonds of earthly love, and the fickle Queen who had lived till then only to gratify her sensual appetites, aspires to be immortal: 'I have immortal longings in me', she says just before she puts the asp to her breast.

But her imagination already expresses the implicit effects of this yearning for immortality when she transposes her lover's great qualities to the supernatural world—his beauty, his calm strength, his terrible wrath, his generosity, his unfading joy, his omnipotence. Antony dead is deified, and the image that presents itself is no longer an earthly image but a dream-image—intense and precise as an hallucination and as far removed from actuality. There is a strange dialogue between Dolabella and Cleopatra in which, without stopping to notice the intruder's presence, she asks surprisingly:

> You laugh when boys or women tell their dreams,
> Is't not your trick?
> > *Antony and Cleopatra,* V, ii, 74 *et seq.*

and immediately goes on (the whole passage needs to be quoted):

> I dream'd there was an emperor Antony:
> O! such another sleep, that I might see
> But such another man! . . .
> His face was as the heavens, and therein stuck
> A sun and moon, which kept their course, and lighted
> The little O, the earth. . . .
> His legs bestrid the ocean; his rear'd arm
> Crested the world; his voice was propertied
> As all the tuned spheres, and that to friends;
> But when he meant to quail and shake the orb,
> He was as rattling thunder. For his bounty
> There was no winter in't, an autumn 'twas
> That grew the more by reaping; his delights
> Were dolphin-like, they show'd his back above
> The element they liv'd in; in his livery
> Walk'd crowns and crownets; realms and islands were
> As plates dropp'd from his pocket.

This portrait of Antony is one of Shakespeare's strangest successes: its luminous metaphorical inconsistency expresses with rare felicity that wonderment of the mind faced with something that can be described only in terms of myth—a wonderment made possible by grief and love. It makes the fabulous world where the incomparable love of Antony and Cleopatra will become eternal, as tangible a reality as the physical world itself. From the very first simile—'his face was as the heavens'—the Antony-myth appears, as powerfully evoked as the Satyr-myth which Victor Hugo requires

some hundreds of lines to develop. At a single stroke
Antony is projected into the heavens with the attributes of
his greatness—the sun and the moon shedding light on this
little globe, the earth.

And as earthly things receive their relatively diminished
value, his giant stature becomes more defined: 'His legs
bestrid the ocean; his rear'd arm Crested the world; his
voice was propertied As all the tuned spheres, and that to
friends; But when he meant to quail and shake the orb, He
was as rattling thunder.' Then suddenly the quality of the
image changes and we pass from the cosmological vision
to the more human scale of the earth's seasons: 'For his
bounty There was no winter in't': autumn, the season of
'mellow fruitfulness', as Keats calls it, befits Antony's inexhaustible gentleness. And the memory of joys associated
with the scale of gentleness takes the forms of dolphins
bounding through the ocean. Finally, the incomparable
grandeur of the man has to be emphasized once more: 'in
his livery Walk'd crowns and crownets; realms and islands
were As plates dropp'd from his pocket.'

Here the fabulous greatness of Antony is purely the product of an ardent imagination which makes the heroine great
to match the hero and paves the way for the sublime
coronation scene of her death: 'Give me my robe, put on my
crown; I have Immortal longings in me. . . .' While expressing the most devouring passion, this speech of Cleopatra's rules out all uneasiness of frustration, and the tender
adoration which gives it its caressing rhythm and ecstasy
puts it already in the supernatural kingdom of eternal
fidelities. How unless by these images could Shakespeare
express that elusive essence, the soul of Cleopatra, which
knows by instinct that other elusive essence, the soul of
Antony, like a cosmic phenomenon making play with the
Creation.

Let us take another emotion, fear. In *Measure for Measure* Claudio, condemned to death, has just seen disappear
the only chance of safety that he could for a space set his
hopes upon. His sister Isabella, vowed to chastity, tells him
in his prison that she has refused to pay Angelo his price
—her virginity—which she considers a treasure more precious than her brother's safety. Fear seizes him then and he
tries to move the cold Isabella by a heart-rending plea and
to convince her that she should yield. This plea is the image
he has of death:

> Ay, but to die and go we know not where;
> To lie in cold obstruction and to rot;

This sensible warm motion to become
A kneaded clod; and the delighted spirit
To bathe in fiery floods, or to reside
In thrilling region of thick-ribbed ice;
To be imprison'd in the viewless winds,
And blown with restless violence round about
The pendant world; or to be worse than worst
Of those that lawless and incertain thoughts
Imagine howling: 'tis too horrible!
The weariest and most loathed worldly life
That age, ache, penury, and imprisonment
Can lay on nature is a paradise
To what we fear of death.

Measure for Measure, III, i, 116-30

This celebrated passage (which, more than any other, defies translation) achieves that perfect alliance of poetic imagination and dramatic movement precipitated by an intense emotion. Clearly Claudio is here using all his powers of persuasion, all the resources of imagination and eloquence. He wants to communicate to Isabella his own master-passion, fear: to prove to her that nothing is more terrible than this horrible unknown thing, death, which Isabella (apparently lacking in imagination) fears less than the loss of her honour. Death and honour are not interchangeable for the brother and sister, for it is Claudio's death that is at stake and Isabella's honour. But death for Claudio wears the terrifying guise of a perceptible void where the threat of a frightened conscience nevertheless subsists. And it is the pangs of this conscience that Claudio tries to put into words. Let Isabella be like him afraid, more afraid of death than of her own dishonour, and Claudio will be served.

To imprison in words this void, the most fleeting of abstracts is caught in the concrete toils of sensual antitheses: *obstruction* is opposed to *motion*, cold to heat, the sensible to the insensible (the 'clod' that the rain and the heavy earth have 'kneaded'). It is by the abstract words 'sensible *warm* motion' that Claudio best and most briefly expresses what is implicit in life—sensibility, heat, movement—and, by a concrete image, what becomes of the living body's remains —'a kneaded clod'. Then comes the turn of the immortal soul which delighted in the earthly life, to undergo its metamorphosis and its unknown but terrifying ordeal. Two expected aspects of hell (rivers of fire and icy solitudes) are evoked in the strange sixth line, 'In thrilling region of thick-ribbed ice.' But this does not exhaust the possibilities: the possibility presents itself to Claudio's mind of a prison of invisible winds blowing the guilty soul, without respite, in a frenzied dance round the globe of the universe sus-

pended in the void. And finally he reaches the end of the
resources of expression, the limit of what thought can conceive with precision, retaining only the 'howling of grief': he
breaks off with the words ' 'tis too horrible!'

Here the function of imagery is indeed to express a
dramatic reality beyond which no further expression is
possible. It conveys the content of an emotion: it is an
ardent idea, the inevitable language of a mind which seizes
upon the only reality that passionately interests it and
interests us: that of a character in a given situation. The
sonorous words, the rhythms themselves are in direct accord with the gasping of the emotion, with the shades of
internal meaning. Everything contributes to the total effect.
It is here that blank verse, which we saw earlier so clumsy
and mechanical, becomes marvellously supple and varied.

I am not an expert in prosody and I have no intention of
appearing to be one by gravely using learned terms. I do
not consider the learning of the prosodists superfluous, but
I say that they have taught me nothing if they confine themselves to offering to me the analysis of a line's rhythm
merely in their learned terms. Study of a verse should always lead to a judgment of its quality and value, just as
study of a painter's tones should be of use to the collector
of pictures. Scansion is one thing, prosody another, and both
are the handmaids of literary criticism. Having said so much,
I can turn back to T. S. Eliot's words at the head of this
chapter and apply them to Shakespeare: 'Few things that
can happen to a nation are more important than the invention of a new form of verse.'

The classical French verse, the alexandrine, bears a whole
civilization, that is, a form of thought and emotion, which
are the classical French thought and emotion. It expresses
one particular world, to which it lends its own precise and
immortal visage. But for Racine's verse, the century of Louis
XIV would have appeared to us, and no doubt to itself also,
quite different. But subsequent French literature, i.e. the
evolution of French civilization, would likewise have been
quite different. Though they have other poetry, and great
poetry, the French cannot think of it except in terms of
alexandrines. It is useless to take it to pieces and belabour
it, it continues to triumph in their Romantic poets, in
Baudelaire, Rimbaud, Valéry and even Aragon. Not that it
is the only possible one, the only expressive verse, but all
other forms derive from its divisions. It is the alexandrine
that represents the utmost poetic power of which the French
language is capable, despite the deceptive breadth of the

ten-syllabled line which has also many claims on our respect.

But if the ten-syllabled line—in spite of the magnificent successes it has had to its credit from Scève to Valéry—remains a minor form of verse, it is because French has crystallized in syllabic scansion whereas accent dominates in English. Chaucer in the fourteenth century borrowed the ten-syllabled line from the French, and this verse with its five strong beats and ten syllables became the great English line. The reason was simple: within each line a three-beat rhythm could and should be substituted for a two-beat rhythm. In more pedantic terms, the anapaestic would replace the iambic rhythm whenever the poet found it necessary. This was an immense advantage and the very nature of the English language made it necessary. For in a strongly accented language the rhythmical sequences can very soon prove monotonous, and moreover they could only strictly be preserved by using monosyllables or disyllables. As soon as a three-syllabled word came into the line, the balance ran the risk of being disturbed. But this danger is an advantage, for the accent is always strong enough to allow the rhythmical unity of the line to be preserved, and thus the way was open for all sorts of patterns.

It is by its rhythm as much as by its images that a verse is expressive. The rhythmical succession is an emotional pattern, showing a purpose, imposing a mood or defining a thought. To keep to simple examples: the trochaic metre (two beats, beginning with a strong one), is the energetic, aggressive rhythm of measured tread; the iambic (its converse, the most frequent) is lighter, more supple, carries the reader to the end of the line; finally, the third metre is a skipping, galloping, flying rhythm: it can express joy, lyric ecstasy, languishing passions, with more persuasive force. It is thanks to the close and varied mixture of these rhythmical possibilities that the English decasyllable—Shakespearian blank verse—became the most perfect instrument of expression.

At the outset it was stiff and mechanical and there is no need to repeat the examples already quoted at the beginning of this chapter. As the complexity of the characters increasingly required a more varied form of expression, the verse served as the docile tool for the needs of emotion and thought. Rhyme at first drew gradually away from the dramatic action for it blocked too severely the development of the thought at the end of the line, tending to make of each line or each couple of lines, an independent, organic unit, in which the poets of the classical school (Dryden, Pope and

the poets of the beginning of the eighteenth century) were
to triumph. Their ambition was to preserve the most complete balance between the syllabic system and the accentual
system. Blank verse, on the other hand, freed from rhyme,
permitted all forms of enjambment and all varieties of
rhythm.

With the disappearance of rhyme and the break-up of
pure iambic rhythm, blank verse was assured of a tremendous
future. The sensibility of the age could knead it—sensibility,
of course, peculiar to each poet but comprising common
features and (as in all great periods) fitting diverse talents
into a single perspective. The transition from one kind of
verse to the other had already taken place at the end of
the sixteenth century. The year 1600 stood at the parting of
the ways: on the one side, regular channels between parallel
banks; on the other, a thousand fruitful streams that, winding capriciously, were to fertilize the future.

Shakespeare in his work knew this development for he,
more than anyone, had taken the whole universe for his
field of experience. It is not surprising that his verse displays the utmost variety. It ranges from the inflexible beat
of the iambic pentameter to the verse-paragraph of *The
Winter's Tale,* for example, where even the most practised
ear would find it difficult to detect the original skeleton of
the blank verse:

> *Perdita:*   . . . O Proserpina!
> For the flowers now that frightened thou let'st fall
> From Dis's waggon! daffodils,
> That come before the swallow dares, and take
> The winds of March with beauty; violets dim,
> But sweeter than the lids of Juno's eyes
> Or Cytherea's breath; pale prime-roses,
> That die unmarried, ere they can behold
> Bright Phoebus in his strength, a malady
> Most incident to maids; bold oxlips and
> The crown imperial; lilies of all kinds,
> The flower-de-luce being one.
>
>   IV, iii, 116-27

I have chosen this passage precisely in order to show
how, even in a simple enumeration, even with the traditional
theme of emblematical flowers to which Shakespeare here
returns, as to the finest epoch of Elizabethan formal poetry,
the medium of expression has been changed. Let me recall
the flower-passage in *A Midsummer Night's Dream*:

> I know a bank whereon the wild thyme blows,
> Where oxlips and the nodding violet grows

> Quite over-canopied with lush woodbine,
> With sweet musk-roses, and with eglantine:
>   II, i, 249-52

The passage from *The Dream* is purely descriptive: it is a framework, stage-scenery painted by Shakespeare to receive his fairy-characters. We find Titania there asleep. Each flower has its expected epithet but has no need to have a personality. The verse flows regularly, having to express only the gentleness of fairy landscape, springing from a calm vision of conventional English scenery. Here the poet's sensibility is not concerned to produce anything but a pleasing decorative picture. Neither the themes of the play nor the character of Oberon nor even, doubtless, the playwright's experience at the time of writing *The Dream,* required more. This explains why the fairy themes, images, verses and music are so fragile, conventionally regular, and exquisite.

But with *The Winter's Tale* it is quite different. The pastoral theme here repeated is charged with human experience, as the Shepherd's speech ('Fie, daughter! When my old wife lived . . .', Act IV, sc. iv) proves; and the flowers and images are no longer mere decorations intended to embellish a description. Their emblematic value also has been superseded and the part they play becomes symbolical. Perdita, King's daughter, and Shepherdess, the queen of the sheep-shearing festival, offers to each visitor the flowers that are appropriate: those of summer to grown men of maturity, and those of spring to Florizel and the young shepherdesses. They are the flowers that Proserpine let fall from Dis's wagon on the day when she was abducted: daffodils and violets, oxlips and lilies, associated at once with spring, fertility, kingship with all its terrors, and the danger that hangs over these rustic nuptials and will cruelly delay their consummation.

The passage quoted is rich in suggestion, in shades of meaning barely hinted at, in muffled tones, which are evidence of a complex experience, hesitant as it were on the threshold of joy yet ready to accept life's sumptuousness in the fullness of love. The enumeration partakes both of ecstatic and of restrained adoration, each flower being so lovely and so full of meaning that Perdita needs a line of melody for each, a flowing, caressing rhythm which extracts every ounce of feeling from the phrase and reaches the highest pitch of emotion in:

> . . . daffodils
> That come before the swallow dares, and take
> The winds of March with beauty . . .
>   . . . violets dim,

But sweeter than the lids of Juno's eyes
Or Cytherea's breath;
                    . . . pale prime-roses,
That die unmarried, ere they can behold
Bright Phoebus in his strength, a malady
Most incident to maids . . .
                    . . . bold oxlips and
The crown imperial . . .
                    . . . lilies of all kinds,
The flower-de-luce being one. . . .

There is a joyous vitality and slightly ironic undertone to
the whole passage, remarkable in the lines that follow where
the flowers that Perdita would like to strew upon her lover's
body are precisely the scattering of love, not of death. From
this movement, these images, the value of these symbols
one can measure the distance that Shakespeare has travelled
since *The Dream*.

We are dealing here with the finest shades of tone. The
seasons and the gods mingle in the music of the words, and
to the charm of the emotional associations attached to the
image of each flower is added the gift of a particular
rhythmical pattern for each melodic phrase. 'It has a dying
fall', as the Duke of Illyria says, and this caressing cadence
—according as it lingers on an accented syllable or is prolonged on a mute one—confers upon the rhythmical pattern
a graceful variety, more subtle than rhyme and free from
the insipidity of the monotonous affectation of 'feminine end-
ings', of which there are far too many in Beaumont and
Fletcher. This extreme example of fine shades and rich
implications shows what a marvellous instrument blank verse
had become in the hands of an expert, sensitive artist.

Many other passages could be similarly analysed, but
that would exceed the limits set to this book. What is
important to emphasize is that this progress in blank verse
proceeded parallel with a progress in Shakespeare's experience and sensibility. The artist requires more supple means
of expression as what he has to say becomes more complex,
delicate and difficult to unravel. Mastery of the language
bears fruit only when accompanied by what must be called
prosodic mastery. This does not mean writing with unfail-
ing virtuosity (minor poets may be, and often are, virtuosi),
but the faculty of finding a form of expression for every
form of sensibility. And the key to the celebrated psychological richness with which Shakespeare is credited lies no
doubt in this marvellous mastery of expression. For him the
one prosodic canon is the canon dictated by inner emotion
when he is in full possession of his genius.

Similarly, there is no canon of melody or language or vocabulary or rhetoric that he cannot subdue to the requirements of the dramatic situation and of the character concerned. Thus the mixture of styles in his last plays is astonishing. The verse of *The Tempest* is perfectly adapted to the precious lyrical fantasies of Ariel's song; Caliban, exposed to the curses and mummery of Stephano and Trinculo, delivers with surprising success the rarest eulogy of the most spiritual of all music: '. . . the isle is full of noises, Sounds and sweet airs, that give delight, and hurt not' (*The Tempest*, Act III, sc. ii); and in Act IV the Goddesses of the Masque speak a language ranging from that of pastoral convention to the rhythmical incantations of the blessings of Ceres and Juno. Prospero's eloquence in his abdication speech (so different from Richard II's!) recalls the finest invocations of a Senecan Medea reduced to the proportions of a human magician: in the superb balance of its lines and the power of its imagery, it anticipates the epic sobriety of Milton's Satan.

And so we pass from academic rhetoric to organic rhetoric, from the set speech to the living metaphor, from the verbal or intellectual play of wits to the dialectic of the heart, from regular prosody to freedom of movement, from splendid monotony to the tragic diversity of the most personal and yet the most universal passions. It was by this vigorous multiplicity that Shakespeare surpassed all other dramatists. He breathed life into the convention and the image, vitalizing the rhythm's power of music and language's power of expression, and found a perfect mould for that sensibility which it is the artist's duty to communicate by what we call a work of art.

There remains the substance communicated; and the next pages examine it briefly in the same spirit as that of the foregoing.

PART THREE

THE THEMES

On a huge hill
Cragged, and steep, Truth stands and he that will
Reach her, about must, and about must go.
JOHN DONNE

THE THEMES

CRITICS HAVE RARELY been able to resist searching Shakespeare's Works in order to discover the man behind them. Most have pursued the inquiry all the more ardently because so many points in his life remain obscure, ambiguous or controversial. Even those for whom material existence is of minor importance have succumbed to the temptation of tracing the biographical pattern which accompanies the curve of the Works, so as to reconstruct a picture of the author's mind and character. They have tried to draw—like the famous seventeenth-century Map of Love, Despair and the Sublime—a chart of his faith, a calculation of his likes and dislikes, or a table of his ideas.

The 'key' to Shakespeare's heart has been sought sometimes in the youthful poems and sonnets, sometimes in the tragedies and sometimes in the last, 'calm' plays. Texts and facts have been collated, categorical and rash conclusions drawn, every allusion subjected to pressure to give up its secret. Here and there Shakespeare has been recognized in some twist taken by the text, in some speech, some judgment on life, on women, on love, upon which (we are assured) this event or that private adventure ('reconstructed', most probably awry) throws an indubitable light. Shakespeare 'believed' this, 'thought' that; 'liked' one thing, 'detested' another—in short, so many commentators have offered us a spiritual or psychological or historical or metaphysical or symbolical biography of the poet that it would be futile to examine them one after the other to refute them; or to attempt yet one more biography.

To say that Shakespeare is found in his Works is a flat banality, but we need to be told what Shakespeare it is that they claim to piece together. Who would dare lay down dogmatically that a portrait of him can be presented with any likelihood of authenticity? No one knows exactly when or why this mystery man came to London. His friendships and his loves are revealed only by a couple of dedications, and his magnificent literary achievements. The precise part that he played in the great Elizabethan scene is known to us only through gossip and some cryptic allusions which are still matter of controversy. No one will ever establish the real reasons for his retirement to Stratford, or the nature of his malady when he was composing the Tragedies of Despair.

Far be it from me to take up the cause of the anti-Stratfordians and to deny Shakespeare's title to the authorship of his own plays! I am well aware that these critics go even further in their ingenious interpretation of the texts, but I believe that their clever detective work is hazardous for all its erudition and subtlety, and that they deduce from fragile data and allusions more meaning than these can perhaps bear. I am, however, just as sceptical as regards those who assert with equal conviction that Shakespeare has written his autobiography in his plays, and that their situations, characters and themes have a close connection with his own adventures.

It is obvious, of course, that personal experience has the same importance as contemporary events for an artist: in fact, this personal experience with which he nourishes his work is part of the larger life and experience of his own age. Betrayal, a happy love affair, or a public calamity, the anxiety of war or the satisfaction of a national victory, may have an equally important influence on him. But what matters for the critic is not the event or experience in itself but the transformation that it undergoes. When one can proceed from the event to the play, it is much easier to explain the play. But it is a far more delicate matter when passing from the play to the event, from the event to the man, by interpreting an allusion twisted to support a satisfactory explanation by accepting 'internal evidence' which often involves merely wishful thinking on the part of the critic.

An allusion capable of various readings, an uncertain fact, a poetic symbol are frequently made to agree, more by straining resemblances (an artificial but attractive game) than by any compulsive force of their own. And the way in

which a creative mind is affected, whether by the historic
event or the personal incident, may take such different and
contradictory forms that critics should remain prudently reserved. The plague in Florence caused Boccaccio to write
escapist tales; Gautier fiddled over his *Emaux et Camées*
while a revolution was breaking out, and Defoe wrote a
Journal of the Plague, the horrors of which he was too
young to have seen. Other writers, however, deliberately
undertook to tell their own story and that of their age,
directly or indirectly.

In its broad lines and by its major themes, a real artist's
work reflects the deeper preoccupations of its own day, and
this is the essential problem. We can say, for example, that
T. S. Eliot's *The Waste Land* offers a moving picture
(though allusive and hard to decipher) of the spiritual disorder that followed the 1914-18 War; but we cannot—
without running the risk of making the poetic smile—infer
his life from this poem. A personal experience translated
into terms of poetry is important only in the form of its
expression and, in itself, does not interest the critic to the
same degree as the biographer or the historian. When later
generations come to study the themes of *The Waste Land*
(supposing present-day critics leave them anything to say!)
they will collate them with similar themes in poems of the
same time, however different their forms of expression, and
will evaluate the extent to which these themes inspired the
men who made use of them. They will have to translate
them into terms that their epoch can understand, and to
show how the poem derived its quality and its importance
from them in the perspective of aesthetic creations.

The same, I believe, applies to Shakespeare the dramatist.
No doubt he leads you into pseudo-critical temptation by
the accent of conviction which rings through so many
speeches of such different characters that, at one time or
another, might well be his own mouthpieces. Nor is it only
this accent of conviction that predisposes us to believe in
the presence of the real man behind the fictitious personage.
It is above all, perhaps, the tone of direct confidence perceived through the familiar and poetic language, the profound quality of the emotion, the special way in which
Shakespeare addresses you through the mouth of the speaker
(dramatic irony) that is perceptible in so many passages.
It seems impossible that these accents should be purely
impersonal, that these themes should not be vital for the
author, that Shakespeare should not have put something of
himself into every important problem that confronted him.

But what we must beware of doing is to conclude that the character and the author are identical, to say for example that Shakespeare is as much Oberon as Theseus, Mercutio as Romeo, as much Ulysses as Troilus (not to mention Thersites!), Ariel, Caliban, Prospero and so on, unless we mean that this is the sort of identification that confuses the Reverend Charles Dodgson, eminent mathematician and Student of Christ Church, with Lewis Carroll, who sets out with Alice to pursue the White Rabbit and passes with her through the Looking-Glass into Wonderland where the unknown quantity is not written equated with x.

For according as one is touched by the grace of this or that sublime or subtle sentence, one builds up a particular image of the poet from each particular particular. Here we are faced with a Protean Shakespeare who vanishes as soon as he is glimpsed, rises from his ashes like the Phoenix, a reflection of the very man who is bent upon reconstructing his own image. The myriad-minded Shakespeare gains in diversity of illusion according to the critic's temperament, culture and doctrines. The image is a composite, confused one, a clever children's puzzle, the strange construction of which soon irritates the grown-up. Emotions and ideas in this extraordinary world stand as mighty opposites, judgments are revoked, convictions cancel each other out, ambiguities are legion; feelings, passions, vices and virtues are intertwined and form the most heterogeneous scene on a background (itself moving and elusive) of beliefs, conventions, acquiescences.

Shakespeare, for example, we are told, was a Catholic, yet someone observes that he never once mentions the Holy Trinity. Again, he is depicted as a democrat, yet he is shown to have detested the mob and to have been more royalist than the King. He believes in the most idealized love, he exalts the perfect union of souls, he makes authentic passion speak unforgettably; yet (treason!) no one has surpassed Shakespeare in covering woman with blazing insults, in depicting base human passions in the most hateful colours, loveless lust, arrogant and sordid lewdness, criminal, baseless jealousy—all inevitable corollaries of what we call love.

Far from exalting military glory, as one might expect after reading *Henry V*, he mocks at and parodies heroes, whether of English birth or of classical antiquity: Hector, after a fine argument demonstrating the mistake of the Trojans in debating whether they should keep Helen, absurdly concludes that she should be kept; and what a stinging satire on war is that farcical counterpart in *Henry IV* where Falstaff serves as an enormous, attractive demoralizing agent. Republican with Brutus, political with Mark Antony, pious and resigned with unhappy, criminal kings; provocative with Coriolanus, blaspheming with Timon, mad with Lear; frequently Machiavellian; hypocritical and lewd with Angelo, chaste and pathetic with his figures of young girls; a melancholy, deranged play-actor with Hamlet, an assassin damned from Hell with Macbeth—Shakespeare is by turns sceptical, bigoted, stoic; he is at once tender, terrible, tolerant; he rages, he dreams, he is cynical. He is Montaigne and Plato, Ovid and Seneca, Petrarch and Machiavelli; a respectable married man, full of wise saws and of superstitions, yet a homosexual and stormy lover; a faithful and prudent friend, a treacherous friend; a fond father, a cruel husband; an unbending creditor, a generous giver;—which picture of him are we to choose?

But these are vain questions and pseudo-problems, perhaps; or, it may be, this is to approach the difficulty from its most deceptive angle because, no doubt, the most immediately human. It is to set course towards an impasse of conjectures, to construct myths which are destroyed as soon as set up. Shakespeare's true personality is the one that is identified with his mysterious and omnipresent poetical power. It is not so much the attitude he adopts towards the problems he poses or the themes he develops; it is the way he treats them, the vibrant tone of his voice, the quality of his images, the modulation of his rhythms which make him so unmistakable—less dry than Ben Jonson, a better lyricist than Marlowe, more vigorous than Webster, as smooth as the acknowledged love-poets, though it cannot be said that the problems he deals with, the themes he treats of, the solutions he proposes have that disconcerting, almost overwhelming originality found in some of the Baroque writers, particularly John Donne.

In Shakespeare we find the whole of his age. He is all his contemporaries at once, yet no confusion is possible: he is strangely detached, unique, supreme. If we must at all costs put to this exciting Drama a question that goes beyond mere aesthetic requirements, let it at least be a question connected with knowledge of the Elizabethan man and consequently with our own age also. It is no longer sufficient to say that Shakespeare's people are those one would like to meet in the street, in a drawing-room, on the battlefield, or anywhere else, and to make friends with them; nor that it would be wonderful to find oneself seated oppo-

site Shakespeare in a tavern and to be captivated by his
talk.

The universe he created obeys certain laws; it characters
are moved by certain passions, tortured by certain problems;
they believe, fear, love, excite themselves, die. As he sees
the play taking shape in his mind, as its men and women
group themselves and move over the stage, within the time
taken by a performance, and in the framework of a dramatic
convention; as the play comes to life by its composition, by
the stirring of its dialogue, becomes real by visible movement, by the sparks struck through its images, by the perception even of an accent, the music of the human voice
—this universe rises out of nothing, is built up and enlarged
and prolonged, is given reality. At this point the image of
a man is defined—no abstract, empty creation, a mere
silhouette, but filled out and solid, of flesh and blood, speaking and acting, and doing these things not like a phantom
from an unknown world, but in a known, substantial, visible
world. Drama is man's place in this world, the part he is
called upon to play in it, the way he plays it and his
reasons for playing it that way.

There is no need for us to put ourselves back in a psychological universe that we have in part repudiated. The problem of *Henry IV* or *Henry V*, of *Hamlet* or *The Tempest*, is
not a psychological problem. The vitality of Hotspur, of
Gloucester, or Coriolanus is not a psychological vitality. The
truth lies in the poetry. Man and his moral and material
universe are transmuted into poetic substance, and the
themes are the substance of which poetry is the expression.
Here, I believe, is the great principle which must in future
—as a result of English critical progress in the last thirty
years—inspire all Shakespearian criticism.

The theme is defined as the subject of a development, but
it is not a pure concept, any more than the development
can be a pure intellectual attitude. Once grasped, it engages
the whole consciousness of the poet in the fusion he effects
between his own personality and the fictitious characters.
That is to say, in poetic objectivity, all development of a
theme includes an emotional reaction towards it, which goes
beyond the mere adherence of the intelligence or the mere
refusal of belief. For a poet, the theme is essentially dramatic and, it may seem childish to add, particularly so for a
dramatic poet. Yet it is through failure to realize this
evident proposition that the incidental has so often been
mistaken for the essential. From the attitude adopted to-

wards contemporary themes, from the way they are treated, from the part they are made to play, arises that conception of man which is the *ultima ratio* of the work of art.

We can now speak of Shakespeare's 'experience', and explain the famous graph of his work which runs from political to moral problems, from anguish to final peace, from experimental word-play to the exhaustive expression of a consciousness that has lived, from the outside to the inside of man. The Works are now seen in all their amazing richness, the characters in their full relief, the poetry sounds in accents never before heard. And there really has been development, an enriching and deepening of knowledge. The secret of Shakespeare's strange attraction, the presence of something that beggars all description and seems to be 'an instinctive knowledge of the roots of being whence the phenomena spring',[1] is to be looked for, no doubt, in the study of the themes.

There are minor themes, ceremonial themes, major themes, symbolical themes; sometimes set out *en clair,* sometimes developed at length and sometimes, on the contrary, lightly touched upon, just suggested; mysterious agents of the subterranean eddies of the soul or of great decisions, but everywhere present, active, solid, a substance without which a play would be only a corpse or an automaton, something empty, dead and rouged like the skeleton in *The Revenger's Tragedy.* It is the theme that supports the (apparently inexplicable) human reality, the starting-point of the poetic transmutation, since each theme poses a conflict which the development of the situation has to solve. And the study of the themes raises so many questions, casts upon the characters, the situations, the images and the style a light so revealing that we are surprised we have remained so long insensible to it.

These themes are simply Bergson's 'immediate data of the consciousness'. From it proceeds a conception of the world and of man's place in Creation. Apart from a 'science', this implies a faith, a policy, a morality and a metaphysic: God, Creation, Man. What the human mind, bending its thoughts upon the universe and upon itself, seeks to know, is a series of certainties, giving a meaning to life, to man's attitude towards God and his fellows and himself. Once more, it is not a question of claiming that there is a philosophy of Shakespeare, of asserting that he wrote his plays in the light of this philosophy. But the passions, attitudes, actions, reflections of the characters are quite naturally con-

[1] Una Ellis-Fermor, *The Jacobean Drama,* p. 249.

ditioned by the intellectual and emotional attitude of the
age towards the problems presented by man's existence in
the universe. Between the Works and the epoch there is an
instinctive and necessary cohesion which lies far beyond a
positive doctrine or faith, which breathes life into the
characters, the dramatic conventions and ideas, and charges
them with meaning. It gives them that tragic character of
a sorrowful questioning which raises nothing less than the
problem of man's destiny, not only in the limited historical
framework of the past but in the infinite perspective of the
universal.

The fundamental idea underlying medieval thought and
continuing down to the end of the sixteenth century was
that there was a necessary and pre-established order and
hierarchy governing the eternal verities that were linked
together like the relations between man and the Creation,
and between man and man. It was from Chaos that Creation
came, to enter a divine order: man in his place, gifted with
reason, in a universe made for him, 'neither angel nor beast',
but capable of achieving a relative balance between his
spiritual aspirations and his material miseries, capable of
realizing a saving unity in the midst of universal harmony.
This idea of order is everywhere present in Shakespeare's
Works, and it finds its completest expression in the famous
speech where Ulysses reproaches the Greeks with their prolonged failure to capture Troy:

> The specialty of rule hath been neglected . . .
> The heavens themselves, the planets, and this centre
> Observe degree, priority and place,
> Insisture, course, proportion, season, form,
> Office, and custom, in all line of order;
> And therefore is the glorious planet Sol
> In noble eminence enthron'd and spher'd
> Amidst the other; whose med'cinable eye
> Corrects the ill aspects of planets evil,
> And posts, like the commandment of a King,
> Sans check, to good and bad: but when the planets
> In evil mixture to disorder wander,
> What plagues, and what portents, what mutiny,
> What raging of the sea, shaking of earth,
> Commotion in the winds, frights, changes, horrors,
> Divert and crack, rend and deracinate
> The unity and married calm of states
> Quite from their fixture! O! when degree is shak'd
> Which is the ladder to all high designs,
> The enterprise is sick. How could communities,
> Degrees in schools, and brotherhoods in cities,
> Peaceful commerce from dividable shores
> The primogenitive and due of birth,

> Prerogative of age, crowns, sceptres, laurels,
> But by degree, stand in authentic place?
> Take but degree away, untune that string
> And hark! what discord follows; each thing meets
> In mere oppugnancy: the bounded waters
> Should lift their bosoms higher than the shores,
> And make a sop of all this solid globe:
> Strength should be lord of imbecility,
> And the rude son should strike his father dead:
> Force should be right; or rather, right and wrong—
> Between whose endless jar justice resides—
> Should lose their names, and so should justice too.
> Then everything includes itself in power,
> Power into will, will into appetite;
> And appetite, a universal wolf,
> So doubly seconded with will and power,
> Must make perforce a universal prey,
> And last eat up himself.
>
> *Troilus and Cressida*, I, iii, 78 *et seq.*

With the cosmic order corresponds an order of the human community, clearly expressed by the Archbishop of Canterbury in *Henry V* (to take but one example) in the detailed comparison that he develops between a hive of bees and a community of men:

> They have a king and officers of sorts . . .

and with it corresponds, also, an order in man's own mind. It is the failure to observe the rules laid down that brings about a disturbance in the equilibrium and calamities both cosmic and human. For there is a close correspondence between the cosmic, natural and human orders, and man the microcosm is subject to the same strict laws as the universe. The tragedy that constantly threatens the fate of kingdoms as of individuals is precisely that of a disequilibrium caused by the forces of disorder weighing down one scale of the balance.

Now, the end of the sixteenth century, like every period of transition, saw the break-up of this harmonious conception of the world which—despite disorders and conflicts that might have endangered it—had not yet been seriously breached. Science, philosophy, morality and politics (or moral politics) gradually undermined this optimistic structure. The new cosmology of Copernicus dethroned the earth from its central position in the universe, and the whole harmony of the spheres became discordant. Montaigne struck a rude blow at man's superiority in the hierarchy of living creatures in his inspired and terrible *Apologie de Raimond Sebond*, and so also, as we saw in an earlier chapter, did the demoralizing influence of Machiavelli. ' "What is truth?" said jesting Pilate, and would not stay for an answer.' Hamlet's conclusion after his meeting with the Ghost—'the time is out of joint'—may serve as a symbol for the whole age. For it was, indeed, a dislocation that was taking place, the framework was crumbling, the equilibrium was destroyed. And it is the adventures of the human soul—abashed, uneasy, hesitant, desperate, in search of a faith, of a new order, of new reasons for hope—that form the substance of tragedy.

When age-old values that have hitherto given a meaning to life threaten to collapse, it is man's destiny that is in question: his very integrity runs the risk of disappearing. Every age more or less clearly feels this anguish and this fear, and finds its own words for them. Sensibility and the power of expression combine to fix in the work of art an image of this disorder, this fever. The artist stamps his own imprint upon this image, even more when its expression takes the form of drama, in which the materials are men and women, to whom these problems present themselves with the urgency of a crisis: for a crisis drives them to act and requires of their consciousness, every time, a personal reflection, a lucid examination of the nature and consequences of their action. The examination may *follow* the action, and the lucidity result only in setting up a new scale of values at the moment of the irrevocable step.

What makes Shakespeare so movingly and uniquely great is the fact that all through his Works he instinctively links his people, from the highest to the lowest, to the political and moral crisis which was painfully bringing the new world to birth. In it man, just because he was man, at grips with his passions, his weaknesses, and his vices, was at least assured of finding a place worthy of him. This infinite diversity was discovered by Montaigne at each step of his wise meditation and of his pitiless self-examination. Shakespeare found it too in the innumerable characters acting in the universe that his dramatist's imagination set in motion on the stage. There is, doubtless, no conceivable situation for a man, no problem to be solved, no reflection, no state of mind, no fluctuation of the consciousness that Shakespeare has not turned to account. He tried to push back the very frontiers of man's liberty to the indeterminate borderline between madness and stoicism, crime and generosity, self-sacrifice and the hardening of the soul in the presence of death. He does it like a man of the end of the sixteenth century, yet something in him transcends his age, perhaps because, after all, the important thing is not how problems are solved but how they are posed, and the intensity with which they present themselves to the man who has to solve them.

The idea of order that we find everywhere in Shakespeare, that haunts his political plays and the great tragedies and even the comedies, is what gives his Works their coherence and their seriousness. There is another idea, too, perceived in many of his images and comparisons, namely that there is a correspondence and even a symbolical likeness between man, the body of the human community, and the universe. It is a nostalgic survival from medieval thought and constitutes the background—still stable though dangerously threatened—before which the human tragedy is played out. A caprice, a passion, a crime may precipitate the forces of confusion which for a while darken the sun, wrap the earth and the soul of man in impenetrable clouds, where free rein is given to violence, injustice and evil, until the moment when the crime is expiated, the evil-doer slain, the forces of disorder vanquished or appeased, and the sun comes out again and the balance of nature is restored.

When passions are unleashed, when night is particularly baleful and the storm violent, the extent of this commotion and the quality of this madness are always described as 'unnatural'. And it is this which is intolerable to Creation, and frightening to the mind, because it means a return to Chaos, the very negation of Creation, where any life is unthinkable and impossible, where suffering has no longer any meaning, for the individual or the community, for king or subject.

Taken as a whole, the historical plays may be considered the illustration—simple at first, but increasingly complex— of this theme of an order compromised and even overthrown by disobedience to natural laws. It can be felt in the early group—the three Parts of *Henry VI*; it is developed and defined in the two Parts of *Henry IV*; and it matters little in this context that *Richard III*, for example, chronologically (if not historically) comes before the solution of the crisis. Already in 1 *Henry VI* (even if Shakespeare was not responsible for the whole play), it is the forces of disorder that create confusion: nobles quarreling round the prince, the absence in this prince of the qualities that really make a king, the maleficent action of the witch Joan who defeats the valour and honour of a Talbot, and who is symbolically continued by the appearance on the scene of the French Margaret, another personification of the forces of witchcraft. The fierce greed of rival Houses, competing for the succession to a generous but pusillanimous King, ravages the fair land of England which has become a bloody battlefield, where treason and crime and rebellion are rampant, and where disorder reaches its culminating point in the symbolical combat between a father and son, on land where the only light comes from a blood-red sun.

But it is also in this chaos where evil triumphs that the damned soul, its symbolical expression, is forged and sharpened—the necessary pure product, the brilliant black pearl, or rather (not to deprive Gloucester of the bestial qualities that his enemies attribute to him), the venomous toad, the misshapen dog, the ignoble devil. We see Gloucester rising and flourishing in the last two Parts of the *Henry VI* trilogy till, in the play devoted solely to him, he attains the zenith of his evil power in the midst of the disorder which he aggravates to his own advantage. Here, all his strength is bent towards establishing and retaining a personal order, based upon and issuing from evil. But the stability of such an order is illusory, and what makes it so is precisely the gradual shrinking of the domain where such an order can prevail. Richard's worst enemy is not the hatred with which he is surrounded on all sides, but the terrible solitude arising from it, and the confrontation with himself which is the only result of his victory:

> What, do I fear myself? there's none else by:
> Richard loves Richard; that is, I am I.
> Is there a murderer here? No. Yes, I am:
> Then fly. What, from myself? Great reason why:
> Lest I revenge. What, myself upon myself?
> Alack, I love myself. Wherefore? For any good
> That I myself have done unto myself?
> O, no! alas, I rather hate myself
> For hateful deeds committed by myself!
> > *Richard III*, V, iii, 183 *et seq.*

Here he becomes conscious of the insoluble contradiction within himself. (There is the same position, the same feeling in Macbeth a little later, but it is expressed with a very different poetic power because Shakespeare had by then developed his dramatic style and enriched his experience.) Night, which had seemed to disappear on Edward IV's accession—

> Now is the winter of our discontent
> Made glorious summer by this sun of York;
> And all the clouds that lour'd upon our house
> In the deep bosom of the ocean buried.
> > I, i, 1

thickens again, and on the morning of the Battle of Bosworth
the sun hides itself:

> *King Richard:*   . . . Ratcliff!
> *Ratcliff:*   My lord?
> *King Richard:*   The sun will not be seen to-day;
>   The sky doth frown and lour upon our army . . .
> V, iii, 284 et seq.

Richmond, the minister of the forces of good, sent by God
to restore order, to make peace and justice reign, to reconcile
the rival Houses and to cure England's malady, calls upon
Almighty God calmly, with religious and submissive accents,
on the eve of a night which will be peopled for him with
beneficent dreams:

> O thou, whose captain I account myself,
> Look on my forces with a gracious eye. . . .
> V, iii, 109

> The sweetest sleep, and fairest-boding dreams
> That ever enter'd in a drowsy head,
> Have I since your departure had, my lords.
> V, iii, 228

Richmond's figure is as yet but an allegory of the ideal King,
scarcely come to life; just as Richard's, despite his ruses, his
agitation and his energy, just because it is too much committed to brutal and immediate action, still falls in complexity far short of the figures that are to come.

The dramatic technique here is affected by the demands
of the Chronicle-play and the Morality—slices of history
packed but still two-dimensional, many of the scenes being
almost ritual in their balance, the symbolical analogy constantly employed, the conflict between the forces of good
and evil much in evidence, and also the reversal of situations.
But in the second trilogy, where the problem remains the
same, we shall find characters and themes considerably enriched—the characters more carefully portrayed, the themes
more complex—thus showing the amazing progress made by
Shakespeare in a few years. Reverting to both the conflict
of order and disorder, and the study of the ideal figure of
a king, he amplifies the tragedy by the ironic and comic
counter-point of his common characters, of whom Falstaff is
the hero. Just as the epilogue of the three Parts of *Henry VI*
is the abortive triumph of the misshapen Richard, so the
prologue to the trilogy of *Henry IV* and *Henry V* is the
short and sad career of Richard II.

Richard II is the story of an initial crime. It also depicts
the figure of a King who draws down upon himself and

upon England a century of civil war and bloody disorders by his immobility at the heart of his illusion. It has been said (and the parallel is attractive) that Richard II foreshadowed Hamlet by his propensity to meditation, by his delight in the play of verbal analogies, by his confusion of the illusory with the real, and by his constant recoil from taking action. But the resemblance is superficial, for, in the first place, Hamlet is more practical than a romantic interpretation of his character would admit; and secondly, because Richard wilfully stereotypes his formal conception of his kingly role, which bears no relation to reality. Archaic in his ideas, he imagines that his Divine Right will put at his disposal cohorts of angels to fight the rebels, whereas his chimerical armies cannot stand up against real soldiers.

Richard's enemy, the realist Bolingbroke, fails to dispel this illusion, even if he puts the angels to flight. But he commits the capital offence of regicide, a crime for which he can make no atonement in spite of his sincerely wishing for a generous and just government. He wears the crown but he embarks upon misfortune and he drags a century of history after him. In his old age, a sick and discouraged monarch, deceived by his son the dissolute companion of Falstaff, and faced with rebellion, his kingdom is in chaos until his death.

Prince Hal, the future Henry V, begins his life in disorder, but he possesses the truly regal qualities that allow him to touch pitch without being defiled. He is without doubt the nearest that Shakespeare gets to an ideal king, and it is he who best plays the part of king. But—and here we have the enrichment of character that distinguishes him from Richmond—this sun is not spotless, this monarch has his defects. Here the theme of royalty is thoroughly treated and the King's character is put to the test by problems that go beyond the mere possession of a crown—problems raised alike by the exercise of power and the internal drama in a man's conscience *qua* King. Prince Hal's conversion is described as miraculous, and it is not untinged by a certain politic calculation which rules out spontaneity in face of his kingly duties. His attitude to Falstaff is marked by an inexplicable hardness that leaves us uneasy: he raises the question of responsibility for the war he has declared in evasive terms, as if to elude it and lay it at France's door, which apparently puts his conscience at rest. But really it is his passion rather than his reason which decides: his anger, once roused, bursts the frail covering of wise humility, and his pride speaks in arrogant terms:

But I will rise there with so full a glory
That I will dazzle all the eyes of France . . .
Henry V, I, ii, 278

He salves his conscience once more by throwing upon the
citizens of Harfleur the responsibility for the pillage and all
the ills unleashed by war. He is fully conscious of them, but
in the famous soliloquy on the night before Agincourt the
conflict between the king and the man in him breaks out:
the King seeks in vain the 'ease of heart' enjoyed by the
common man, and feels the weight of the remorse that oppressed the conscience of his father.

While making the necessary concessions to patriotic feeling and to the King's renown, Shakespeare lets us see in
Henry's meditations and soliloquies—through the unstudied
answers of the soldiers whom he talks to before the battle,
and also through the cynical reflections of the dead Falstaff's
disreputable followers—that the political problem, linked
with the moral problem, is far from being solved by a
victorious campaign and a marriage with happy consequences for the country. It is not with Richard II that Hamlet should be compared but with Henry V, because of this
element of uneasiness that hardly ever leaves him, because
of his sombre views of human nature, because of the continual questionings of an anxious mind constantly opposing
violence with self-mastery, generosity with the implacable
character of the sovereign's impersonal duties, and unbridled
passions with the harmonious balance that is the nostalgic and
inaccessible ideal towards which both king and subject
desperately strive. Already in King Henry lurk disturbingly
the evil spirits which will develop in the great tragedies.
Already also the problem presents itself of the real and the
apparent, which is much more than a psychological problem
since on its solution—whether by a mere intellectual attitude
or by the assumption of effective responsibility in action—
depends ultimately the meaning that man gives to life itself.

From play to play, moreover, the themes become more
and more closely associated with the characters and the
situations. Each drama, each comedy raises one or more
problems—not only those of the particular play but those
resulting from an ever more serious application of thought,
seconded by emotion, to the infinitely various aspects of
the human condition. Here, I can only touch upon this
evolution, which would call for a whole volume to itself,
and make a few points in passing, before reaching the goal
where Shakespeare thought fit to stop. He seeks to attain
the deepest and most authentic human reality. An experi-

mental play, like *Love's Labour's Lost* belonging to his first
period, shows this concern already, despite its apparently
flippant subject.

Four men have formed the plan to devote every hour of
their life to study, neglecting all other human needs. However noble the aim—Navarre will be the wonder of the
world!—this wilful confinement does not withstand the assaults of passion: the quartet are not immune against love.
And when, shamefacedly, they recognize themselves for-
sworn, it is to love that the cleverest of them gives the
credit of leading man to his full development:

> But love, first learned in a lady's eyes,
> Lives not alone immured in the brain,
> But, with the motion of all elements,
> Courses as swift as thought in every power,
> And gives to every power a double power,
> Above their functions and their offices . . .
> *Love's Labour's Lost,* IV, iii, 327 *et seq.*

Here, however, love seems to be mere badinage, though the
comedy ends on a grave note and Rosaline prefers to put
Berowne to the test of suffering (she sends him to a hospi-
tal) rather than to that of knowledge. Integrity of soul,
nevertheless, is not in question here, any more than it will be
in *Romeo and Juliet* where nothing can hurt their faith,
their optimism or the splendour of their love, in spite of
the 'lamentable' failure of these perfect lovers. The cause
of this failure lies outside themselves: they will be for ever
'star-cross'd' lovers, and they die without a malediction on
their lips. Evil has not yet penetrated into the nature of the
character—the evil and the consciousness of it which make
the rebels of the great tragedies.

It is a commonplace that Shakespeare's plays grow gradually more sombre at the beginning of the seventeenth
century, and that this was equally true of other playwrights.
The melancholy Jaques of *As You Like It,* an ambiguous
character whom Shakespeare treats with irony rather than
sympathy, lacks vitality and balance. One would make reservations about Antonio in *The Merchant of Venice* or about
the strange heroine of *All's Well that Ends Well.* In *The
Merchant,* that disturbing character Shylock soon carries
the plot to the dangerous point where it skirts tragedy. Between the themes of the apparent and the real, of material
wealth and spiritual wealth, emerges the central theme of
the play—that of Grace, the daughter of universal harmony,

challenged by the blind letter of the Law, which is invoked
to serve cruelty and the spirit of revenge. In this struggle
between the brute and the angel, the angel is still triumphant
—not without a mocking smile—over all dangers.

Even Shakespeare's brilliant comedies are not free from
a certain veiled anxiety, and perhaps the current view,
which ranks them high in the amused light-heartedness and
indifference to serious problems that seemed to mark the
poet's mind when he composed them, should be revised.
Much Ado About Nothing is a far more serious play than is
commonly supposed, even if Hero's death is mere pretence
and the 'villain' simply an extra, not very deeply studied,
and even if the comedy ends with a reconciliation all round.
On reflection we see Benedict and Beatrice as something
more than the accomplished fencers they are taken to be,
and their lively passages of arms reflect on the surface a
much less carefree attitude towards their own problems and
those of their friends.

As for *Twelfth Night*, smooth and delightful though its
atmosphere may be, it is not without uneasiness: the tone
of some of its scenes is only on the fringe of comedy and
echoes of it in an aggravated form recur in later plays. I
think the attitude of the French towards Shakespeare's comedies has been largely conditioned by their attitude towards
Alfred de Musset's plays. It is curious to notice how, having
been told so often that Musset is the French playwright
who comes nearest to Shakespeare, they have ended by
transferring their opinion of the imitator to the original.
The resemblance is, indeed, wholly superficial and it would
be rash to press the analogy between them too far. The
poverty of Musset's thought, for all the scintillating quality
of his wit and the skill of his technique which looks so
natural, should make the critic chary of forcing a comparison.

The note of gravity is clearer, and the importance attached
to major themes is more evident, in the tragedy of *Julius
Caesar*, where we must not be misled by the so-called
'Roman' atmosphere. In this play what is involved is not
merely a problem of Roman politics, the Roman character
of which is merely accidental. It is, once more (though with
what profound resonances in Brutus), the theme of the conflict between order and disorder, good and evil, presented
as a struggle between the sentiment of honour and the
attraction of a crime committed for a 'noble reason'. It is
no mere chance that brings the words 'honour', 'honest',
'honourable' so often to the lips of the characters, sometimes in their positive meaning, sometimes negatively and

steeped in accumulated and destructive irony. In this un-happy hero—Brutus, I mean—purity of intention is tarnished by contact with political reality and the search for liberty becomes involved in the bloody entanglements which follow the murder of the dictator and destroy all honour, peace of mind and public order.

In an atmosphere heavy with storm, superstition and presages, Brutus's pure conscience struggles and succumbs to the evil insinuations which represent the death of that unattractive and even tainted hero, Julius Caesar, as the only solution consonant with the principles of justice and liberty. The whole tragedy is nothing but the slow degrada-tion of Brutus's conscience, before and after the crime, although he does not forfeit our esteem and admiration. Brutus's scruples bring upon him defeat after defeat, and the nightmare-vision of *Julius Caesar* anticipates *Macbeth*, the tragedy that followed it closely in point of time. In *Macbeth*, too, night is the vast, redoubtable womb in which seeds of evil and phantoms proliferate. Here the soul is as-sailed while the body shivers, and here, through the strangest contrasts—avowed terror, longing for harmony, a desire for escape, refuge in individual stoicism when all is lost—through disorder unleashed, the coming order is prepared which will put to rout the chimeras of evil temporarily vic-torious.

But *Julius Caesar* does not appear to be a universal tragedy, perhaps because it insists too much on the theme of pure honour, perhaps because the whole tragedy—despite the grandeur of certain passages—remains too much the state-ment of an individual drama, closely linked with a famous historical event, and made impersonal by the very fact of this celebrity. *Hamlet* comes first among the greatest of Shakespeare's dramas that can claim to be at once extremely individual and universal. Here the struggle between man and his destiny, man and the pitfalls of evil, man and his phantoms, his temptations, his contradictions, takes place on a high plane where it can claim to stand symbolically for mankind.

Starting with a trivial incident, centering the action on revenge, Shakespeare writes a huge tragedy—huge but im-perfect, for it starts off in all directions, and all efforts to reduce it to unity fail in spite of the central figure. But this very imperfection is the sign of a new and deeper interest, the effect of a conception of the world and of man's nature that is overwhelming, that constantly bursts the bonds of

ordinary dramatic technique. For the drama is in Hamlet's
mind, and all the external excitement, all the structural incidents of the play are reduced to the symbolical representation of an internal excitement which no decision can allay.
The underlying theme under the pretext of vengeance is
simply man's own nature faced with the moral and metaphysical problems whereby it is defined—love, time, death,
perhaps even the principle of identity, the whole problem of
existence summed up in 'To be or not to be'.

The shock Hamlet receives from the death of his father
and his mother's remarriage releases a battery of questions
fatal to his peace of mind, which is further corroded by
the revelations of the Ghost. The world changes colour, life's
meaning changes, love is stripped of its spirituality, woman
of her virtue; the state loses its stability, heaven and earth
their joys. By the sudden irruption of evil, the world becomes meaningless, gentleness turns to bitterness, reason to
madness. The malady is contagious, spreading from man to
the kingdom, from the kingdom to the vault of heaven:

> . . . it goes so heavily with my disposition that this goodly
> frame, the earth, seems to me a sterile promontory; this most
> excellent canopy, the air, look you, this brave o'erhanging
> firmament, this majestical roof fretted with golden fire, why,
> it appears no other thing to me but a foul and pestilent con-
> gregation of vapours.
>
> *Hamlet,* II, ii, 316 *et seq.*

Hamlet eagerly questions the human, social and cosmological order, since something has happened to dislocate his
conscience and damage his faith. The shock he has received
pushes him to the pitiless logic of doubt; his hypersensitivity
(he is melancholic) now harbours disgust and contempt;
his keen intellect pitilessly analyses the values (now falsified
by the intrusion of the impossible, the unthinkable) of that
harmonious world where once he himself was

> The expectancy and rose of the fair state,
> The glass of fashion and the mould of form . . .
>   III, i, 161-2

The work of destruction goes on apace, with a trembling
rage that spares nothing.

It is curious to see the sustained insistence with which
Hamlet in his numerous soliloquies constantly supports his
reasoning with antitheses which are only in appearance
figures of rhetoric. At the back of his mind he always has
a longing for a noble, spiritual framework which his reason
instantly repudiates, and he indulges in the game of skittles

with a savage joy, a crafty wickedness, an intellectual ruth-
lessness which make this prodigious display of mental gym-
nastics an excellent justification for those who hold that
Hamlet is mad. But he is not. He remains master of his
simulation, and it is his keen intelligence that is so disconcerting. He has an acute understanding of evil and consequently a hatred of evil, borrowing from evil its own
weapons to defeat it with, and having no other resource
than to do evil.

Suddenly reason becomes passion's slave and sovereign
man degenerates into an evil-doing beast. Hence the un-
matched cruelty, the blasphemies and the crimes in this
tragedy. The scene with Ophelia and the later scene with
Gertrude are hard to bear. Even Othello's frenzied bullying
and abusing and murdering of the innocent Desdemona seem
less painful than the invective with which Hamlet chooses
to insult Ophelia. Desdemona's lot is less cruel than Ophelia's, for her death is merely an injustice against which
reason rebels, pleading justice. But Ophelia's fate cannot be
atoned for, even by reason, for the evil is the defilement of
the soul, the pollution of innocence by the conscienceless.

As for the scene with Gertrude, it goes beyond the limits
of what drama can do: sex-hatred here breaks out in language never till then heard and matched only by certain
modern novelists, particularly American. It is intolerable because the nauseating sarcasm is turned by Hamlet against
his own mother, because the violence of the sensitive imagination attributes to the being who of all others should be
above reproach, the bestiality and hypocrisy of a prostitute.
Hamlet lingers hatefully upon the musty smell of soiled
sheets, the foetid sweat of an incest that is a desecration,
and it requires the intervention of the Ghost to recall him
to some decency.

Here Hamlet goes too far, and the shifting chaos of a disordered brain seems, in his horror of sexual excess, to revert
to a line of resistance so coherent that it has made some
critics argue that his was a pure mind in shocked revolt. I
do not believe it. The touchstone of the character is his
wrathful identification with man's twofold nature, revealed
by his mother's misconduct (misconduct in regard to the
unwritten but traditional normal morality), and it is expressed in these generalities perceived, apparently for the
first time, acutely and intolerably, by a personal awareness:

What a piece of work is a man! How noble in reason! How
infinite in faculty! in form, in moving, how express and admirable! in action how like an angel! in apprehension how

like a god! the beauty of the world! the paragon of animals!
And yet, to me, what is this quintessence of dust? man delights
not me.

II, ii, 323, et seq.

'And yet to me'—it is the personal reaction, constantly introduced in this striking form peculiar to Hamlet's *volte-
faces,* as if a hot iron were being plunged into the wound.
It gives the character a mordancy, the internal conflict an
intolerable reality, which have made Hamlet under the most
diverse forms haunt men's memory ever since his creation.
Ridiculously he has been made out to be a romantic figure,
as if he could be reduced to a grandiloquent and sentimental
attitude. Hamlet, on the contrary, is the essential anti-
romantic: his clear-sightedness and his brutality fling him
wildly against any illusion. His negative cast of mind refuses to fall into the trap of idealized appearance, and if
he makes some play with bombast it is, as it were, for a
recoil, so as to give more pungency to the sarcasm which
turns against himself.

But in this disordered excitement human experience
deepens. Psychologically Hamlet becomes wiser and more
resigned as the play advances. He comes to see that his
mortal sickness, which threatens his country no less dangerously ('there's something rotten in the State of Denmark'),
none the less assures continuity of life and the solidity of
the State. As for him, the game is over, 'the rest is silence'.
But Fortinbras perhaps will achieve what Hamlet has missed.

Hamlet's experience, however unsatisfactory, leads Shakespeare to still profounder depths, to yet darker caverns.
Hamlet, after all, ends on a note which does not rule out
optimism. The inevitable death of the Prince of Denmark
is merely one unhappy incident amongst others, in an adventure from which a philosophy emerges, roughly similar
to that of the historical plays. The difference is that the
theme of disorder has invaded the mind and become the
hero's personal affair. But the poetry of doubt and abuse is
still contained within limits which the following plays will
press back. Similarly, the apprehension by the poet's consciousness of the complexity of the human condition was
to throw him into the tantalizing irresolution of the problem-
comedies, *Troilus and Cressida* and *Measure for Measure,*
only to issue in ultimate negation.

Troilus and Cressida is a play with many facets, and recent critics have quite rightly underlined its ambiguity.
Over the two great themes of Love and War situations de-

velop which are the most likely to confuse the reader's mind.
It is not the actual nature of war that is involved here, as it
might be in the historical plays: it is the reason for war's
outbreak, the way war is waged, its aims, and the catastrophes it brings in its wake. The problem is examined from
the twofold point of view of the responsible leaders and of
the satirical spirit personified by Thersites. He is not im-
plicated in the tragic adventure but observes it from the
outside, and transcends it, not like a Falstaff with his vitality
individualized by vigorous humour, but with that acidity and
aridity of the sarcastic function to which he is confined, like
Apemantus in *Timon of Athens*, the philosopher of ill-
humour and hatred.

The Greeks have gone to war to avenge the insult to
Menelaus. The honour of the race is at stake. For a similar
reason the Trojans withstand the siege. But honour has no
valid object on which to base itself. An unworthy woman,
a prostitute, is the reason for the fighting. Such is Thersites's
view. And those who fight? They are kings and generals who
have lost all sense of discipline, proud egoists like Achilles,
garrulous old men like Nestor, bovine and conceited fools
like Ajax. And on the Trojan side, in spite of the pure
heroism of Hector and the furious idealism of Troilus, men
who idolize honour yet seek in vain a reasonable justification
for the adoration of their myth.

For Helen's sovereign beauty, which had once thrown
Faustus almost into ecstasy, is a mere illusion, covering corruption, or rather emptiness, for the corruption is not so
much in her as all around her. It is reason which has become cynicism, Time which devours life whose instants
one would like to see eternal, society and the laws imposed
by men which stand in the way of all self-realization. The
apparatus of chivalry, the challenges, the gloves thrown
down, the single combats—a ritual degraded alike by the
failure to observe a code formerly sacred, and by the unworthiness of the cause for which it is set in motion—is
an absurd (and, when one comes to think of it, sad) parody
of the great scenes in *Richard II*. Scoffed at by the Greeks,
the spirit of chivalry remains alive in the Trojans, but it no
longer has a worthy object.

A whole world is breaking up on the windy plains of
Troy. Everywhere disorder and confusion reign supreme.
Ulysses with his clear mind sets himself with great subtlety
to diagnose the malady. This war bears within it the seeds
of its own disintegration—a 'phoney war' one might call it,
in which everything (honour, the art of government, the

conduct of operations) goes by the board. The great speech
of Ulysses, already quoted, is more than a fine political
lesson that might bear fruit: it is a moral lesson, a useless
warning given by clear-sightedness to men so immersed in
their pride that they destroy each other before destroying
themselves. In both camps the morale of the army is undermined by wavering and uncertainty. The anarchy that
Ulysses so much dreads is a moral as well as a military anarchy: it engenders the chaos in which treachery flourishes.

To say that we have in *Troilus* a parody of the heroic
world is not enough. Parody is a matter of treatment rather
than of conception. It is a deliberate exercise in style, but
conception cannot stop at the surface of things or have only
a negative aspect. When Shakespeare wrote *Troilus* he was
as much a master of his thought as of his style and technique. The infamous way in which Achilles causes the murder
of the disarmed Hector is the sign of an appalling decay
of faith no less than a parody of the famous combat between these two valiant warriors. And the Trojans are
hardly any better, despite their romantic heroism, their cult
of honour, their love of beauty, their ideals disproved by
the facts and by reason. This State is more dangerously
rotten than the Kingdom of Denmark. The prophecies of
Cassandra sound the death-knell of Ilion, but the trumpets
of the Greeks do not sound for a victory over the ruins.
The last noises of the battle under the threatened walls are
cries of lamentation for the death of Hector, and the curses
of Troilus against Pandarus as he storms and rages, seeking
a heroic death in battle to deliver him from love. It is to
Pandarus that the last words of the play are given: 'a goodly
medicine for my aching bones.'

It is, indeed, significant that there should be so many
metaphors taken from illness and digestion. On the one side
there is the loud-mouthed Thersites, the professional scoffer,
the embodiment of cynicism, who reduces the grand design
of the War of Troy to a struggle for a whore and a cuckold,
and who spits the pox, scabs and running sores in the face
of everyone. On the other side, there is the shady character
of Pandarus, the heroes' pimp, full of goodwill and good
humour. The one sees nothing in human nature but stupidity,
pride, useless cruelty, instinctive and arrogant bestiality. The
other is in a good mood only when he can further illicit
amours; he is at ease only in immorality. The hateful
Thersites, a growling dog and a poltroon; the go-between
Pandarus—such are the finished products of the fine Greek
intelligence and of Trojan idealism.

Against the pseudo-heroic background of the 'epic' we
see the lovers, Troilus and Cressida, strangely degraded
copies of Romeo and Juliet. In them there is the same youth
and ardour, but what a difference! Troilus is sincere, faithful, hot-headed, and calls himself 'as true as truth's simplicity
and simpler than the infancy of truth': [2] he is not deceived
by the ambitious aspirations of human love, and (far from
reasoning like Romeo who regards Destiny alone as responsible for his complete failure) Troilus finds in himself
—before Destiny intervenes—the explanation of his secret
fears: 'this is the monstrosity in love, lady, that the will
is infinite, and the execution confined; that the desire is
boundless, and the act a slave to limit.' [3]

In *Romeo and Juliet* physical love is referred to only in
the broad, healthy twaddle of a woman of the people, the
Nurse; in *Troilus* it is conveyed through the innuendoes of
Pandarus. In the one play the lovers invoke the stars and
listen to the nightingale's song; in the other, they are
equally ardent to be united, but their passion is no longer
that of the celestial bodies. The tone and images employed
by Troilus in his great speeches have an intensity of a very
different flavour. Flavour is the right word, for metaphors
derived from the sense of taste are the most numerous.[4]
And in this taste we have a foretaste of corruption. Sensuality is stirred in prospect and fears to be too soon sated:

> I am giddy: expectation whirls me round.
> The imaginary relish is so sweet
> That it enchants my sense. What will it be
> When that the watery palate tastes indeed
> Love's thrice-repured nectar? death, I fear me . . .
> > *Troilus and Cressida*, III, ii, 17 *et seq.*

The expectation that gnaws Troilus gives his imagination
so acute a vision that his impatience takes the form of even
more than usually precious metaphors:

> . . . . O that her hand,
> In whose comparisons all whites are ink
> Writing their own reproach.
> > I, i, 57-9

and reopens the wounds of love till they are made intolerable: 'Instead of oil and balm', he says to Pandarus boasting
Cressida's charms to him, 'Thou lay'st in every gash that
love hath given me The knife that made it' (I, i, 63). The

---

[2] *Troilus and Cressida*, III, ii, 176.
[3] ibid., III, ii, 87.
[4] See the excellent article by D. A. Traversi in *Scrutiny*, December 1938.

violent metaphor replacing the traditional arrow by the
knife (has ever Cupid wounded his victims with knife-
stabs?) reveals his intolerable anxiety. The shadow of the
approaching treachery is already thrown into the uneasy
mind of Troilus.

On her side Cressida is already an experienced coquette
('Women are angels, wooing: Things won are done'), prof-
ligate, almost *blasée*. She pretends to be accessible only
through the intercession of the ribald, leering, vicious Pandarus, uncomfortably. She is all hesitation:

> I have a kind of self resides with you,
> But an unkind self, that itself will leave,
> To be another's fool.
>
> III, ii, 154-6

But during this capital scene of Act III she raises herself
to the point of uttering a great vow of fidelity that tries to
sound as sincere as Troilus's. She calls down upon herself
already an anathema ('If I be false . . . Yea, let them say,
to stick the heart of falsehood, "As false as Cressid"') for
her infidelity is already near: she *is* unfaithfulness and knows
it.

In the cold dawn that follows the marvelous but all too
brief night, the uneasy banter of Pandarus, the urgent appeals of the messengers of Fate who come to demand the
daughter of Calchas, the vows renewed in haste and without
conviction, the coarse boasting of the coxcomb Diomedes,
Troilus's bitter reflections on Time:

> Injurious time now with a robber's haste
> Crams his rich thievery up . . .
>
> IV, iv, 42-3

all this gives the abrupt separation of the lovers a strangely
embarrassed character of potential catastrophe and disconcerting irony. The devastating part played by Time in the
tragedy of *Troilus* has been remarked upon: [5]

> Throughout this play, in compressed metaphor, in self-
> conscious and detailed analysis, and thence to dialogue and
> incident, we have a philosophy of love which regards it as
> essentially un-at-home in time, and incapable of continued
> concrete embodiment in the difficult flux of events. The love-
> interest turns on this theme: the theme of immediate value,
> killed, or apparently killed, by time. [6]

And Mr. Traversi, comparing this theme with that of the

[5] G. Wilson Knight and D. A. Traversi.
[6] G. Wilson Knight, *The Wheel of Fire*, p. 67-8 (new edition 1949).

Sonnets, writes: 'The tragedy consists less in the personal
suffering of Troilus than in the overriding influence exercised
by Time upon human relationship and feelings.' [7]

For it looks as if the psychological problem of Cressida's
treachery cannot be solved by the mere assertion of her
inconstancy. The study of the characters here, once again
—as so often, indeed almost always in Shakespeare—is subordinated to a conception of human relationships.

How can a moral judgment be passed on Cressida if she is
convicted beforehand of the frailty of her feelings? Nevertheless, the scene of the instantaneous effecting of her treachery—where she accepts unblushingly the kisses of all the
Greek leaders—is painful; and still worse is the scene where
Troilus is present with Ulysses at the shameful simpering
of the woman who has pledged him her word. One can
understand the sarcasm of Thersites and the cautious words
of Ulysses. Troilus may ask himself the question, 'This, she?'
and answer with the irreconcilable: 'This is and is not
Cressida.' Tortured love here presents a problem of identity
which the play fails to solve. Or rather, reason loses itself
when confronted with the opposed data of remembered appearance and present reality, as if love itself, subject to
Time's uncertainties and to those of accident and of personality, were incapable—except in a simplified vision of
its essence, whether Petrarchan idealism or the fornication
desired by Thersites and Pandarus—of attaining that purity
of object and function which gives it a positive sense.

The complexity of its nature is surrounded by aggravating
circumstances which few poets till then had been willing to
see. For, in addition to the metaphysical problem which
the amorists and Shakespeare himself in the Sonnets raised
in the fervour of a passion which aspires to complete unity
and fulfilment, there is the equally insoluble conflict of the
unworthiness that may exist at the very core of love's aspirations. Troilus's only remaining way out of his predicament
is to throw himself again into the frenzy of the accursed,
hopeless war in which Troy will collapse in ruins over the
conception of a world destroyed.

Powerful, well constructed and varied, this play offers a
remarkable unity of design and atmosphere. It is the product
of a mind which has constantly drawn further away from
the peaceful solutions which his age offered him at the
outset of his career, and which with growing experience
came to be filled with a settled uneasiness.

[7] D. A. Traversi, *Scrutiny*, December 1938, p. 308.

Measure for Measure passes for a comedy but it is the arch-problem play. Its atmosphere is even more oppressive: there is nothing heroic, nothing romantic to lighten it. Everything in it is fraught with consequences, meticulously concerted and arranged. The moral preoccupation is evident from one end of the play to the other but, serious though it may be, it seems ill defined and gives rise to divergent interpretations. It was long considered a failure as a play— as lacking internal unity, expressing the blackest pessimism and showing how little interest Shakespeare took in his subject. Modern critics take the opposite view. Wilson Knight has no hesitation in comparing the Duke with Christ. C. J. Sisson declares that the spirit of the play is 'profoundly Christian'. It is ardently admired for similar reasons by D. A. Traversi, F. R. Leavis and Miss M. C. Bradbrook. Finally, Roy W. Battenhouse has gone so far as to base his interpretation of *Measure for Measure* on the Christian doctrine of the Atonement.

Yet it is difficult to breathe in the prison air, with its musty atmosphere reminiscent of brothel bedrooms and their stuffy, uniform curtains. Some of the characters, Angelo in particular, carry about with them the unpleasant starchy smell of their ruffs, of mouldering parchment; Angelo can even be detected, like the devil, by his foul breath. The friar's cowl, like the novice's veil, appear suspect, just as the jokes are forced, the situations intolerable, the ending altogether too artificially contrived. It is as if the play had to be retrieved from its false situation, its house of ill fame, by means of an edifying end, difficult to stage, so as to show that all hope is not lost. The chief personages, and some of the minor ones too, are bad characters, bad to know, people of bad faith and bad will. The play cannot possibly be made out a tragedy, although death haunts their minds and hovers in the wings, and the title refers to the scales of justice and the equating of a brother's life with a sister's chastity. Moral arguments may be plentifully employed in it, and ethical introspection pressed as far as it will go, but it is hard to believe, as Wilson Knight would have us do, that the numerous and profound Gospel echoes of *Measure for Measure* cannot be understood unless one re-reads St. John or St. Matthew.

The problem of government, which seems at the outset to be once more the problem that the Duke wants to solve, is posed in terms so special that he cannot remain as definite and as pure a character to the end of the play. Imagine a conflict between lust and the State—a virtuous State (or

one that would like to be virtuous)—which causes houses
of ill fame to be closed and decrees death for the crime
of fornication but applies the law in strange ways. The
philosopher-Duke wants to see the experiment at work; he
delegates his powers of life and death to a carefully chosen
deputy so that he himself may wander at will through the
worst of the streets, the palace corridors and the prison-
cells. Authority is concealed in a friar's cowl and acts by
proxy against human nature, which is sentenced in advance
to the disgrace of punishment for an infamous crime.

The straitest-laced, the apparently noblest of the State
officials, on whom is laid the duty and the honour of enforcing the law, suddenly takes fire and is caught in his own
trap, like a clumsy hunter. The hypocrite—as keen in cir-
cumventing his own law as he had been inflexible in applying
it—offers death with one hand and dishonour with the
other. He is possessed by the demon of lust. Never before
had it spoken so categorically:

> I have begun;
> And now I give my sensual race the rein:
> Fit thy consent to my sharp appetite;
> Lay by all nicety and prolixious blushes,
> That banish what they sue for . . .
>> *Measure for Measure,* II, iv, 160-4

Angelo threatens with a harshness that terrifies himself:

> . . . redeem thy brother
> By yielding up thy body to my will,
> Or else he must not only die the death,
> But thy unkindness shall his death draw out
> To lingering sufferance.
>> II, 164-8

He flees even before the reply reaches him, and gives the
order of execution. His tormented conscience, his pride, his
exacting Pharisaism have ruined him. To save appearances,
virtue relies on appearances—but, there too, the core is
rotten.

The dramatic interest of this play is, moreover, divided.
Will Claudio, the sinner filled with terrible anguish at the
prospect of death, pay for the general corruption? Will
Isabella, leaving her convent, succeed in moving the pity of
Angelo when he proposes to her his disgraceful bargain?
Will the Duke's deputy, with his icy virtue, burning with the
very lust which it is his duty to punish in others, have
Claudio's head or Isabella's virtue? And the experimenting
Duke—'the old fantastical Duke of dark corners'—sets the
pace. Never had a plot depended so much on a single

character, and the same thing was to be true again of *The Tempest*, though there at any rate the 'Soveraign Plasmator', as Sir Thomas Urquhart calls God,[8] is a magician. Here, the Duke tries to restore a precarious balance. He is full of arguments, maxims, advice, secret orders, in vain exhorting Claudio to courage:

> Reason thus with life:
> If I do lose thee, I do lose a thing
> That none but fools would keep . . .
>   III, i, 6-8

or scheming with Isabella how to save her virtue by a substitution unworthy of her virtue, and with the Provost of the prison a substitution of heads so as to round off neatly the final distribution of rewards and penalties, in which he tries to persuade us (without much success) that his authority can restore order in his State and make justice supreme in a world condemned.

But it would seem that no repentance can redeem the criminal hypocrisy of Angelo (whose name is an ironical contradiction of his nature), no docility in marriage can allay our mistrust of the insensitive Isabella, whose religious vocation is as questionable as her feeling of outraged virtue. As for Claudio, no happy ending can make us forget his egoism and physical cowardice in the presence of death ('Aye, but to die . . .'). These people are either too human or not human enough; even the wisdom of the philosopher-Duke is a too conscious attempt to give arbitrary behaviour the guise of benevolence. He is incapable of true generosity towards Lucio who has offended him personally; and Lucio is not wholly contemptible: he is at least true to the brotherhood of sinners, and the ardour with which he defends Claudio at the most dangerous moment is to his credit.

By comparison with these, the disreputable company of pimps and bawds of whom the play from time to time gives us a glimpse, seems more respectable. For they at least are sincere to the point of cynicism and do not seek to be believed. The Duke's decree ruins them and it is not in the name of virtue that they protest. But the other characters merely fill us with mistrust or repulsion. Shakespeare has made them so equivocal or contemptible, has placed them in situations so clearly calculated to bring out only their unattractive or shady sides, that the play's major themes, far from being those of justice, of honour or love, seem to be those of ugliness, of sin and villainy. The conflict between

[8] Rabelais, II, 8.

instinct and reason, good intentions and the mass of resistance
offered by the complex of vices, touches here the lowest
depths if not of tragedy at least of demoralization.

The ideal of order and generosity may inspire the philosopher-Duke's experiment, guiding step by step the ups and
downs of his complicated scenario, and may give this sententious moralizer a paternal, benevolent and merciful tone.
None the less, the feeling of uneasiness that grips us from
the moment that the play begins to move, does not leave us
even when it has ended happily. Evil here is shameful,
slimy, insinuating: it is the negation of all innocence, all
integrity. Judge and prisoner are alike suspect; the chaste
and the licentious equally repulsive, life and death alike
unreal and undesirable. All nobility seems to be excluded
from a life that contains a thousand underhand deaths, from
a death which prolongs the horrors of life and magnifies
them tenfold. Both life and death here are apprehended in
profoundly ambiguous terms, and it is no exaggeration to
say, as Miss Ellis-Fermor does,[9] that we have touched the
lowest point of cynicism and disgust.

Or, on reflection, we may be attracted by the mirage of a
symbolical interpretation of the play and regard it as a
dramatic picture of the story of the Atonement.[10] The sovereign in disguise mingles with his people, just as God de-
scended to earth to wage war upon Satan and to deliver
Creation from the bondage of evil. He leaves to His deputy
(Angelo) the application of the Law but at the same time
undertakes to moderate its rigours. Thus two great principles
enter into conflict—that of the Law and that of Grace. The
Law will be the instrument whereby Grace can manifest
itself, and Grace after a dramatic struggle will triumph. The
pseudo-just are shown to be sinners; they will be unmasked
and punished. The sinners had in them sufficient Grace to
be forgiven and redeemed. Thus the sacrifice of the Prince
of Love will have borne its fruit.

The symbolism of the names (Mariana=Mary+Anne—
the Virgin and her Mother; Angelo=Angel—Satan is a fallen
angel; the Duke, Vicentio=Conqueror, etc.); the numerous
biblical images (star of the morning, shepherd, sinner, ran-
som); the parable themes, notably those of the Miraculous
Draught of Fishes, of the Bridegroom, of the Temptation, of
Sin; the justification of the lie and of disguising for the ends

[9] *The Jacobean Drama*, p. 263.
[10] As do Wilson Knight (*The Wheel of Fire*) and Roy W. Battenhouse
(*P.M.L.A.*, December 1946, pp. 1029-59: '*Measure for Measure* and the
Christian Doctrine of the Atonement').

of salvation; the incidents of the plot (Isabella the saint inter-
ceding for the sinner, receiving the proposal of her spiritual
death, rejecting the temptation to do a wicked deed for a
good cause, then agreeing to save her honour and her
brother, on the Duke's advice, by a manœuvre which can
be symbolically interpreted as a ruse of the Divine Spirit
fighting the Devil with his own weapons, so as at last to
reap her reward in the form of marriage with the symbolical
Bridegroom): all this points to a supernatural context, which
gives the play a richer and higher meaning.

Nothing would be lacking, not even the temptation of
Grace in an Isabella who, at the moment when the tragic
alternative is presented to her, is incapable of a movement
of charity. But her conversation with the Duke (Act III, sc.
i) renders her more prone to human feelings and makes her
accept the substitution of Mariana which saves her from
dishonour and at the same time redeems the threatened
sinner. 'The hand that hath made you fair hath made you
good', says the Duke, 'the goodness that is cheap in beauty
makes beauty brief in goodness; but grace, being the soul
of your complexion shall keep the body of it ever fair.' These
words easily lend themselves to a supernatural interpretation
of the word grace. Enriched by Grace the spiritual life will
attain the fullness in which changeless mystical beauty pro-
tects the body from all defilement, and Isabella consenting
to the good Friar's suggestions is unconsciously preparing for
the perfect union which the Duke offers her at the end:
'What's mine is yours, and what is yours is mine.'

Thus understood, *Measure for Measure* takes its place in
the tradition of the Mysteries and the Morality plays. On
the temporal plane the Duke, full of indulgence and of
loving concern, can act with gentleness by persuasion, and
his keen intelligence guides virtue through the mire of vice;
he can also use his royal authority to ensure for each his
due reward. On the supernatural plane, he symbolizes the
ideal Prince who strives to put an end to the world's disorder
by his spirit of Justice, of Charity, of Wisdom. And Wilson
Knight concludes: 'The play should be read not as a picture
of normal human affairs but as a parable, like the Parables
of Jesus.'

This double interpretation, whether one likes it or not,
enlarges the scope of *Measure for Measure* considerably and
makes possible at least two conclusions. The first, historical,
namely that we should not try to describe too rigidly the
moral or philosophical 'curve' of Shakespeare's Works. The
most probable chronological order in the canon gives: *Merry*

Wives of Windsor and *Troilus and Cressida,* 1600; *Twelfth
Night,* 1602; *All's Well That Ends Well* and *Measure for
Measure,* 1604. It was a period of uncertainty, of instability,
when the poet passed from one theme to another, from one
mood to another, questioning the world indefatigably, addressing himself to every kind of problem with a keen, clear
intelligence, seeking to form a coherent vision at the cost
of painful experience. Any classification of the plays in this
central period that tried to reach a theoretical assessment
would therefore be arbitrary. There is chronologically no
compact group of 'dark plays' except for *Othello, Macbeth*
and *King Lear,* which all come round about 1606.

But the critic is not entitled for the convenience of his
demonstration to require that poets should divide their output into sections thus clearly defined. A theme, an attitude
may well be resumed, contradicted or rejoined at the will of
the creative mind. The infinite complexity of work like
Shakespeare's refuses to be contained within a geometrical
graph.

And the second conclusion is this: The peculiar characteristic and function of poetic drama is to include not merely
words, deeds and structure, but a shifting implication, a
margin of uncertainty between the surface meaning and the
overriding intention, between matter and spirit. The poet
speaks to us in turns by bright or dark signs, and poetic
experience, like religious experience, expresses itself through
the indirect channels of image, metaphor and symbol. They
are all devices for reaching his goal, which is to state a
lasting human truth that can be felt through the various
aspects of beauty. It is not surprising, therefore, that Shakespeare's plays have given rise to such diverse interpretations,
each of which is an enrichment of the experience of reader
or spectator. The diversity of themes and means of expression
in Shakespeare are so rich indeed that after three centuries
they are still far from having been fully explored. We are
only just beginning to see clearly. *Measure for Measure,* on
which I have dwelt at some length, is a typical example of
this many-sidedness, which should make the critic at once
bold and prudent.

Yet in *Measure for Measure* we are far from Cleopatra's
immortal longings. Even if one accepts the Christian interpretation of the play, it still, by its structure and subject,
clings too closely to the temporal and the earthly to be anything but a stage on the journey through the kingdom of
evil which has worse to follow. What on reflection strikes us
most, when we have given the parable-interpretation every

chance, is the absence of tragic grandeur alike in good and evil in *Measure for Measure.* But with *Othello,* which belongs to much the same period, the aesthetic quality changes: here we enter a tragic universe where nobility and grandeur speak with unmistakable accents.

A domestic tragedy with clear outlines, like *Macbeth* and *The Tempest,* the closest to classical structure, by its unity of theme, action and atmosphere if not of style, *Othello* has the straight-forwardness of a psychological study and at the same time the character of a moral crisis of despair. This tragedy, which brings on the stage living people whose greatness does not depend on their symbolical function (even Iago is too strongly individualized to pass for a mere symbol of the traditional Machiavelli or of the spirit of evil), is the first of Shakespeare's tragedies to soar with such ease to the sublime.

The psychological crisis entails a moral crisis, and this goes beyond ordinary criminal jealousy. Yet there is no explicit comment or direct allusion to weaken the dramatic tension which continues right up to the final suicide. In *Othello* there are no dialectics of explanation or demonstration (not even, again, in Iago's speeches), and the role of the intellect remains subordinate to that of the passion which inflames Othello's imagination and drives him to act. Great as Iago's importance may be, and however nicely calculated his machinations (he has been regarded as the diabolical intelligence working with subtle application to break up a moral order that he detests), it is the Moor who carries upon his shoulders the whole weight of the drama. It can no longer be represented as simply a study of baseless jealousy, provoked by the exercise of diabolical power which in its turn is started by the combined passions of envy and hate.

It is not certain that there is an intended opposition between the intelligence of Iago and the unconscious stupidity of Othello, or that the ravages of jealousy are caused solely by a childish credulity fostered by a master-slanderer. Iago, indeed, possesses all the traits of the Renaissance villain: he reveals himself openly either by his asides to the audience or in his scenes with Roderigo in which he lets us completely into his plans. His crude tactics are managed with an imperturbable economy of means, and his efforts to make his terrible hatred plausible are hardly convincing. One still wonders which is uppermost in him—envy, spite, jealousy or ambition. It is hate that makes his calculations so shrewd, his mind so clear, his intuitions penetrating. But at bottom the motive matters little. The mask he wears—the unassailable armour of flashing honesty—conceals the quickest and cleverest of brains serving a negative passion bent upon destruction. There is no temptation in him to use soft insinuations. He proceeds by direct blows and intimidation. It is his cynicism that compels Roderigo's admiration:

> Virtue! a fig! 'tis in ourselves that we are thus, or thus. Our bodies are our gardens, to the which our wills are gardeners.
>
> *Othello,* I, iii, 323-5

The vulgar brutality of his comparisons and his vocabulary, the arrogant presumption of his affirmations, would give him away with anyone but such a basely jealous and petty creature as Roderigo. In his language there is something suspiciously staccato, incomplete and also exaggerated. To Othello he talks differently: he is cautious in planting his calumnies; he can be terse in his accusing suggestions, as if always hesitating to advance them or as if he was on the point of withdrawing what he had just advanced. His masterpiece is the first exclamation that injects the poison: 'Ha! I like not that!' He is a man of scruples, 'honest' because scrupulous. He is rarely lyrical but blazes when he is so ('the green-eyed monster' is his phrase). It may be unconscious imitation of Othello on Iago's part or merely that Shakespeare does not bother about realism of language when he has to express infinite longing mingled with uneasiness. But the fact remains that he gives Iago the finest poetry in the whole play. Satisfied hatred breaks out into the rich melody of Iago's triumphant ecstasy:

> . . . Not poppy, nor mandragora,
> Nor all the drowsy syrups of the world,
> Shall ever medicine thee to that sweet sleep
> Which thou ow'dst yesterday.
>
> III, iii, 331-4

Never before had hatred exulted with such accents. We should no doubt have to go back to Medea defying Jason, to find a sadism of such poetic quality. Here Iago steeps himself in what Wilson Knight calls 'the music of *Othello*'. But this voluptuous fluidity is rare with him: more often his joy is voiced dryly, even when he is wrought up like a torturer racking his victim's flesh until he becomes unconscious. Incisive, cynical, brutal, he carries on this strange dialogue of the executioner and the condemned man heard, as it were, through a fog of blood and tears. Iago speaks with the assurance of one who knows what he wants and intends to achieve it. Othello, on the other hand, is blinded with grief and anger, quivering with impotent rage and misery. The more smoothly Iago lies, the more sincere he appears.

At times they exchange their tones, like fencers picking up each other's foils. Then it is Iago who rises to the grand style, while Othello drops into vulgar, staccato, stammering prose:

> Witness, you ever-burning lights above!
> You elements that clip us round about!
> Witness that here Iago doth give up
> The execution of his wit, hands, heart,
> To wrong'd Othello's service!
>   III, iii, 464-8

cries the Ancient; and Othello, tortured beyond endurance, exclaims:

> Lie with her! lie on her! We say, lie on her when they belie her. Lie with her! that's fulsome. Handkerchief—confessions—handkerchief! To confess, and be hanged for his labour. First, to be hanged, and then to confess: I tremble at it. . . .
>   IV, i, 37-42.

Iago, when he is unmasked, hurls a final challenge and then falls silent:

> Demand me nothing: what you know, you know:
> From this time forth, I never will speak word.
>   V, ii, 302-3.

One can well imagine that he, under torture, will keep silence.

The spirit of evil? No doubt, Evil is in possession of all his intellectual faculties, of his aggressive character, vigorous and merciless. Yet, because he is evil, he has imagination enough only to hate what is beyond him, namely the good: Othello, the 'noble hero', Desdemona, 'the innocent victim', and their perfect union, their romantic marriage, their attachment based on their admiration for, their adoration of, each other. Is that what Shakespeare wanted to destroy? Othello is indubitably presented in the noblest colours: brave, completely devoted to the State, full of an elevated love that, in the happy days of its zenith, is tarnished by no sensuality. He speaks as great men do, hardly raising his voice, always calm, radiant, dignified, until the moment when uneasiness undermines this nobility. Then the imposing rhetoric of Act I—'Most potent, grave, and reverend signiors'—is succeeded by the anguish, the breathless rhythm, the furious imprecations, the repulsive images of the scenes where the monster gnaws at his heart:

> I had rather be a toad
> And live upon the vapour of a dungeon,
> Than keep a corner in the thing I love
> For others' uses.

III, iii, 270-3

Arise black vengeance, from the hollow hell!
Yield up, O love! thy crown and hearted throne,
To tyrannous hate. Swell, bosom, with thy fraught,
For 'tis of aspics' tongues!

448-51

Othello will recover his nobility of attitude and language only when his calm returns and the evil spirit is exorcized. The green-eyed monster suddenly loses its consistency and its power, and falls at his feet like a skin sloughed off. But he has had to pass the supreme test: he has had to kill the thing he loved. For Othello has never ceased to love Desdemona and the act of the justiciary coincides with an act of love. The terrible scenes in which Othello brutally insults Desdemona are the result less of rage than of his mind's being blinded by fear of chaos. The man of war has lost the taste for war: 'the plumed troop, the neighing steed, the ear-piercing fife'—all this will never again delight him. 'Othello's occupation's gone!' He feels the abyss yawning at his feet and it is dizziness that makes him demented.

The emptiness that takes possession of him is really the absence of his love:

> . . . Perdition catch my soul
> But I do love thee! and when I love thee not
> Chaos is come again.

III, iii, 90-2

This was a love that strengthened his life. His unworthiness now overthrows his faith:

> If she be false, O! then heaven mocks itself.
> I'll not believe it.

III, iii, 277-8

Suffering, then, increases his stature till he reaches a height never yet attained by any commoner as hero. Othello is not the head of a State; his fall will not bring disorder upon the city. But the upheaval started by his personal tragedy has very wide repercussions in the human consciousness. Here is love which kills without ceasing to be love, tenderness which forces itself to be cruel while still tender: 'I will kill thee And love thee after' (Act V, sc. ii, l. 18); and notice this extraordinary answer, a few seconds before the crime:

> *Othello:*   Think on thy sins.
> *Desdemona:* They are loves I bear to you.
> *Othello:*   Ay, and for that thou diest.
>   V, ii, 40-1.

Here is the pathetic absurdity of justice and of love. It is
not sufficient that the law's officer should fall upon the innocent: the judicial error must be loaded with the whole
weight of the executioner's desperate tenderness for his victim, and of the victim for her executioner. The interaction
between the apparent and the real takes once more a tragic
turn and ends in the reality of death. Once the awful deed
has been done—and Othello approaches it slowly like a man
who is choking for breath and whose every gesture is one of
suffering, whose every image is a torture—he expects the
whole universe to be appalled by it:

> Methinks it should be now a huge eclipse
> Of sun and moon . . .
>   V, ii, 98-9

He has become the centre of a tragic world, as he had
been the centre of a warlike world when he was spectacularly
promoted by a happy decision of the whole Senate. Othello—
so sure of himself, so easy to deceive, so tender and so fierce
—has always been something of an actor. He is conscious of
his position as compared with that of his entourage: to some,
kind or haughty; with others, noble or respectful. He is
aware of his greatness as he is aware of his shame. He plays
his part; he almost plays *a* part. As soon as he appears and
opens his mouth, all listen; when he commands, all obey.
Between him and them there is an imperceptible dividing-
line, which they do not cross. Enforcing the law to the very
end, even upon himself, he does not miss his final scene in
which once more he displays a supreme serenity, a clear
awareness of services done, a scrupulous sense of honour, a
rich, nostalgic imagination and a feeling for the drama of
situation:

> And say, besides, that in Aleppo once
> Where a malignant and a turban'd Turk
> Beat a Venetian and traduc'd the state,
> I took by the throat the circumcised dog
> And smote him, thus.   (*stabs himself*)
>   V, ii, 351-4

This suicide of Othello's is the only logical conclusion of
the tragedy in which Desdemona is the pearl which the base
Indian cast away, richer than all his tribe. It is an absurd
world in which innocence is thus struck down, calumny

destroys the noblest of minds, and justice is overwhelmed in a travesty of itself. 'Blood! blood! blood!'—'Fool! fool! fool!' cries Othello—bestiality, folly—yet it is no more than an episode in a tragic story that will experience forms of excess. Despite the remarkable discretion of the metaphysical proportions, the significance of the play is immense. Moreover, it is an accomplished work of art. One hears it, like Ludovico, with a heavy heart.

We come now to a trio of dark plays, of approximately the same date, of kindred themes, terrible in their character, and magnificent in their poetry—a feature inseparable from the dramatic movement illuminating their desolate world which is indubitably dominated by evil. Yet each stands alone in its grandeur, wrapped in its own atmosphere, and the colours of night are different in each. In *Macbeth* it is a night of blood; in *King Lear* a night patterned with pallid lightning and traversed by squalls of madness; with *Timon of Athens* a night of anger, a tragedy *par excellence* of commination. We have now reached the lowest flood-level: absolute evil in *Macbeth*, the most grotesque aberration in *Lear*, the most universal hatred of the human species in *Timon*.

For *Macbeth* presents the complete triumph of evil, evil in its pure state, so to speak, evil without reason or issue. It is a great poem of death and of darkness, set under the maleficent vault of the witches' evil chanting, and it opens upon a midnight hell. Blood, ghosts, a desperate struggle—and then death. An extraordinary poem, hallucinatory from one end to the other, a compact mass of words, images, sounds, all associated with the poetic function of darkness and death. Round the major theme—that of the confusion of values ('fair is foul and foul is fair') are gradually grouped all the factors that create chaos, all the symbols that carry within them the promise of evil, all the menace that is hidden in the poisoned air of a sick and accursed country. Everywhere there is uncertainty, ambiguity, indecision accompanying the tragic rise of the hero who climbs the arid slopes towards the Castle of Despair.

In the nightmare world of blood and Fate, where the dice are loaded with the supernatural and the unnatural, the floating image of a dagger haunts Macbeth, whose eyes are fixed on the massive gold of a crown. Haughty and contemptuous beneath the crenellated walls, there waits a woman with steely eyes, who forges the tragic chain of the crimes to come. Here, love is out of place, as indeed is any other human feeling. It is customary to speak of the hesitating ambition of Macbeth, and of the harsher, more exacting

ambition of his wife. Yes, both desire the crown, and their
complicity admits a community of aim. But ambition is not
the least mystery of this inhuman pair who isolate themselves in a world where there is no longer anything human,
in the sense that Montaigne used the word, emanating from
them or touching them. The poetry of evil springs without
the need of any motive likely to satisfy the psychologist, and
closes upon the characters like some black monster which
stifles men's souls and invades the universe.

To lay the stress upon ambition and its consequences
would be to reduce *Macbeth* to a domestic tragedy, whereas
it is pre-eminently a nocturne of despair. The lighting of the
play varies, so to speak, from twilight to darkness. Between
the shadows and nightfall are released the evil forces which
will bend or tighten up men's wills, spread terror everywhere,
harbour dark designs, create nightmares, provoke hallucination, drive wild beasts to savagery, arm the criminal's hand,
summon the witches' sabbath, and the ghosts, with just
enough light for blood to be visible on the ghastly flesh.

The play opens in the half-light of a symbolical tempest
in which the three fatal sisters—neither women nor men—
after declaring the confusion-theme in a few flashing lines,
confront Macbeth with his destiny. The first vision we have
then is of a man, covered with blood, coming to report the
battle, of which the issue was long uncertain, and Macbeth's
superhuman exploits. Already Macbeth is assuming gigantic
stature, a familiar of death, making great flourishes with a
sword bathed in blood. Rebellion and treason preside over
the carnage, in epic terms, and the honourable heritage that
falls to Macbeth as a result of the massacre rings ambiguously
like a trick of fate as valour's accomplice.

What a strange threat is this title of Cawdor which the
King so trustingly confers on the brave general! In this
Serjeant's scene, as it is called, the essential themes of the
whole play are defined, the images come thick and fast,
creating the atmosphere of battle and confusion. It ends with
Duncan's line: 'What he hath lost noble Macbeth hath won',
which is an ironical, because unconscious, echo of the very
words used by the witches to assign his hour to the chosen
victim. The battle, honour, the crown have been lost and
won; the crown, peace and life have been won and lost.

Similarly, there is the leitmotif of the trickery of the opposed aspects of reality. Macbeth (also unconsciously) repeats the antithetical terms employed by the witches in
unison—'So foul and fair a day I have not seen'—referring
to the bitter fighting and the joy of victory, the corpses

piled up, death of friends, survivors' acclamations, danger faced or evaded, the doubtful issue of the day under a low ceiling of cloud and rumbling thunder, followed in the evening by an unlooked-for gleam of light. But the line refers also to all that the future holds—success and failure, pitfalls, deceptive appearances and equivocations.

Macbeth is meeting with his first surprise. People always imagine that one excitement is stronger than any that went before. Macbeth will know a long series of days which will be both fouler and fairer than their predecessors, and every time his alarm will increase. The witches who appear to the victorious generals, recognizing them and greeting them, with predictions that contain a grain of truth, start in Macbeth a process of illusory reasoning which will never stop. It is always by a surprise shock that catastrophes begin. The time comes when one's mind becomes all at once aware of a revelation that will change the course of destiny. The Ghost in *Hamlet,* Iago's 'I like not that', and here the coincidence of a truth and a prediction which will come true in the near future.

To be hailed as Glamis is already something noteworthy. To be Cawdor in the teeth of all probability startles Macbeth still more. But the promise of kingship makes his 'seated heart knock at [his] ribs'. In his aside which is noticed by Banquo, that dangerous witness, we see the whole of Macbeth: torn between fear and the temptings of imagination, burning with desire to anticipate the future, and perceiving all the possibilities in a flash. To the very end he will be deceived by appearances. His mind is incapable of distinguishing between the possible and the impossible, the real and the chimerical, the keen desire and the actual fact. The defect in him is this fundamental inability to avoid being the sport of the façade of things—a defect that is perhaps not Macbeth's alone but a universal human failing.

Never has the protagonist of a poetic drama been faced with such anxious choices, such torturing alternatives, so alarming in their continuity. Never were they accompanied by so prolonged a vision of harrowing prospects. Macbeth pretends to leave matters in the hands of Destiny—'come what come may, Time and the hour runs through the roughest day'—and abandons to fate the consequences which later, but in vain, he will try to bend to his will. King Duncan, for his part, solves the problem briskly, yet his part is to make the same mistake with the same assurance. His reflection on the execution of Cawdor—

There's no art
To find the mind's construction in the face.
He was a gentleman on whom I built
An absolute trust.

I, iv, 11-14.

is fraught with unconscious and tragic irony. He transfers to
Macbeth the confidence of which Cawdor was unworthy, and
with what noble words he assures him of his gratitude! Innocence and loyalty are doomed in advance to lose in this
struggle against the forces of evil which will pass brutally
over to the attack.

The supernatural element which at the outset might have
seemed purely conventional and capable of a symbolical interpretation, invades the drama from the moment that we first
see Lady Macbeth. Then it sheds all its grotesquely human
concomitants (the rags of the witches, their beards, their
ugliness) and moves on to a strictly dehumanized plane. She
is forthright in speech and at a stroke she is in command
of the future. Her imperious tone is prophetic. Challenging
Destiny, she dispels reticences with a hiss of contempt, and
word by word she treads the path towards evil's apotheosis.
Her wild invocation to the spirits that foment thoughts of
death, her sublime prayer to cruelty, her appeal to be
changed from woman to wild beast, her address to night
the accomplice of crime, are stages in this process of damnation. Words here operate like an incantation of black magic,
uttered with complete lucidity.

Lady Macbeth eliminates everything that might deprive
evil of its specific harmfulness. Without hatred, without commination, without any motive except the mirage of the gold
crown, she forges for herself an inner armour of calculated
violence and insensibility, deaf to the solicitations of pity.
Her first speech is so concentrated that it seems to defy
analysis. It is perhaps the first time that Shakespeare has
put so much into so few words, and this taut richness, this
extreme tension of expression, is a characteristic of the whole
play. A wealth of poetry and dramatic interest are fused:
together they rise to the highest summits of Shakespeare's
art, especially in the first two acts of *Macbeth* where the
pathos and the poetry are inseparable.

Hardly has Lady Macbeth uttered her incantation when
Macbeth appears, to receive from her the fatal counsel of
duplicity: 'Look like the innocent flower, But be the serpent
under't' (Act I, sc. v, l. 65). He has taken the short cut
and plunged headlong into the inferno. Yet he has not made
the choice, he has not lost (nor ever will lose) the feeling

of the duality of a world where he must incessantly move
or drift into fear while still remembering the peace he once
had known. The mask of loyalty which hardens on his face
barely conceals its contortions. There is the same symbolism
in Inverness Castle where the atmosphere is pure and martlets
haunt the air, but the darkest designs are hatched within its
walls.

Nevertheless, the struggle between angel and demon goes
on in his conscience. Scene vii is a fine metaphysical poem,
beginning hesitatingly in abstractions, with Macbeth spec-
ulating on the uneasy idea of justice and punishment, and
ending in the expression in concrete terms of his highly
charged imagination. (In point of fact this soliloquy should
not be taken literally as voicing the personal scruples of a
man driven to an evil deed and fearing its consequences, but
as having a bearing by anticipation on the sequel of the
impersonal tragedy of which Macbeth's career is the symbol.)
The combat between the sensible forms of good and evil
ends in the projection, almost in the form of a vision, of the
sentiment of pity.

In the linking of the ideas and the images all through the
soliloquy, there is something ornate in the Baroque movement, a rush of concepts and metaphors, reminiscent of that
style at its most impure and perhaps its most attractive—an
identification, under the feverish pressure of the mind in
travail, of pity with its object, which gives the passage an
extraordinary force:

> Besides, this Duncan
> Hath borne his faculties so meek, hath been
> So clear in his great office, that his virtues
> Will plead like angels trumpet-tongu'd against
> The deep damnation of his taking off;
> And pity, like a naked new-born babe,
> Striding the blast, or heaven's cherubin, hors'd
> Upon the sightless couriers of the air,
> Shall blow the horrid deed in every eye,
> That tears shall drown the wind.
>
> I, vii, 16-25.

For the time being these delirious words, by their insistence
on the horror of the deed that is being plotted, give the
victory to the weakening forces of good. The balance is re-
dressed by an increased hardening in Lady Macbeth's pitiless
will-power. The last outpost of pity's resistance—that tender
and sensitive part of the heart which still refuses to yield—
is brutally crushed. Lady Macbeth's prayer of incantation has
certainly had its effect. Crueller than Clytemnestra, calmer

than Medea, she has not a drop of 'the milk of human kindness' left that is not changed to gall. The horror produced by
her cold declaration—

> I have given suck, and know
> How tender 'tis to love the babe that milks me:
> I would, while it was smiling in my face,
> Have pluck'd my nipple from his boneless gums,
> And dash'd the brains out, had I so sworn as you
> Have done to this——
>
> I, vii, 54-9.

exceeds all that the imagination of the cruellest heroines of
tragedy ever conceived. Here the aggressive realism of the
evocation has a frightful sound, but it is also because the
language reaches such a degree of precision, such thick-set
force, by the hail of consonants and the cadence of the lines,
that each word stings to the quick. Macbeth's admiring comment, 'Bring forth men-children only', is the resigned admission of his defeat. Lady Macbeth has done more than
vanquish his last scruples: she has raised herself to a pinnacle
of pure evil from which no tragic heroine has since dethroned her.

But Macbeth has still to attain to complete villainy. The
fever never leaves him; hallucinations throng his heated
brain, giving him the clearest insight into his crime. He sees
a living dagger on which are 'gouts of blood'. The famous
soliloquy is another triumph of incantation, for it is with
words that the haggard Macbeth whips up his courage to
the point of doing the repugnant deed. He needs the poetic
connivance of darkness and, even more than the brew his
wife has prepared for him, it is the verbal potion he swallows
that gives him the necessary intoxication. Night delivers up
to him the dearest of its furtive phantoms, those that make
palpable the thickness, the mystery, the horror hidden in
that part of the hemisphere where shadows alternate with
the day:

> Now o'er the one half-world
> Nature seems dead, and wicked dreams abuse
> The curtain'd sleep; witchcraft celebrates
> Pale Hecate's offerings; and wither'd murder
> Alarum'd by his sentinel, the wolf,
> Whose howl's his watch, thus with his stealthy pace,
> With Tarquin's ravishing strides, towards his design
> Moves like a ghost.
>
> II, i, 49-56.

Macbeth's exit leaves on the stage a terrifying emptiness
for a few seconds, an indescribably moving suspense, which

is prolonged after Lady Macbeth's arrival, until he returns.
In the dialogue that follows, breathless, hurried, whispered
between the dishevelled criminal and his cynical accomplice,
both of them are sweating fear, despite Lady Macbeth's
superhuman self-control, so great was the tension preceding
the crime. It is Macbeth who collapses, and here again what
he says is the result of dream-delirium and hallucination. The
slow litany of the benefits of sleep, an ancient theme if ever
there was one, assumes on his lips the despairing accent of a
dying groan, and the murder of an old man in his sleep
stands for the murder of deified Sleep. The 'sleep no more'
rings under the arches of the castle and echoes without end
through all the bloody career of the hero. When he looks
at his hands he has the fixed stare of madness, and his
imagination magnifies their stain to the size of an ocean:

> What hands are here! Ha! they pluck out mine eyes.
> Will all great Neptune's ocean wash this blood
> Clean from my hand? No, this my hand will rather
> The multitudinous seas incarnadine . . .
>
> II, ii, 60-3.

Lady Macbeth, though she takes a more realist view of the
bloodstains—'A little water clears us of this deed'—admits
that she did not dare plunge the dagger into Duncan's body,
he was so like her father. It is the only *conscious* weakness
that she shows in all the play. Her will is strained to breaking-point in these superhuman minutes, and she arranges
without flagging all the plans for putting suspicion off the
scent.

But the crime committed is so odious, so contrary to
natural laws, that it becomes the symbolical gesture which
will unleash chaos. Already we have seen, with *Julius Caesar*,
how crime, even when committed for 'noble reasons', inevitably entailed confusion in the State, and the downfall of
the criminal. This determinism of evil is aggravated in
Macbeth and will be further aggravated in *King Lear*. Already at the moment when the deed is done, the disturbance
of the elements resembles a prophetic exultation: 'The night
has been unruly.' Lennox declares; strange death-cries have
been heard, the owl has cried all night, chimneys have
fallen and the feverish earth has trembled. Later, the Old
Man who acts as Chorus, and Ross, tell each other of even
stranger portents. On the morrow of the crime the darkness
continued by day as if daylight were ashamed to appear.
And Duncan's horses, those fine, noble animals, catching the
madness in the air, rebelled against man and ran wild from
their stalls, attempting to devour each other. Macduff's thrice-

repeated cry of 'horror!' on discovering the crime, rings
through the night announcing it as a desecration:

> Confusion now hath made his masterpiece!
> Most sacrilegious murder hath broke ope
> The Lord's anointed temple, and stole thence
> The life o' the building!

II, iii, 72-5.

When we see Macbeth again, in the next act, the violence
done to Nature condemns him to the long agony of suffering
that his crime entails, and the subterranean working of evil
is now operating in a soul wholly possessed by the fatality
of evil. He is isolated, making his decision alone, and Lady
Macbeth virtually disappears from the scene: she receives
only ambiguous confidences and she tries in vain to save
appearances in the banqueting scene by pleading an affliction
of the mind in Macbeth when her counsels fail. In the end
she is the defenceless victim of that insidious terror which
formerly she so haughtily repudiated. The spring of her will
breaks in the jealous solitude into which the necessity of the
criminal deed implacably throws the murderer. Each is the
prey of his own terrors which drive the one to frenzied action, the other to the obscure vagaries of an obsessed conscience, driving it finally to suicide.

But the poetic themes, whether connected with the preparation of the crime, its accomplishment, or its consequences,
always present the same features, and always have the same
importance. They are the inmost substance of the tragedy
and cannot be isolated from the action or from the study
of the characters. This is why Macbeth's scene with the murderers, which paves the way for the ambush in which Banquo
is to lose his life (a scene which it has been said is unnecessary for the action or which could be much shorter) is of
capital importance (Act III, sc. i). The theme of the Chain
of Being in the scale of Nature, illustrated by the catalogue
of dogs, has its share of the secret irony of evil. And the
theme of sickness, which will reappear in connection with the
sickness of the soul, has a symbolical value. Shakespeare often
employs it in contrast with the nostalgic and underlying
theme of health, the harmony of body and soul and of the
State that Macbeth desperately hopes for but knows is beyond his reach. There is also, always, the recurrent theme of
confusion, uncertainty, ambiguity between the being and the
seeming, the sure and the doubtful, the violence of the wish
and the fragility of its realization.

Terror in face of crime, like terror in shrinking from crime,
is reflected in language that derives all its effects from the

personal symbolism of a Macbeth who is at the mercy of the
mysterious power of the poet in him. The restrained and
quivering dialogue between Macbeth and Lady Macbeth in
the thick twilight in which Banquo's murder is to be carried
out, is perhaps the richest in mystery of the whole tragedy.
It begins with the baffling metaphor of the snake which has
so much intrigued the critics:

> We have scotch'd the snake, not kill'd it:
> She'll close and be herself, whilst our poor malice
> Remains in danger of her former tooth.
> III, ii, 13-15.

What is this snake? Does it stand for Duncan whose posterity
is in safety (for the King's sons have escaped) and, like a
serpent, can bite again? Or is it evil itself in the obscure
form of the danger involved in the survival of a witness?
The snake is in general (and in this very play) associated
with treachery, with the trap laid by Destiny in innocent
forms, and it arouses fear and repulsion. But this does not
make sense.

L. C. Knights suggests that the snake is 'the natural order
that Macbeth has infringed' but which will be cured of its
wound and recover its vitality. The word 'snake' must in
that case be loaded with all the hatred that Macbeth feels
for this 'natural order', for this harmony of things which
will ultimately drive out the fomentor of this disorder, as in
a human being the foreign body is assimilated or rejected. In
the next line, moreover, this hatred bursts out: Macbeth
hopes to see the destruction of the universe rather than live
in the terror of the return to the natural order—and the
ascending rhythm, quickening up to the fourth foot, is expressive of this violence: 'But let the frame of things disjoint,
both the worlds suffer.' (III, ii, 16.)

Then, there is Macbeth's indescribable longing for sleep.
The evocation of the blessed state of the dead Duncan, contained in the slow, weary rhythm of the following lines,
conveys all Macbeth's lassitude, all his sullen envy of a
Duncan now out of reach, whose serenity brings no peace
to Macbeth:

> Duncan is in his grave;
> After life's fitful fever he sleeps well;
> Treason has done his worst: nor steel, nor poison
> Malice domestic, foreign levy, nothing
> Can touch him further.
> III, ii, 22-6.

And the evening falls, while preparations go forward for the

banquet, the symbol of rejoicing, and for the murder of
Banquo—the honoured guest who will appear but as a bloody
ghost. Again Macbeth mutters an invocation to night; for
night is his favourite region where alone he is at ease and
where pity (identified with the day) cannot enter. He calls
upon night in tender accents, and the thickening of the light
is almost voluptuous. The beasts that are familiars of night
are already on the move: the solitary raven, whose flight is
heavily directed towards the dark wood, becomes the symbol
of the crime: it floats over the castle and will swoop down
on it, on a Banquo marked out by Destiny. The lyrical emotion that seizes Macbeth, incomprehensible to Lady Macbeth,
halts abruptly at the finding of the necessary links between
the crimes:

> Come seeling night,
> Scarf up the tender eye of pitiful day,
> And with thy bloody and invisible hand,
> Cancel and tear to pieces that great bond
> Which keeps me pale. Light thickens, and the crow
> Makes wing to the rooky wood,
> Good things of day begin to droop and drowse,
> While night's black agents to their preys do rouse.
> Thou marvell'st at my words: but hold thee still;
> Things bad begun make strong themselves by ill.
>   III, ii, 46-55.

For Banquo's murder is only the second in the series.
Others will follow until the most hardened of murderers is
nauseated by the pools of blood. Even a butcher will weary
of slaughter. The outbursts of anger in the banqueting scene,
the challenge thrown out to the most terrible monsters (the
Hyrcanian tiger, the Russian bear, the horned rhinoceros)
fail to allay the terror of Macbeth who is petrified by the
supernatural as he becomes its prey. Death is no more death
if corpses can rise from their graves and drive men from their
places! Here, delirium reaches fever-pitch: the style is halting,
the images violent; the thought proceeds by leaps and bounds
and expresses itself by exclamations. Pallor and fearful grimaces, gasping, a burning fever of the brain—everything
points to a physical disorder parallel with the mental disorder. The whole man is possessed.

Hence Macbeth's only possible recourse against terror and
nightmares is to plunge still deeper into blasphemy and
crime, to call down upon the whole world the chaos in which
he has himself foundered. During his visit to the Witches
(Act IV, sc. i) Macbeth hurls at the supernatural world his
ultimatum of despair:

> Though you untie the winds and let them fight
> Against the churches . . .
> . . . though the treasure
> Of Nature's germens tumble all together,
> Even till destruction sicken, answer me.
>
> IV, i, 52.

'Till destruction sicken'—it is an appeal to the absolute of evil, but it is also an admission of failure. The universe continually shrinks round Macbeth. The enigmatic apparitions, the terrifying symbols, and even the equivocal language by which the evil spirits take a malign pleasure in plaguing his mind, all trace round him a circle which it will soon be impossible to cross, or rather, a circle he can break out of only by plunging to his death.

We see a gradual hardening of Macbeth's soul which has supped so full of horrors that 'I have almost forgot the taste of fears'. (V, v, 59.) He grows insensitive (as in his strange reply when he is told of his loved accomplice's death), and he goes out to meet his last combat with an admission of the inevitable uselessness of his effort and of life itself. There is logic in the conclusion expressed with infinite weariness in his famous lines:

> Tomorrow, and tomorrow, and tomorrow,
> Creeps in this petty pace from day to day,
> To the last syllable of recorded time;
> And all our yesterdays have lighted fools
> The way to dusty death. Out, out, brief candle!
> Life's but a walking shadow, a poor player
> That struts and frets his hour upon the stage,
> And then is heard no more; it is a tale
> Told by an idiot, full of sound and fury
> Signifying nothing.
>
> V, v, 19-28.

Here we have the haunting theme of Time (the most imperative of all to the Elizabethan mind) and that of Death; the metaphor of the flame that one blows out, the metaphor of the shadowy actor on the world's stage, and lastly the final judgment of a man in his unsanctified death-agony upon the noisy, mad agitation of a now meaningless existence. Intelligence in its turn yields to the fantastic conspiracy hatched by all-powerful Evil. All that remains is the obstinate courage of the bear tied to the stake, dying, like a Senecan hero, with a snarl.

Macbeth's world is a world of deceit, of fear, of death, wholly given up to supernatural fraud which works in the shadow, in night's caverns, in the flickering twilight between a ghost and an hallucination, where the screams are screams of fright, invocations are poetic frenzy and prophecies are equivocal. There is not a line without its symbolical meaning, not an image that does not cause a shudder, not an ambiguity that does not conceal a menace in its irony. A triumph of concentrated lyricism, this play bears some resemblance to a Morality of despair, constantly longing for a divine order and universal health which have been ravaged by experience of Evil.

In *Macbeth* revolt occupies no place in the metaphysical form it will have in *King Lear*: in the hero it is a challenge without appeal, thrown down to the very madness of an unforgiveable act when he is being driven to failure; but pity, kindness, tenderness shed a fixed and veiled light, glimpsed from time to time through the nightmare-mists of the tragedy. Such is the miracle of the poetry that Shakespeare's most intensely dark drama seems the richest in concrete poetry, pressed to the breaking-point, and we are so much caught by the mirage of the tragic vision that we end by imagining it our own. The very excess of evil's triumph paves the way for the establishment in the near future of positive values which poetic experience must still wait some time to see ripen.

Despite the complete victory of evil in the darkness of its night, *Macbeth* is still a tragedy with clear-cut outlines, organized and coherent, in which all the developments follow each other with strict poetic logic. *King Lear,* on the other hand, seems the Tragedy of Disorder in its unbounded confusion. The characters, the action, the poetry—all are stamped by a tremendous effort to reach out beyond the facts of the real world to the vague regions of the Absolute, and to bring there the shock of destruction. The world of *Hamlet* gives off a dry stench of sulphur and death; that of *Macbeth* is all dark and clammy with blood; in *Othello,* in spite of the blazing storm that scatters the Turkish fleet, Mephistopheles is at work on an island in a suffocating ante-chamber hung with black velvet. In *King Lear* the high wind of madness howls in the night, over an endless heath, uprooting oak and reed with the same furious blast. Compared with *Lear* the other tragedies seem to us rational, well composed, cut to Man's measure. In *Lear* there are no longer any frontiers between the sublime and the ridiculous, between the sane and the insane, between man and beast, perhaps even between man and God. Everything is swept away in the whirlwind of a tempest that symbolizes a world out of joint.

Hamlet, Macbeth and Othello presented personal problems, which it was for them to solve as far as men could solve them; and they bore objectively if they wished it the responsibility for their own fate. Hamlet and Macbeth are clear-sighted to the point of disgusting themselves; Othello may be the victim of his own mistake, but at least this mistake is psychologically explicable and does not involve the fundamental validity of deluded reason. Everything may take place in a sick world, but the meaning of the world itself is not to be reduced to unthinkable nonsense. In *King Lear* the indictment of the ordered universe dislocates the very foundations of reason. Transitions, shades of meaning, logical sequences—all yield to the brutal assault. The play is not closely knit like *Macbeth*, where every image, every word, every rhythm contributes to the total effect, but in one and the same direction.

Yet *Lear* is just as compact, in spite of the violent cleaving of the themes and the strong contrasts or analogies which sway the reader alternately from irony to imprecation, from absurdity to sublimity, illuminating a whole scene or suddenly fathoming its meaning, now stammering in exasperation, now rambling incalculably. We do not penetrate Lear's world: we look upon it from without, horrified spectators of a cataclysm that nothing can stay.

In the first place, the characters in this more than in any of Shakespeare's plays are difficult to match with the credible and the real. Curiously unreal, their psychology remains elementary: it is as if they had been roughed out, with broad strokes, from some obstinate material on conventional lines, though their vitality is indisputable. Lear, immense in stature, dominates the play—Lear and Cordelia, for the drama is between them: a senile King, derived from Kyd's Hieronimo, who passes from blindness to lucidity by dreadful stages of madness; a daughter, like Iphigenia, doomed from the very first to suffer injustice and death. Lear's continual anger, which puts his robust temper at the service of an infantile folly and drives him to make discoveries by tragic revelations, contrasts with the calm dignity of Cordelia whose restraint and reserve always leave the pure treasure of her feelings unexpressed.

Between these extremes there is the Fool, always leaping from the ridiculous to the sublime and back again. His is the shimmering and disordered awareness of the situation and the characters. Then there are the minor characters who fill the tragedy with incidents and noise. Strongly contrasted and opposed, either ironically underlining, or on the fringe of the central theme and the principal characters, they are all tarnished, incomplete or disreputable in some part or other of their nature. None of them attains the allegorical perfection of evil.

In this gallery of portraits, sardonic or severe, it is that pair of monsters, Regan and Goneril, who excel all others in their black-heartedness: they are cruel, avaricious hypocrites; jealousy changes them to tigresses when they lust after the same man, and they are capable of committing murder and even suicide. Cornwall has the cold hardness and insensitivity of the single-track mind. Edmund, an envious bastard, a debauched Machiavelli, plays with eagerness and vigour the tragic traitor, ready, when he fails, to make the final gesture of generosity that is the less convincing for being the more expected. Albany, in whose veins there is some milk of human kindness, is weak and indecisive, too flabby to have any influence on events. Kent, forthright in his devotion, has a rough soul and a maladroit goodness. Gloucester, credulous and passionate, capable of joking in bad taste, makes the same mistake as Lear, and thereby loses his honour and his life. Edgar, the legitimate son, prefers to fly rather than to fight, to take refuge in the pretence of physical and mental degradation.

Add one or two characters, like the gentleman or Curan who plays the part of Chorus—and in this list, curiously enough, each shines with a lustre of his own, imposes his personality despite the radical unreality which strikes us at first sight in them. All are astonishingly individualized as if they were in search of some Absolute towards which the internal force of their character was impelling them, and as if moreover all the elements of the play to which they give life contributed in their turn to make them more intensely real. There is a sort of interaction between the personages and the incidents, a symbolical correspondence, the effect of which from the purely technical point of view is to create a complete unity of atmosphere between all these contrasted opposites.

The central theme of Lear's madness is underlined and coloured by the relative, functional or simulated madness of the people round him: the Fool, a professional madcap; Edgar, who assumes madness as a disguise; Gloucester and Kent who reach the very limit of what the human frame can endure before they go really mad. To this wilful or instinctive disorder of the reason is added the disorder of the elements which amplifies the oscillations between the opposite poles of a stable, human universe and a hell of universal discord where the simplest propositions become monstrous to the intelligence. Madness is nothing but a conception of the world individualized to breaking-point and constantly colliding with the massive obstacle of everyday realities. What characterizes it dramatically is irresponsibility and the tension of mental states. What provokes it is also, dramatically, the sudden revelation of a reality underlying appearances in which one had believed, heart and soul—a reality that brings everything into question. Nobody goes mad unless predisposed to madness, for madness and reason are linked together by the intensity of the inner life before and after the mental derangement.

Those who are passionately involved in a faith, a devotion or love, which gives life a meaning for them, cannot withstand, without disturbance of their mental balance, the emotional shock of this unexpected revelation. It is a too painful amputation, an intolerable traumatism which unleashes chaos. The phrase 'mad with grief' means simply this, if it means anything. Madness as employed by the playwrights is usually set on the emotional plane, with extravagance of language and violence of behaviour. They do not necessarily throw new light upon the shadowy zone that subsists even in a normal conception of the world. But what separates Hieronimo from Lear is the fact that the latter's madness passes from the emotional to the intellectual and, indeed, the metaphysical plane. It is not the sudden disappearance of someone dear to him that drives Lear demented, but the realization of his mistake, that is, the revelation of an irreconcilable difference between what he believed to be real and what lay hidden beneath the appearances.

The part played by error in the tragic hero's career is so important that it is surprising to find it has not been methodically investigated. Lear is doubly mistaken: he takes for love the simulation of it, and he takes for indifference the true love whose expression cannot compete with that of dissimulation. The reversal of values that takes place in proportion as he is led to attribute truth to each appearance —this is his tragic purgation, and it is the subject of the play. The purgation is effected by madness, that is, once again, by the suddenness with which a counter-reality ironically assails Lear. Hence, the whole world, and his gods, are brought into question under the repeated, furious blows of evil's deadliest weapons.

The very violence done to reason in the first incident of
the play sweeps away at a stroke all the reservations which
the critical mind might make. We are precipitated into an
incredible world where there is no longer room for the
slightest incredulity. This extravagant kingdom, situated outside time and space (in spite of a symbolical realism which
in places still attaches us to firm ground), where the most
solemn pomp presides over the partition of property and
affections, is not a State rotten like Denmark's. It is at the
arbitrary mercy of a fundamentally illogical King, who proceeds to bring about chaos by his dictates. The evil springs
from his intelligence, at once delusive and deluded, which
decides without discernment between hypocrisy and sin-
cerity and chooses with blind obstinacy to load wickedness
with honours and to strip virtue of them.

Lear's fierce anger, caused by Kent's protest, is the first
indication of the climate of the tragedy. Passions are brought
to the highest pitch of tension; the extravagance of the
curses upon Cordelia and the banishment of Kent set the
tone for the outbursts to come. But already the persistent
irony of the reality he ignores accompanies softly the aberration of Lear's presumptuous decisions. 'Thy truth be then
thy dower', he exclaims furiously to Cordelia, and it will
indeed be her only dowry. Here the curse contains a pathetic
element of truth just as, later, there will be the lightning of
blinding truth in the extravagance of language. 'He always
loved our sister most', says Goneril to Regan after the
division of the kingdom, 'and with what poor judgment he
hath now cast her off appears too grossly'. (I, i, 293.) Here
is his initial folly.

The tension rises from scene to scene as the scales are
torn from the King's eyes: his 'poor judgment' is enriched
by his demented experience and dramatic irony itself assumes the acute form of violent opposition between the
ridiculous and the sublime in a desperate situation. Lear is
doomed to put off the old man—a spiritual stripping that
must follow the physical denuding through which he goes.
His angry outburst against Goneril (I, iv), his irritated
amazement on seeing Kent in the stocks (II, iv), the accumulation of insults, each of which fans the hope that
Lear clings to stubbornly, so that he takes as real what
crumbles more and more away—all lead to the conclusion
'O fool! I shall go mad!' (II, iv, 289). It is then that Lear
turns his back squarely on the past and abominates his own
mistake. Rage and hatred take possession of him. He rushes
out into the night which is falling, by the only door that

remains open—the door leading to the bare heath with all its liberating ecstasies.

Darkness of the night, darkness of the mind—they are complementary and in their midst the uncontrollable forces of sky and passion combine in a mad rout. It is no longer the equivocal heath of *Macbeth* where evil spells assail man with scoffing temptations. It is the perfect void where man can grow in stature to match the elements of Nature, where his curses can outroar the thunder, where the challenge thrown down to his own nature leads to the tragic cry at the supreme moment when he tears off his garments: 'Off, off, you lendings.' Man then appears in all his primitive nakedness, abandoned to the misery of his animal condition, wild, demoniac, torn by passion, lashed by the wind, drenched by the rain, cowering from the lightning and from the earth as it quakes beneath his feet.

As his reason breaks up, unsubstantial truths fall away in rags and out of the confusion of the converging strains of madness a new scale of values gradually emerges. The Fool may offer his bauble to Kent who sides with those who fall into disgrace, may concede to Lear the only title that remains to him—the Fool's—and may propose his paradoxes, his songs and sallies in sarcastic exchange for outworn articles of faith, while Edgar in the portrait he draws of himself combines the features of symbolical animals whose vicious passions make up the image of man: 'hog in sloth, fox in stealth, wolf in greediness, dog in madness, lion in prey' (III, iv, 93), and seeks to define himself by the most repellent attributes: 'What are you there?' asks Gloucester, 'Your names?' and Edgar replies (III, iv, 132): 'Poor Tom; that eats the swimming frog; the toad, the tadpole, the wall-newt, and the water; that in the fury of his heart, when the foul fiend rages, eats cow-dung for sallets; swallows the old rat and the ditch-dog; drinks the green mantle of the standing pool', etc. This loathsome vision of the animality to which, it seems, man must resign himself to belong when the noblest of his functions, reason, flinches before reality, has become the only possible reply to the outrage it has suffered.

In his passionate revolt Lear willingly identifies himself also with the animals, and his sympathy is immediately aroused for 'poor Tom'. After his curses, after the apostrophe to the elements, after the incoherent parody of justice which draws from Edgar secret tears, the balm of sleep will come to the relief of an utterly exhausted Lear and will mark the dividing line between reason and madness. When Lear again appears, fantastically dressed with flowers, the dramatic symbol of madness, he comes into a world that will disappoint him no more. The bitter taste of his former rage is still in his mouth. The temperature of his brusque sarcasm has gone down. He embroiders upon the sensual theme, 'Let copulation thrive!' (IV, vi, 117) and utters unconsciously cruel words about the blinding of Gloucester. But over all this there plays the light of a new knowledge containing fragments of old truths revalued and associated with the disparate parts of a world that is seeking cohesion.

Lear can no longer be disappointed, but he can still suffer. He has learned suffering, and resignation has settled upon his aching body and his mutilated mind. In this third stage of his madness he is calm and clear-minded, and he accepts the trial that he has still to undergo. This crushed and impotent sick giant, who used to clench his fist in wild defiance of the heavens, and who made the blasted heath ring with his curses, is now no more than a helpless old man tended by Cordelia. He awakens to the strains of soft music, a symbol of spiritual reconciliation, and he is surrounded by the pure love of his daughter whom he has found again at last. Cordelia's tenderness shines forth in the pathos of this moment when love comes into its own and pride, anger and hatred retreat. She appears in his eyes as spirit—'You are a spirit, I know; when did you die?' (IV, vii, 49)—she *is* a spirit, the very symbol of love threatened but indestructible, the love that Lear had ignored.

Like all redemptions, Lear's is effected by love, to be followed shortly by the supreme sacrifice which is also the supreme knowledge. Lear finds at last his real clear-sightedness and expresses it humbly and hesitatingly:

> . . . Pray do not mock me:
> I am a very foolish fond old man,
> Fourscore and upward, not an hour more or less;
> And, to deal plainly,
> I fear I am not in my perfect mind.
> Methinks I should know you and know this man;
> Yet I am doubtful: for I am mainly ignorant
> What place this is and all the skill I have
> Remembers not these garments; nor I know not
> Where I did lodge last night. Do not laugh at me;
> For, as I am a man, I think this lady
> To be my child Cordelia.

IV, vii, 59-70.

And he asks her pardon:

> . . . You must bear with me.
> Pray you now, forget and forgive: I am old and foolish.

IV, vii, 85.

The reconciliation is complete: they are in perfect communion. But storms still rock the kingdom and chaos does not relent. The initial injustice which started the disorder will bear fruit to the very end. Greed and hatred have not yet wreaked all their destruction. The world from which Lear has detached himself in spirit continues none the less the prey of evil forces, and injustice inevitably pursues purity at the moment of her greatest moral triumph. It is significant that in the deadly excitement of the fifth act, when the she-wolves are killing each other, when Edmund's trumpet prophetically sounds the victory of good over evil, when evil itself is finally touched by Grace in the presence of death, we have to see the ignominious end of the most radiant symbol of love and innocence. Cordelia is found hanged in her prison at the very moment when she was about to be released—a cruel sport of chance, but necessary, for this death (the only logical issue for the view of the world on which the tragedy is based) allows Lear's soul in the end to be sublimated.

Leaning over his daughter's dead body, Lear asks the question to which there is no reply: 'Why should a dog, a horse, a rat have life, And thou no breath at all?' (V, iii, 309-9), followed by the stammered 'Never, never, never, never, never!' and by the mysterious exclamation that accompanies his heartbreak and opens the magic casements through which the soul wings its flight, 'Look on her, look, her lips, Look there, look there!' Lear's torture is over. He is released from the wheel of fire to which his mistake had bound him. His thunderous quarrel with the universe ends on the highest spiritual note. The grievous purgation of the arrogant, storming King leads to the unknown bourn where hope surely lies. The terrifying, bestial world traversed by the dangerous shadows of evil passions seems in the end unreal. The very extravagance of evil, in its most hateful forms, exhausts the possibility of the reign of chaos.

The personal tragedy of Lear and Cordelia, profoundly human though it still is, rises to the universal plane. Intolerable suffering first undermines reason and the abyss into which it can fall seems ever deeper. But there comes a time for pity, a limit where evil spends itself, and, like a beneficent wave, love bathes the heart and clears the sight. Lear may die after Cordelia, but it is a serene death which the dramatist opposes to intolerable injustice, and perhaps we should see in this play with its culmination of revolt, cruelty and rage, the promise of victory over disorder which by its very excess has wearied the forces of evil.

But there are still two tragedies at the end of Shakespeare's 'dark period', one of them (*Coriolanus*) raising political problems, the other (*Timon of Athens*) going far beyond *King Lear* in its loud invective and the extraordinary power of its hate-theme. Both tell the story of the fall of a hero impressive in his qualities of mind and character but a rebel against the society in which he lives. Coriolanus's career ends in dramatic failure, and three-fifths of *Timon* are filled with misanthropic rage, yet neither tragedy leaves one with the oppressive feeling of disillusionment or despair produced by the great plays preceding them. The reason, no doubt, is that both these heroes are imperfect in the sense that their noisy charges against their own country and against humanity lack the real justification that the other heroes had through their suffering or the nobility of their natures. Coriolanus sins through excess of pride and individualism, so that he appears a superb war-machine and offers a deformed and debased (because selfish) image of the sentiment of honour. Timon, who is kindness personified, takes on an allegorical air of hatred when he has ceased to play the part of the generous man. There is in both of them a deformation, a shrinking of the human person, and an inconsistency of behaviour which, despite their magnificent and varied dramatic rhetoric, impairs the emotion they might arouse in us and leaves us unsatisfied.

For the debate which sets the tragic hero against his entourage or against himself and which in the great plays formed the material of human drama transmuted into poetry, is absent from these two tragedies or is so abruptly resolved that it fails in its essential duty of moving us. Coriolanus is presented to us all of a piece—the brave soldier, of superhuman boldness and strength (he surpasses both the elder and the younger Horace of Corneille), but also of superhuman insensibility. The portrait frequently drawn of him to try to justify his attitudes, to explain him in the eyes of ordinary men, makes him out a monster of war, happy only in fighting and killing, and pressing military virtues to a point hardly to be reconciled with normal humanity. Look at Cominius's praise of Coriolanus to the Senate:

> . . . His pupil age
> Man-enter'd thus, he waxed like a sea,
> And in the brunt of seventeen battles since
> He lurch'd all swords of the garland. For this last,
> Before and in Corioli, let me say,
> I cannot speak him home: he stopp'd the fliers,
> And by his rare example made the coward
> Turn terror into sport: as weeds before

> A vessel under sail, so men obey'd
> And fell below his stem: his sword, death's stamp,
> Where it did mark, it took; from face to foot
> He was a thing of blood, whose every motion
> Was tim'd with dying cries: alone he enter'd
> The mortal gate of the city, which he painted
> With shunless destiny; aidless came off,
> And with a sudden re-enforcement struck
> Corioli like a planet. Now all's his:
> When by and by the din of war 'gan pierce
> His ready sense; then straight his doubled spirit
> Re-quicken'd what in flesh was fatigate,
> And to the battle came he; where he did
> Run reeking o'er the lives of men, as if
> 'Twere a perpetual spoil . . .

II, ii, 103-25.

Here, indeed, we have such a vigorous and colourful portrayal of the warrior's temperament as only the Shakespeare of the final period could give us. The splendid images, the rapid movement, the very exaltation of the speaker whose tone, rhythm and words depict this incomparable soldier in action: everything contributes to stir our sensibility. But side by side with the extraordinary vitality of the fighting man we see the unconscious brutality of blind strength which makes courage a superfluous virtue. The courage of Macbeth who has no fear of death by the sword and who, like Coriolanus, scatters images of death all through his speeches, is humanized by his terror of the mysteries of night and death. Antony, another superhuman, cosmic warrior, is great alike in generosity and boldness. But Coriolanus is merely drunk with blows given and wounds received, with the pride of being a Roman soldier, with contempt for the people. He rails against any shackles of love, of peaceful, politically organized civil life. He regards everything as base and unworthy unless it be military exploits, rashness and joy of battle.

All this is so obvious that wise old Menenius trembles every time Coriolanus is to appear except on the battlefield. I am surprised that, some years ago,[11] he should have been exploited for a political cause and presented as the victim of a mob incapable of appreciating his virtues. 'There is no more mercy in him than there is milk in a male tiger', (V, iv, 31) says Menenius, and indeed Coriolanus is quite ready to sack Rome, forgetting that he is her son. If he yields to the petition of his mother who comes to exhort him to spare the city, it is much more out of pride than of pity. His insolence would make him the equal of a god

[11] At the Comédie-Française before the Riots of February 1934.

were he immortal with a throne in heaven. His capitulation, followed closely by his ignominious fall, is not the act of a god nor of a pure hero.

But this does not mean that the tribunes are not detestable or that Shakespeare intends us to have unmixed admiration for the Roman mob. The exaltation that comes of victory in the dangers of war, the implacable pride that follows it and leads, in Coriolanus as in Aufidius, to pretence and treason, are to some extent encouraged even in their excesses by the craven behaviour of the crowd and the blackmail to which the heroes have to resort to make them heroic. Shakespeare does not come down on the side of either plebeians or patricians. It is significant that the fable told by Menenius to allay the revolt is that of the Belly. For if the populace is inconsistent, disorderly, evil-smelling and ungrateful, the patricians, selfish and satisfied in their sloth, are typified by the stomach 'I' the midst o' the body, idle and unactive, Still cupboarding the viand, never bearing Like labour with the rest'. (I, i, 104-6.) On the one hand, vulgarity, vice, baseness, sly and tyrannical demands; on the other, the repletion of the satiated animal, the arrogance that dehumanizes, the insolent affectation of a superiority that allows the sense of responsibility to slumber in the egotistical enjoyment of privileges maintained by custom and intimidation.

Coriolanus is not the tragedy of an immaculate hero rejected and repudiated by the ungrateful mob, nor that of a people betrayed by its leaders. It is the tragedy of an imperfect political and social State, as it appeared to the poetic conscience of an artist rich in human experience. Shakespeare turns into drama a complex situation—that of the Roman society in which Coriolanus moves. The warriors and the politicians are not set against each other as symbols of two ideal conceptions of life, any more than the plebeians and patricians represent the antithesis between one social and political conception and another, between which a choice has to be made. A pervading irony—perceptible through the exaggerated imagery, in the words spoken by the most contemptible characters and in the very futility of Coriolanus's disordered career—gives the play an implicit richness which precludes its being used to illustrate any one thesis. All that can be said is that it is destructive rather than constructive, and so must be included (in spite of its great beauties) in the period of disillusionment.

This period is now closed in the angry, hateful outbursts of Timon of Athens, the most openly declared, most categorical and universal misanthrope in the whole gallery of

Shakespeare's malcontents. Timon, the most generous of
men, becomes the bitterest enemy of the human species and
passes from the extremity of kindliness to the opposite extreme of detestation. The drama of this radical conversion
is simplified to such a degree that it looks like an arbitrary
precipitation of events for the sole purpose of condemning
the whole of humanity. For the transition from one position
to the other, carefully though it is prepared by the gradual-
ness of Timon's disappointment, is followed by effects so
rapid and violent that the tragedy looks like a parable or
fable. There is no strictly personal tragedy as in *King Lear*,
where the bonds of affection between one character and
another are so powerful that their sudden severance staggers
the consciousness and completely changes one's vision of
the world and lifts the hero from the individual to the universal plane.

Timon trusts all men indiscriminately and equally repudiates and curses all men indiscriminately. The lyrical richness of the early scenes combines magnificent sensuousness
with a joyous extravagance. Jewels, works of art, love, feasts,
music—all contribute to present Athenian civilization as the
perfection of humane, settled dignity, friendship and nobility, as opposed to the lyrical vengeance of passions suddenly released. The world of Timon's princely liberality is
too good to be true. He distributes gifts and benefits with
a godlike prodigality, as if his earthly possessions were as
inexhaustible as his stores of love for his fellow-men. All
recognize his nobility, admire his disinterestedness. In the
fullness of his heart Timon may weep tears of joy. He is
so happy in dispensing kindness that his tenderness over-
flows. In this golden atmosphere, glowing with jewels, full
of the joyful hum of banquets, hands are stretched out,
hearts are exchanged, cups circulate—what a tempting vision
of an earthly Paradise, and how the generous Timon can
afford to smile at the sarcastic warnings of the cynical Apemantus!

Apemantus, the embittered philosopher, has no illusions to
feed on: he has seen through the general hypocrisy. This
world, that Timon conceives in his own image—noble,
generous, grateful—appears to Apemantus in all its hideous
bestiality and for him the Athenians are apes and monkeys.
Just as Thersites leeringly stripped the heroic Greek Staff
of its false aura of grandeur, so Apemantus with his
sarcasm and insults tears off the veneer that covers rottenness of body and mind. He precedes Timon in hatred and
disgust, he revels in his awareness of an ugly truth still

concealed from Timon, he battens upon his contempt for humanity. This prophetic voice of cynicism rings through the play from one end to the other, and he gloats with satisfaction. Apemantus foresees the ingratitude of Timon's 'friends' with an insulting jubilation at the very moment when Timon is most triumphant in gentle confidence and forgives the insulter. His dramatic role is important and complex, for his hateful clear-sightedness leads to the opening of Timon's eyes, although later the quality of his hate will be contrasted with Timon's. Moreover, his attitude to Timon sets off the unalterable attachment of the servants to their master, an attachment that still, and unwillingly, ennobles the lofty figure of the Athenian.

When Timon is warned of the first effects of his prodigality, he exclaims 'you shall perceive how you Mistake my fortunes: I am wealthy in my friends'. (II, ii, 193-4.) Wealthy indeed! He is abruptly ruined and collapses, without any intermediate stage except the short scene where he is at bay and offers his heart and blood in exchange for the gold he no longer possesses. Then his rage breaks out and hatred takes possession of him. In no play have we ever seen such a sudden and complete change of front. Timon cuts himself off from the whole of humanity. Standing before the walls of Athens which he has just left, a gigantic figure of solitude and hate, he utters his first curse—more absolute than Lear's, more assured than Medea's of old. This wild rhetoric, pursued with rigorous logic, omits no form in which chaos can be invoked upon the world that Timon repudiates. Every positive value finds its opposite, every virtue its antithesis, every element its foe. He curses the very order of society, the equilibrium of human nature, health, purity and innocence.

From every quarter of the compass the City is assailed by the birds of ill omen summoned by Timon's powerful voice:

> Piety and fear,
> Religion to the gods, peace, justice, truth,
> Domestic awe, night-rest and neighbourhood,
> Instruction, manners, mysteries and trades,
> Degrees, observances, customs and laws,
> Decline to your confounding contraries,
> And let confusion live!

IV, i, 15-21.

Timon passionately invokes all those evils which Ulysses in his fear of disorder was so afraid of, those catastrophes which a ruler's crime can unleash upon a society. Nothing escapes his malediction. What he hopes to see is universal

confusion, the total disintegration of the human order. Never
before had a character spoken in these terms. Possibly not
even a god would. Timon by his hatred passes beyond the
human pale. He enters a vast solitude on the verge of the
animal world, having ruled out all possible compromise with
human nature. The one creature excepted from his curse is
his Steward, and even this is out of a derisory remnant of
pity. He extirpates from his being anything that might still
link him with the race of men; he feeds on vile roots, digs
his own grave, and drives away with maledictions those
who visit him out of curiosity or pity. He bids Alcibiades
and his army destroy the ungrateful city root and branch,
and drown its inhabitants in blood. He gives Phrynia and
Timandra who accompany the general, the task of cor-
rupting his flesh to the bone, and evokes the terrifying
spectre of venereal disease. He engages in a bitter argument with Apemantus, turning his insolent pity to derision,
reproaching him with his baseness, his poverty, his sordid
love of life—this to Apemantus, the despiser of men, whose
clear-sighted hatred had foreseen Timon's fall!

But Timon detests Apemantus above all men because
Apemantus's hate arises from his fundamental villainy,
whereas Timon's own is provoked by the outrages which
his magnanimous spirit has suffered. Timon places himself
below humanity out of disgust at having felt himself above
it, and at having belonged to the great race of disinterested
and generous men. While Apemantus rejoices in the intellectual satisfaction of seeing his hateful prophecies come
true, Timon plunges deeper and deeper into irremediable
despair. The one returns like a dog to his vomit; the other
ends by being overcome like Macbeth by an immense
weariness: 'I am sick of this false world' (IV, iii, 378), and
for him there is no way out but death. He associates all
nature with his malediction because it likewise is corrupt.
The beasts devour and kill each other, like the stars which
fight in their courses in the sky. The universal law is that of
deceit and theft. There is nothing in all Creation that can
bring the least ray of hope, the least appeasement. Timon
will die hemmed in on all sides by evil infinite.

His cursing dies down, however, when there remains
nothing to curse, and he prepares himself for the dissolution
of death. This death of Timon, which nothing causes unless
it be the tragic movement of the play towards this ineluctable
end, has the moving grandeur of waves that subside after
a furious storm. Here the rhythm of the verse recalls the
grave nostalgia of the royal deaths of Macbeth and Othello:

> my long sickness
> Of health and living now begins to mend,
> And nothing brings me all things.
>
> V, i, 191-3.

Nothingness brings him everything. After his failure, it is of death that he asks all benefits. His anger, his cursing, his rejection of love are dissolved in eternal absence; reconciled with earth, he hurls at detested mankind the crowning insult of an epitaph which bids them depart and leave his body to be guarded by the mighty voice of the sea. For it is before the symbolic sea that Timon has dug his grave:

> . . . say to Athens,
> Timon hath made his everlasting mansion
> Upon the beached verge of the salt flood,
> Who once a day with his embossed froth
> The turbulent surge shall cover . . .
>
> V, i, 219-23.

The moving sea, blind and shapeless, mountains of rage and a placid pool of indifference—it is the perennial symbol of eternity, of chaos and of beauty.

But the tragedy could not end on this purely negative note. One man, Flavius the good servant, has escaped Timon's general malediction and he represents the possibility of redemption for the accursed city. Another, young and fair, Alcibiades, driven like him from Athens, receives from Destiny the mission to serve as a link between the past and the future, between vice and virtue, curses and hopes. It is he who might be the instrument of Timon's hate and chastise the insolent and the wicked. The Senators humbly beg him to spare the City, as they had in vain begged Timon to forgive and return. Timon had been the height of honour, the fine flower of their civilization. The treasures of his love had not been realized; they had been confused with earthly treasures, finding their natural symbol in gold.

Timon's defeat is converted into victory after his death. Fear of chastisement makes the ungrateful repent, makes the guilty old men bow their heads and all the City tremble. The Senators plead guilty, offer to be decimated, sue for pity. Pardon and love come into their own again. Alcibiades returns, not as the bloodthirsty avenger Timon had wished him to be, but

> . . . like a shepherd,
> Approach the fold and cull th' infected forth,
> But kill not all together.
>
> V, iv, 42-4.

Between the ideal world which Timon took for real, and the world of corruption which, failing the other, was to his mind the only possible one, it is the normal world that comes to life again, that Alcibiades will rule with the olive-branch and the sword, a world where peace follows war and reduces the chance of war: the eternal see-saw of good and evil, where good, as Timon had hoped, will at least ripen the fruitful treasures of life even if it cannot become an absolute value.

The death of Timon of Athens is the death of the universe of Hamlet, Macbeth and Lear. A resplendent and final death, the symbol of rebirths henceforth possible. In this play Shakespeare has gone to the utmost limits of his tragic view of the world, and his mouthpiece has, once more, but for the last time, penetrated to the depths of despair. Because, as I indicated in approaching this tragedy, his hero knows no personal, intimate conflict, limited to a well-defined affection; because, in other words, the play is situated outside all the psychological crises which alone are supposed to be capable of producing masterpieces—*Timon* has rarely been given the place that it deserves, among the very highest. To say that 'the dramatic value of the play is as slight as its poetic value' [12] is to my mind a serious mistake. The major themes to which Shakespeare gave poetic life in the preceding plays marked by the same spirit are here developed with the same abundance of images, the same imperious rhythms, the same tone of grave, profound conviction. The diptych of good and evil, the multiple significance of gold, the themes of death and ingratitude, the cosmic symbols of the stars, the tempest and the sea, stand out here with amazing prominence.

Timon, indeed, is of more than human stature and his mighty voice is like a trumpet of denunciation, sounding unbearably on the Day of Judgment. But in his immense solitude, a giant in hate as in love, he is the redoubtable symbol of despair. Without Timon's malediction and death, the curve of the play would not have been complete. Released from the finite in evil, the Shakespearian experiment can be pursued beyond the absolute nothingness which is for Timon the sovereign good. One could not remain in this appalling emptiness after a complete repudiation of Creation and of oneself without losing one's whole sense of substantial existence. But, again, the supreme adventure had to be attempted which leads to the unimaginable so that

[12] *Timon of Athens* (Edition Belles Lettres—preface by F. C. Danchin, p. xxiii).

the spirit might be renewed if life continued after the plunge into the abyss. Timon's metaphysical position is untenable, but it had to be adopted so that Alcibiades could be given the victory—the victory of the world's youth, heralding the victories of Love.

Difficult though it may be to establish precisely the various dates when this group of tragedies was composed, one likes to think that logically *Antony and Cleopatra* is the sumptuous transition leading to the last plays and to silence. The Roman world of *Coriolanus* is a warlike world, sordid and unstable and, when one thinks of it, rather confined. The Greek world of *Timon* calls for curses, and the sun veils its head in shame while Timon plunges into nothingness. But a resplendent sun rises upon the world of Cleopatra— the sun of immortality.

The play, of course, is a tragedy: we see the collapse of an empire, the ruin of an incomparable general, the death of a queen unrivalled for the seductiveness of her charm. Antony and Cleopatra are the victims of love, of war, of fortune. They reigned over one-third of the ancient world at the summit of power and glory—he an *imperator* whose triumphs were unnumbered, she a queen who 'beggared all description'. Passion possesses them and exalts them above ordinary mortals, but no longer in the anguish and the hardening of themselves, no longer to make of them the tortured, rebellious demons of negation and evil. And the glorious architecture of this happiness collapses, the empire breaks up, the armies and navies flee, the general runs upon his sword, the queen seeks refuge in suicide. It is in appearance a complete failure—Death once more seems the great victor.

But it is only in appearance. There is a striking contrast between the world of *Antony and Cleopatra* and that of the previous tragedies. The Shakespearian planet has emerged from the zone of shadow and entered the light. Its course is now bathed in a prodigious effulgence and clouds of golden dust. On the surface of the planet there is still agitation, contention, disorder on a cosmic scale the amplitude of which fills us with amazement. But the clouds scatter: the earthly reverse no longer leads to the metaphysical impasse where in former plays the hero was destroyed. There is no longer a spiritual cataclysm. On the contrary, Antony's death is a triumph and Cleopatra's a transfiguration.

How is such a thing possible? We are warned at the outset of Antony's greatness and his weakness, but immediately
also we see the tragic horizon extend over the limitless space
of the heavens. The first twenty lines, the two replies of
hero and heroine, give the scope of the stage on which
the drama is to be played out—a scope that defies the
imagination. Here are the characters posed in their exact
relationship: Mars in armour, a gypsy's slave, one of the
triple pillars of the world become 'a strumpet's fool'. But immediately we have this passage:

> *Cleopatra:* If it be love indeed, tell me how much.
> *Antony:* There's beggary in the love that can be reckon'd.
> *Cleopatra:* I'll set a bourn how far to be belov'd.
> *Antony:* Then must thou needs find out new heaven, new earth.
> I, i, 14-17.

This gives the measure and dimensions of the universe that
contains the lovers, the measure also of their ambition. Antony holds a third of the world, and this world is too small
for his love. Deliberately he sacrifices this petty space for
his immense passion:

> Let Rome in Tiber melt, and the wide arch
> Of the rang'd empire fall! Here is my space.
> I, i, 33-4.

Never before had sensuality attained this magnificence,
never so arrogated to itself the privileges of a spatial universe, unless it were in the metaphysical conceits of Donne
in his quest for a hidden absolute. But no play could be
further from the metaphysical quest in language than *Antony and Cleopatra*. None gives more the impression of a
constant sublimation, an inevitable transfer of the deeper life
of the senses to a mythical and superhuman plane. Cosmic
images abound in it, effortlessly studding the terrestrial universe and conferring upon it celestial dimensions and prestige. That empire which extends from Rome to Athens and
from Athens to the banks of the Nile is merely the accidental
theatre of an adventure which ends on the confines of the
stars.

Against this glorious vast background, moving and varied,
stands out the figure of Antony, increasingly lofty and magnificent, great in boldness and beauty, greater still in defeat
and in the face of death. For him there is no destructive
conflict. He has made his choice of love which deifies and
has rejected in advance all motives of revolt and despair. If

passion burns him up and destroys him, if it costs him his
empire and makes him a coward at the decisive moment
when his destiny is at stake, he is not belittled; evil does not
degrade him. His terrible wrath, his surrender to tenderness,
his errors in generalship, even his suicide which fails—all
leave the hero intact. It is love that keeps him on these
heights and, one must add, his eroticism. Antony is the
perfect erotic hero, the sublime revenge of love over Angelo,
over the hypocrites, the sexually impotent and perverted,
the melancholy and the jealous. Between woman and the
world, between love and action, Antony chooses to realize
himself fully through the communion of the flesh:

> . . . The nobleness of life
> Is to do thus; when such a mutual pair (*Embracing*)
> And such a twain can do 't . . .
>
> I, i, 36-8.

His is no political intellect, coldly constructing his plans
like the pale and severe Caesar; nor is he a military leader
who intoxicates himself with the noise of battle. Glory and
power have attraction for him only in so far as they are
dedicated to Cleopatra and allow such perfect expressions
of love between these two beings who are transfigured by
their complete surrender to its bondage. It is not the shame
of his flight which overwhelms the hero, for he is greater
than adversity. It is the news of Cleopatra's death, which
deprives him of all will to resist despair, of all love of life:

Antony:	Dead then?
Mardian:	Dead.
Antony:	Unarm, Eros; the long day's task is done,
	And we must sleep.

> IV, xii, 34-5.

We saw him magnificent in love, epic in combat, furious
under insults to the point of exulting in the revenge (already erotic) that he takes by flogging Caesar's messenger.
We saw his outburst against the elusive Cleopatra—a possession always lost and always regained—and now, not by
a supreme effort of will, like Corneille's heroes, but with
incomparable ease, he is impatient to resume elsewhere the
interrupted dialogue of love. For this love there is no death
possible, no degradation, no absence. This is what gives a
meaning to life and death. He does not die in order to
escape, he dies to rejoin Cleopatra, to deny their separation.
He leaves a world that has become empty since she no longer
inhabits it, a life that has no object because it is no longer

Cleopatra's. Nobility and magic incorruptible have taken
up their abode on other shores, and there one must go:

> . . . off, pluck off:
> The seven-fold shield of Ajax cannot keep
> The battery from my heart. O! cleave, my sides;
> Heart, once be stronger than thy continent,
> Crack thy frail case! Apace, Eros, apace.
> No more a soldier; bruised pieces, go;
> You have been nobly borne. From me awhile (*Exit Eros*)
> I will o'ertake thee, Cleopatra, and
> Weep for my pardon. So it must be, for now
> All length is torture; since the torch is out,
> Lie down, and stray no further. Now all labour
> Mars what it does; yea, very force entangles
> Itself with strength; seal then, and all is done.
> Eros!—I come, my queen.—Eros!—Stay for me:
> Where souls do couch on flowers, we'll hand in hand,
> And with our sprightly port make the ghosts gaze;
> Dido and her Aeneas shall want troops,
> And all the haunt be ours. Come, Eros! Eros!
>   IV, xii, 37-54.

Here love transfigures the tragic climate and incidentally
we can see how far Shakespeare has come since the death
of Romeo, perhaps even since Othello's. Here there is no
posing: the hero does not see himself in a dramatic light;
he does not, like Romeo, weave poetry out of frail flesh
and accuse the inauspicious stars; he does not, like Othello,
take pleasure in the effect that the news of his death will
have on those who hear it. Antony is wholly possessed by
his longing to rejoin Cleopatra. He has a vision of the
Elysium in store for them. He thinks of the next world in
terms of the miracle of their love.

Cleopatra is the ideal partner of a lover built on this
heroic scale—not that my purpose is to study her character
here: others have done that, have even done nothing but
that—she is the feminine aspect which gives the heroic
pair their reasons of immortality. She is the radiant pole
of feminine attraction, with the same shameless candour as
Antony's. She is the 'enchanting queen' who 'beggars all
description', a mythical symbol of the seduction that always
feeds desire, for whom empires are built and collapse, and
who remains for ever the incorruptible figure on her galley
with purple sails, dragging the amorous winds in her wake.
She is Woman in her maturity, hardly regretting her lost
youth—'My salad days when I was green in judgment'
(I, v, 73-4)—she is all consenting to desire—'O happy horse,
to bear the weight of Antony!' (I, v, 21); furiously jealous

(she, too, flogs the messengers), and ready to depopulate
Egypt in order to send couriers to Antony. But, above all,
she has the same conception as Antony of love's transfiguring
power, the same faith and exultation. It is her ardent imagination that endows Antony with qualities which lift him
above mankind and make him the equal of the gods.
Adoration and grief produce these extraordinary images
which do not belong to the usual poetic vocabulary of
eroticism but borrow from Elizabethan cosmology their
power of evocation:

> . . . O! see my women, (*Antony dies*)
> The crown o' the earth doth melt. My lord!
> O! wither'd is the garland of the war,
> The soldier's pole is fall'n; young boys and girls
> Are level now with men; the odds is gone
> And there is nothing left remarkable
> Beneath the visiting moon.
>
> IV, xiii, 62-8.

And let us remember the wonderful portrait of Antony already quoted (p. 167), where he appears with the gigantic
proportions and supernatural attributes which mark him out
for a place in the fabled gallery of mythological metamor-
phoses:

> His face was as the heavens and therein stuck
> A sun and moon . . .
>
> V, ii, 79-80.

The reality of this vision is so great and so vivid in her
eyes that imagination, she adds, is here defeated by Nature
which alone could have conceived and formed such a man,
a prodigy of Creation. She, too, strives with her whole
being to rejoin Antony on the fields of asphodel, and she
regards death as a passage towards love. In her duel with
Caesar her victory will be the asp. In these last scenes
where she foils Caesar of the only booty that would have
made it worth her appearing in his train, she is preparing a
different triumph, for places still more sacred than Imperial
Rome. She has restored to Antony his cosmic grandeur and
she is going to raise herself to his level. The death of Cleopatra is one of the greatest moments in the drama of the
whole world. The intensity of these minutes exceeds anything that Shakespeare had ever written. The Egyptian queen,
of infinite variety, the sensual, frivolous woman who fled
from Actium embarks again for Cydnus to meet Antony. It
is a death scene planned with care in which woman and
queen rival each other in courage and naturalness. It is
the accomplishment of a rite—royal funeral pomp—yet there

is the joyous ecstasy of impatient love, sure of its consummation.

The grandeur of this death lies not in the pride of its
pomp, but in the certainty of the identity of love with immortality, in this amazing alliance of nobility and simplicity,
of the queen and the woman, which in her final speech
works like magic:

> Give me my robe, put on my crown; I have
> Immortal longings in me . . .
>
> V, ii, 282-3.

The eastern star dies down to earthly eyes but lights up for
others. The sleep that the asp gives is the sleep of love.

The underlying significance of *Antony and Cleopatra,*
therefore, is to my mind that Shakespeare has recovered his
calm of spirit. The heavy covering of lead that weighed
down the universe is lifted, the horror of death dispelled,
the triumph of evil is no longer the only reward promised to
human passions, revolt no longer the only possible attitude
against indifferent or cruel gods. Shakespeare's tragic experience has gone full circle, and the first reconciliation takes
place in a brilliant world, loud with the clash of arms,
traversed by grandiose political ambitions but made poetic
by an immortal love. Man this time accepts his condition,
measures his weaknesses without disgust, but knows his
grandeur also. The impossible task of being oneself no
longer ends in failure because the true spirituality of man
which so many storms had obscured, ends by coming to
light.

This does not mean that evil has been finally laid low,
or that the serpent will no longer dare show his head, but
it does mean that he is no longer assured of being always
the only victor. The exultation of this discovery makes every
line of *Antony and Cleopatra* quiver and rise with every
step the heroes take towards death. But we are still in a
tragic universe where revelation is possible and complete
only in the supreme test of abandoning a finite for an
infinite world. It is reassuring that the passage should be
made with the sense of eternity. But this is perhaps only
the first step towards a new and even more exalting vision
of life. In what are called 'the last plays' of Shakespeare it
is this new, final and reassuring vision that is given us.

In *Pericles, Cymbeline, The Winter's Tale* and *The
Tempest* evil is far from having disappeared, of course. But

it is no longer the only sovereign. They are not, as is sometimes suggested, escapist plays in which the enervating influence of Beaumont and Fletcher inclines Shakespeare to prefer the unlikely and the unreal to the tragic reality and to weave dreams upon the warp of entirely imaginary adventures. Nor can the increased taste of the public for masques and romantic drama provide an adequate explanation. Shakespeare through his heroes has also undergone his purgation. His experience in the poetic representation of evil is as wide and deep as human experience can go. He has acquired an acute knowledge of life's complexity, and no problem is foreign to him. But what has always appealed to him with constant tenacity is the haunting sense of order and equilibrium which can be attained only by crushing the forces of evil and by the triumph of good.

All the tragedies, however desperate, end on a symbolical indication that a better order will be restored. One cannot end with chaos, even if the restored order is merely a fragile truce. Tragedy proceeds between these two truces, necessary links in the chain of misfortune. 'Full of sound and fury', it shows man crushed by fate, the slave of his passions, a victim doomed to die. Man struggles, strives, revolts, curses, renounces and disappears. But Fortinbras follows Hamlet, and Albany, King Lear. The successors are not the equals of their predecessors but they assure continuity of life. Life gains at every step.

So does poetic experience. Shakespeare is sufficiently master of his art to laugh at the captious remarks of the critics. His technique is his own and his supreme characteristic is his absolute freedom. By this I mean his remarkable ease in employing the conventions of the theatre in his day. People have spoken of negligence in his construction, in his presentation of the characters, in the general structure of his last plays. But to my mind they show merely a sovereign acquiescence to the demands of his genius. This, it may be objected, explains nothing, but there is nothing to explain. His imagination moves in the wide open spaces before him by exploring the earthly and the divine world of the last Roman and Eastern tragedy which offered him continents, seas, heavens and the next world. He was free in the choice of incidents to pass from history to poetry, from the individual to the symbol, from realism to magic, from science to alchemy. He is given an unfinished play, he takes over the characters, conducts them through the most romantic adventures, retaining only the favourite themes which he transposes upon a different plane of reality. The last three acts of *Pericles* in which his hand can be seen, are, from the point of view of pure logic, a masterpiece of improbability. But it is a willing, genial improbability, without any perversity.

Here, indeed, we are in the magic kingdom where Prospero will shortly be absolute master. But this magic is merely the poetic apotheosis of a new conception of life. It is merely an aesthetic means of illustrating his recovered faith in man's destiny, no longer thanks to victory *by* death but without death and apart altogether from it. As his career draws to a close Shakespeare turned back to his youth, and his implicit theme is always that of fertility, resurrection, joy of life. It is remarkable that the attractive symbols of these plays should be young girls or young women, for whom misfortune lies in wait, but love also awaits them and will make them its own for an indisputable triumph. Marina, Imogen, Perdita, Miranda—all so assured of the integrity of their souls, pass unspotted and without despairing through the various trials which fate, chance, greed or the ill will of man impose on them. They speak, and their calm utterance disarms the cruel play of falsehood and outrage. Or else it is an animated discussion in which they become heated and defend themselves with the vigorous conviction that their instinctive sense of integrity gives them: Marina in the house of the prostitutes, Imogen meeting the assaults of Cloten and the treachery of Iachimo, Perdita facing the wrath of Polixenes, or Miranda facing Prospero's. The tragedy is *their* tragedy, it is their defence against what remains of hostility in the world, of hypocrisy, jealousy, and impure desire. They strive against what would stifle them, subject and abase them. They fight for their integrity and for the rights of youth and life.

What is there surprising if in this new vision of the world, the older generations are sacrificed? It is the parents who raise the storms by their lack of forsight, their sudden blindness, some crime they have committed, victims as they are of old servitudes of evil. For them there have to be trials before regeneration. But always it is as much a regeneration lying in their acceptance of the young who have been in danger, as a remorse for their error. Pericles loses and recovers Thaisa and Marina, Cymbeline his sons, Posthumus his wife, Leontes, the prey of 'the green-eyed monster' like Othello, weeps with joy at the resurrection of Hermione and the return of Perdita; Prospero, finally, the

most clear-sighted and self-controlled of the sinners and the
most merciful also, carefully prepares for Miranda's happiness and the return to his Duchy.

Again, what is there surprising if the themes of spring,
fertility, and palpitating sensuous life flourish everywhere?
The pastoral universe of Bohemia opposed to the more refined life of the Court of Sicilia is the place where the
redemption is prepared. That of Wales, wild and flowery,
is the counterpart of the corrupt world of Cymbeline's Court.
Prospero's isle is the literally magic spot where the revenge
of kindness and pardon is plotted. The part played by flowers
in *The Winter's Tale,* by music and song in *The Tempest,*
by the funeral dirge in *Cymbeline,* the lyrical outbursts
everywhere, powerfully contribute to create this new atmosphere which finds its most perfect expression in *The
Tempest.* The gods are called in to help, to give the earthly
union their blessing. Better still, spirits take human shape
and are yoked to the work of regeneration.

It is perfectly logical to find Prospero the magician in the
last of Shakespeare's plays. His genius required that the
most powerful of symbols and the most serene of plays
should crown his career. But here everything is symbolic,
beginning with the title—the Shakespearian tempest that is
found in every play and is here merely a flashing prologue,
of which Prospero is the supreme regulator. It is significant
that the tragic central theme of the play should be the old
theme of revenge. For Prospero is a frustrated man who
takes revenge. The victim of treachery, he runs to the very
last the risk of succumbing again to it. But his revenge would
have no meaning if it were merely the punishment of criminals. His power, his magic would be pointless. This man,
all-powerful, terrible in his wrath, who enslaves the bestial
and the unsubstantial spirit, cannot rest until he has brought
about the regeneration of his enemies. It is the supreme victory, that of spirit over matter, of music over chaos, of
love over hatred; in a word, of man over himself.

Prospero wants to be the magician who can work fruitful
wonders, directed not towards motionless ecstasy but towards
the future. He gives Ariel his liberty and his greatest anger
is reserved for the impossible Caliban who does not wholly
belong to human kind, or at least not yet. Should we see
in this exclusion the final irony of the dramatist since he
cannot bring himself to make Caliban an antipathetic personage, devoid of all sensibility? For it is Caliban who is
most aware of the poetry of the isle, whom music affects
with the purest felicity. This miry monster, neither man nor

fish, son of the blue-eyed hag Sycorax, seeking desperately
to recover his kingdom even at the cost of allying himself
with a clown and a drunkard—may be a devil on whom
Prospero's kindness is lost, yet he is not perhaps inaccessible
to Grace: he leaves the stage with words of repentance. Will
Prospero take him back to his recovered Duchy or leave
him in full possession of his isle?

Prospero at all events returns of his own free will to the
human condition. He strips himself of his magician's mantle,
breaks his magic wand and promises to drown his book
'deeper than did ever plummet sound'. Let us avoid facile
speculation on the meaning of this abjuration. A poetic
testament? Very well. But a reconciliation with man would
be more exact or at least more satisfactory for anyone who
seeks to give Shakespeare's Works a complete and harmonious meaning. If *The Tempest* contains a final message, it
can only be this. In Prospero's view there is no heart-
rending conflict. There is the knowledge of good and evil,
the admission of suffering and animality; but violence and
cruelty give way in the end to clemency. Prospero, unlike
Antony and Cleopatra, has no thought of the after-life, or
if he alludes to it, it is to conclude that life and death are
both alike unreal:

> We are such stuff
> As dreams are made on; and our little life
> Is rounded with a sleep.   IV, i, 156-8.

It might almost be Macbeth speaking. Almost! It is a
tragic admission that comes after an explosion of anger.
But it is not inspired by despair. It implies on the contrary
a positive faith in the value of life as it is, with all its im-
perfections but also with all its beauties. It is after having
called up the spirits to bless the marriage-rites that Prospero
chooses to show the marvelling eyes of Miranda real human
beings of flesh and bone. And then comes that unforgettable
exclamation which is a cry of faith:

> O, wonder!
> How many goodly creatures are there here!
> How beauteous mankind is! O brave new world,
> That has such people in't.

INDEX

DRAMABOOKS

Hill and Wang has established **DRAMABOOKS** as a permanent library of the great classics of the theatre of all countries, in an attractive, low-priced format.

PLAYS

MD 1   *Christopher Marlowe* edited by Havelock Ellis. Introduction by John Addington Symonds
(Tamburlaine the Great, Parts I & II, Doctor Faustus, The Jew of Malta, Edward the Second)

MD 2   *William Congreve* edited by Alexander Charles Ewald. Introduction by Macaulay (Complete Plays)

MD 3   *Webster and Tourneur* Introduction by John Addington Symonds
(The White Devil, The Duchess of Malfi, The Atheist's Tragedy, The Revenger's Tragedy)

MD 4   *John Ford* edited by Havelock Ellis
(The Lover's Melancholy, 'Tis Pity She's a Whore, The Broken Heart, Love's Sacrifice, Perkin Warbeck)

MD 5   *Richard Brinsley Sheridan* edited with an Introduction by Louis Kronenberger
(The Rivals, St. Patrick's Day, The Duenna, A Trip to Scarborough, The School for Scandal, The Critic)

MD 6   *Camille and Other Plays* edited, with an Introduction to the well-made play by Stephen S. Stanton
(Scribe: A Peculiar Position, and The Glass of Water; Sardou: A Scrap of Paper; Dumas, *fils*: Camille; Augier: Olympe's Marriage)

MD 7   *John Dryden* edited, and with an Introduction by George Saintsbury
(The Conquest of Granada, Parts I & II, Marriage à la Mode, Aureng-Zebe)

MD 8   *Ben Jonson* edited, with an Introduction and Notes, by Brinsley Nicholson and C. H. Herford
(Volpone, Epicoene, The Alchemist)

MD 9   *Oliver Goldsmith* edited by George Pierce Baker with an Introduction by Austin Dobson
(The Good Natur'd Man, She Stoops to Conquer, An Essay on the Theatre, A Register of Scotch Marriages)

MD 10   *Jean Anouilh* Volume 1
(Antigone, Eurydice, The Rehearsal, Romeo and Jeannette, The Ermine)

MD 11   *Let's Get a Divorce! and Other Plays,* edited, and with an Introduction on The Psychology of Farce by Eric Bentley
(Labiche: A Trip Abroad, and Célimare; Sardou: Let's Get a Divorce!; Courteline, These Cornfields; Feydeau: Keep an Eye on Amélie; Prévert: A United Family; Achard: essay on Feydeau)

PLAYS *(continued)*

CRITICISM